Community and Trinity in Africa

Community and Trinity in Africa recasts the African tradition of community from a theological perspective. Ibrahim S. Bitrus explains the new Trinitarian hermeneutics of God as the fundamental framework for constructing an authentic African tradition of community.

The book explores the tripartite structural evils of the patriarchal tradition, the Big Man/Woman syndrome, and ethnic-religious nepotism, which distort the African tradition of community. It analyzes Trinitarian proposals that liberate the distorted African tradition of community and concludes that an authentic African tradition of community is one that embodies individuality without libertarian individualism, communality without patriarchy, and mutual multi-ethnic and religious relations without nepotism and domination.

Arguing that the communion of the Triune God is not a moral ideal, but a gift that restructures the church and society, this book is an essential read for scholars of African Christianity and Christian theology.

Ibrahim S. Bitrus earned his PhD in Systematic Theology at Luther Seminary, USA and is currently the Nigerian Theologian in Residence for the Minneapolis Area Synod of the ELCA.

Routledge Studies on Religion in Africa and the Diaspora
Series Editors: Fassil Demissie and Sandra Jackson

1 Community and Trinity in Africa
Ibrahim S. Bitrus

Community and Trinity in Africa

Ibrahim S. Bitrus

LONDON AND NEW YORK

First published 2018 by Routledge

2 Park Square, Milton Park, Abingdon, Oxfordshire OX14 4RN

52 Vanderbilt Avenue, New York, NY 10017

Routledge is an imprint of the Taylor & Francis Group, an informa business

First issued in paperback 2020

Copyright © 2018 Ibrahim S. Bitrus

The right of Ibrahim S. Bitrus to be identified as author of this work has been asserted by him in accordance with sections 77 and 78 of the Copyright, Designs and Patents Act 1988.

All rights reserved. No part of this book may be reprinted or reproduced or utilised in any form or by any electronic, mechanical, or other means, now known or hereafter invented, including photocopying and recording, or in any information storage or retrieval system, without permission in writing from the publishers.

Notice:
Product or corporate names may be trademarks or registered trademarks, and are used only for identification and explanation without intent to infringe.

British Library Cataloguing-in-Publication Data
A catalogue record for this book is available from the British Library

Library of Congress Cataloging-in-Publication Data
Names: Bitrus, Ibrahim S., author.
Title: Community and Trinity in Africa / Ibrahim S. Bitrus.
Other titles: Routledge studies on religion in Africa and the diaspora ; 1.
Description: New York : Routledge, 2017. | Series: Routledge studies on religion in Africa and the diaspora ; 1 | Includes bibliographical references and index.
Identifiers: LCCN 2017014516 | ISBN 9781138240643 (hardback) | ISBN 9781315283135 (ebook)
Subjects: LCSH: Trinity—History of doctrines. | Communities—Africa. | Communities—Nigeria. | Communities—Religious aspects—Christianity. | Equality—Africa. | Equality—Religious aspects—Christianity. | Patriarchy—Africa. | Power (Social sciences)—Africa.
Classification: LCC BT109 .B58 2017 | DDC 231.044096—dc23
LC record available at https://lccn.loc.gov/2017014516

ISBN: 978-1-138-24064-3 (hbk)
ISBN: 978-0-367-34114-5 (pbk)

Typeset in Times New Roman
by Apex CoVantage, LLC

This book is dedicated to my brother Nakesemeni Bitrus and my parents, Martha and Bitrus Maaji.

Contents

Foreword	ix
Preface	xii

1 Introduction 1
Background to community and Trinity 1
Purpose, significance, and procedure adopted 7
Scope and limitation of the book 9
The African tradition of community: what is it? 11
Evolution of Nigeria as a nation-state 16
Bibliography 25

2 Major African communal structural evils 28
Destructive patriarchal complex 28
The "Big Man" syndrome 33
Ethnic and religious nepotism 46
Summary and conclusion 55
Bibliography 62

3 The "amazing history" of the Trinity 67
Mainline Eastern Trinitarian thinkers 68
Mainline Western Trinitarian thinkers 80
*Eclipse and renaissance of Trinitarian theology in
  the early modern period 97*
Contemporary African hermeneutics of the Trinity 109
Summary and conclusion 120
Bibliography 131

4 The new hermeneutics of the Trinity 134
Starting point of the new Trinitarian theology 134
*Hermeneutics of Trinitarian mutual relations
  of the Triune God 142*

viii *Contents*

Hermeneutics of the unity of the Triune God 150
The Trinitarian communion: a moral ideal 156
Summary and conclusion 159
Bibliography 165

5   An authentic African tradition of community   166
The Lord's supper and the perichoretic life of God 166
Dismantling the patriarchal complex 169
The true Big Man: newariga diksen 172
The gift of ethnic and religious diversity 179
Perichoretic theological education 183
Summary and conclusion 185
Suggestions for further research 188
Bibliography 190

Index   192

Foreword

In *Community and Trinity in Africa*, Dr Ibrahim Bitrus accomplishes what no other Nigerian Christian theologian has yet to do. He demonstrates that the Triune God's sacramental offer of God's own perichoretic life of personal and shared communion is that abundant divine Gift that eschatologically transforms and consummates the desire of the nations. This bears immediate implications for Africa.

Bitrus imagines recent social Trinitarian reflection as a post-colonial, dialogical intersectionality located deeply within African social soils. He engages the general African tradition of community through a case study of Nigeria, where he finds both social abundance and systemic oppression, and he probes both. His accomplishment, therefore, is not one of high-level academic scholarship alone – it is that! – but is an accomplishment of social, political, and ecclesial courage as well. In the face of structural evil, the Triune God always calls prophetic courage into existence to accompany serious, scholarly sapiential reflection. Dr Bitrus acts from that call. His hope clearly lies in the everlasting and ongoing promise of God's triune emancipatory communion for the African continent, indeed for the entire creation.

Bitrus plots a three-part drama, doing so in a non-linear manner across his five chapters. Moreover, this drama, after all is said and done, is the Triune God's own dramatic life together with the peoples of Africa, and finally with all nations on the face of the earth. In Part One of the drama, he digs deeply into three structural evils rooted in Nigerian soil with their devastating consequences for human flourishing. He critically examines the complexes of Nigerian patriarchy, the tradition of the "Big Man" syndrome, and the heritage of Nigerian nepotism in both ethnic and religious garbs.

In Part Two of the drama, Bitrus explores God's being as perichoretic communion of three mutually beloved persons whose love sacramentally overflows becoming Nigeria's, Africa's, and the world's own eschatological reality ahead of time. He unfolds the drama by way of a fruitful journey through the history of Christian Trinitarian reflection, both ancient and contemporary, both Western and Eastern. Two turning points in the drama are critical. First, he takes readers on a fruitful journey through the history of Christian Trinitarian reflection, both Western and Eastern, both ancient and contemporary. This journey brings him into dialogue with an otherwise diverse and globally distributed group of Roman

x   *Foreword*

Catholic, Orthodox, and Protestant theologians in the late twentieth and early twenty-first centuries who explore social Trinitarian reflection, as it is usually referred to. Here the ancient Greek notion of perichoresis (Greek: περιχωρεσισ), which Bitrus elucidates, comes to the fore. Second, he brings his own Lutheran sacramental heritage to bear on social Trinitarian reflection and the difference that this sacramental heritage offers for the Trinitarian journey toward "an authentic African tradition of community," as he puts it.

Bitrus confesses both of these turning points as crucial to his own Christian confession of faith and life. In regards to the first turning point, he shows how the social Trinitarian theologians have gone a long way already toward overcoming the Western waning of Trinitarian theology. This Western waning had been happening since the eighteenth century, and had been continually gaining ground in the everyday life of Christian confessions and churches throughout the West, and wherever the West's colonial supremacy held sway. Both Roman Catholic and Protestant theologians, with certain exceptions, had been devolving the doctrine of the Trinity in at least two general ways. On the one hand, they had reduced the doctrine of the Trinity to a mathematical mystery not to be engaged either reflectively or practically, especially by church laity or even by local clergy, but only to be heeded under the panoptic gaze of authoritarian promulgation. On the other hand, and perhaps even worse, theologians had surrendered altogether God's life as triune in favor of various tepid versions of moral and experiential monarchical monotheisms. Both of these devolutions, these travesties, left spiritual life of Western Christianity only a step or so removed from outright, full-blown Enlightenment deism. Moreover, it is no mere coincidence that this Western waning of Trinitarian theology in favor of an authoritarian mathematical mystery or of moral and experiential monarchical monotheisms coincided with Western colonialism. These devolutions actually capacitated colonialism. Indeed, the rapid rise of African Christianity did not happen without the colonial imprint of Western monarchical monotheisms. Against these phenomena, Bitrus confesses that God's triune perichoretic communion transforms colonialist ways of life together across all dimensions of life.

In regards to the second turning point in Part Two of the drama, Bitrus draws from his own Lutheran sacramental heritage. He does this in order to overcome prevalent and problematic tendencies among social Trinitarian theologians, whom he otherwise admires, to imagine God's triune being as merely a model to be weakly imitated or a utopian ideal only faintly achievable or a coercive ideology enforced through shame or other disciplinary measures. God's own triune communion is none of these. Rather, God's own being as communion is God's own sacramental offer to the world and to Africa.

Here is the entry into Part Three of the drama, and is finally why God's sacramental offer of God's own personal, open, and transforming communion represents God's own shared way toward an authentic African tradition of community. In Part Three, Bitrus conveys the emancipatory implications that God's sacramental Gift of Trinitarian communion promises for Africa in the face of the three systemic evils that he exposed in Part One of the drama. I won't divulge how he unfolds this concluding part of the drama but leave it to the reader to discover the surprises for herself or himself, and then to imagine how God's sacramental Gift can emancipate Trinitarian communion in one's own, perhaps quite different, contexts.

Dr Ibrahim Bitrus is a Nigerian theological educator. As an epilogue, so to speak, to his three-part drama of Trinity and community in Africa, he reflects on the implications of this drama for the future of theological education. Here as well he offers not only Africans but also those of us in the West, where theological education is facing massive adaptive challenges, an opportunity to listen closely because we especially need decolonization toward innovative emancipatory practices.

by
Gary M. Simpson

Preface

My journey as a contemporary Trinitarian theologian developed over time. It all began with reading of the Trinity in Karl Barth's *Church Dogmatics*. I soon discovered, with much admiration, that Barth had the longest treatises on the Trinity since St Thomas Aquinas. The more I studied the doctrine of the Trinity, the more I fell in love with the doctrine. The research disabused my mind of the widespread belief that the Trinity is simply a "mystery". It dawned on me that the Trinity is not an inscrutable belief about an abstract God, so to speak. Rather, the Trinity is a pragmatic doctrine that grasps and expresses an unfathomable relationship of a tangible Triune God with humans and the world, a Trinitarian relationship that is accomplished by Christ and established through the Spirit. My initial vision was to develop a Trinitarian theology to provide Christians with the framework to image the Trinitarian life of the Triune God in living and treating one another as equal but distinct persons in their family, church, and societal life. Though the vision was not realized, the extensive work I did on Barth's Trinity in my M.Th. thesis led me to probe into contemporary Trinitarian theology, research that further boosted my interest and love for the Trinity.

My concern was to explore the hermeneutics of the contemporary Trinitarian theologians and how it might salvage Nigeria from contextual issues such as oppressive hierarchical leadership, patriarchy, ethno-religious sentiment, and ecological degradation. I thought that the doctrine of the Trinity, when rightly understood and applied, holds the possible key to transforming interpersonal relations in the family, church, and society. In my doctoral dissertation, I explicated the new hermeneutics of the Triune God and its radical significance for the African community. But I experienced a paradigm shift in my Trinitarian thinking at this point. I moved away from my previous claims that the Trinity is only a model or a transformative principle. Instead, I have perceived that the Trinitarian communion of God is a gift. That is, the Triune God is the Gift, and not the new Trinitarian hermeneutics of God itself. The new hermeneutics of the Trinity is merely our human framework that attempts to grasp and interpret the gift of the Trinitarian communion.

The aim of this book is to recast the African tradition of community in Africa with specific reference to Nigeria. Much work has been done about the African

Preface xiii

tradition of community, but there has been little to no work done to recast the tradition from a theological perspective. Though the African tradition of community bears, however faintly, the vestige of the Triune God, the tradition has been romanticized, despite being distorted by systemic problems. What this means is that there is a faint image of the Trinitarian communion in the African tradition of community. As a result, this book explicates the Trinitarian communion of God as the fundamental framework for recasting the African tradition of community. The thesis of this book is that the Trinitarian communion of God is not a moral ideal, but a transformative gift. This gift, which is mediated through Eucharistic practice, empowers Christians to liberate the African community from its tripartite structural evils of patriarchy, the Big Man syndrome, and ethno-religious nepotism. I propose that a transformed African tradition of community is a tradition of community that embodies individuality without libertarian individualism, communality without patriarchy, and mutual multi-ethnic and religious relations without nepotism and domination. This is the fruit of the gift of God's perichoretic communion.

The book is a conjunction of African Studies and the new hermeneutic of the Trinity, both of which command an increasing academic research interest. It is intended primarily for undergraduate and graduate students of African Studies, Christian theology, philosophy and religion in Africa, and the African diaspora around the world. Church pastors and leaders of the global church of Christ will find the book informative, insightful, and imaginative for other contexts.

There are many people who made the writing of this book a reality, whom I would like to thank. To begin with, I would like to express my deep appreciation to my doctoral advisor, Professor Gary Simpson, for his untiring guidance, critique, invaluable suggestions, and for writing the foreword. I couldn't have done this work without his continuous support, patience, and immense insights! In addition, I would like to thank my friend Rev. Dr Bradley Holt for painstakingly reading the manuscript and lending critical and insightful comments and counsel. His unflinching support and recommendation to the publisher made the publication of this book a reality. I can't thank him enough. My sincere thanks also go to the Associate Director of The Center for Writing and Research at Luther Seminary, St Paul, Peter Susag, for his thorough reading, correcting, and editing of the manuscript. His contribution to giving the book its required scholarly form and standard is enormous!

I would like to express my profound gratitude to his grace, Rt Rev. Dr Nemuel Babba, the Archbishop of the Lutheran Church of Christ in Nigeria (LCCN). I would also like to express my appreciation to the Evangelical Lutheran Church in America, the Global Mission Institute at Luther Seminary, and Lutheran World Federation for their scholarship support. I owe an unending gratitude to my friends, Gary and Deana Sande, Lawrence and Janet Crosby, and Alan and Kristina Perry, Shirley Ann Heyer, Craig Pederson, and the Minneapolis Area Synod for their tremendous spiritual, moral, and financial support. The support that they gave my family made our stay in St Paul a home away from home. I am also indebted to close friends: Rev. Amson A. Hamman, Dimas Makka and Ishaku Solomon, and my students at Bronnum Lutheran Seminary for encouraging me to write a book. Above all, I would like to thank my wife, Julecy Bitrus, who stood by me, giving me exceptional support at all the stages of my scholarly journey. I couldn't have published this book without her profound support and patience and that of our children, Pasy, Tunary, Falnyi, and Titveren.

1   Introduction

Background to community and Trinity

God as the Trinity precedes, creates, and sustains community. Nonetheless, the Trinity cannot be known apart from community. There can't be any knowledge of the Trinity without community and vice versa. Why? Because the Trinity is given and made known to us in the context of community. Community and the Trinity are distinct, but inseparable, realities. Community is not only the vestige of the Triune God, but it is also the epistemic locus of the Trinity. As a vestige of the Trinity, community bears the innate relational character of the Triune God, however imperfectly. Community is the network of human and non-human relationships marred by sin and structural evils. The Trinity is the free, just, and loving communion of three distinct co-equal divine persons, a communion that also embraces both humanity and the world. But the Trinitarian communion is not a moral ideal, but a gift to community. Consequently, the Trinity has what it takes to critique and salvage the tradition of community in Africa from sin and structural evils, albeit not devoid of human agency. In other words, the Trinitarian communion of God rooted in the economy of salvation, recently rediscovered in the new Trinitarian hermeneutics[1] of God, is a paradigmatic gift. It correlates, critiques, and reconstructs this romanticized key concept of African philosophy and theology. Yet, the nonchalant attitude toward the doctrine of the Trinity in African Christian theology over the years has in many ways been responsible for the absence of a perichoretic[2] Trinitarian critique and reconstruction of the African tradition of community.

The African practice of community is undoubtedly the most celebrated thought in African theology and philosophy. There is no other African scholar who expresses this claim better than Kwesi Abotsia Dickson. The African concept[3] of community, according to Dickson, is a "characteristic of African life to which attention has been drawn again and again by both African and non-African writers on Africa. Indeed, to many this characteristic defines Africanness."[4] The fundamental dictum on which this *radical* conception of the African way of life rests is "I am who I am because of who we are." But there is little to no work that has been done to recast such a concept, and even when there is, the work done is a philosophical rather than theological reconstruction. For example, critiquing the radical philosophical African concept

2 *Introduction*

of community for affirming the ontological primacy of the community over the autonomy of its individual members, Kwame Gyekye proposes a *moderate* notion of an African community which strikes a balance between the communal and autonomous being of its individual members.[5] Gyekye concurs with radical proponents of the African concept of community that it is the community that confers personhood on the individual. Gyekye rightly argues that there are essential personal attributes such as rationality, virtue, and freedom, which constitute personhood. The community cannot create them in individuals, but only discover and nurture them. But the potential shortcoming of his philosophical re-conceptualization of African community is his failure to call into question structural issues ingrained in the African practice of community, which constrain the successful discovering and development of these essential personal attributes. What is needed is the Trinitarian theological reconstruction of the African concept of community. The key to this Trinitarian reconstruction is the paradigmatic gift of the perichoretic communion of the Triune God for recasting the African tradition of community.

But the new Trinitarian theology, which teaches this amazing gift of God's perichoretic communion, is often neglected in the mainstream of African theology. According to Mika Vähäkangas,

> The Holy Trinity has not gained much attention among African theologians. Even in those cases when it has been discussed, it has sometimes been briefly mentioned almost as if it were a necessary evil . . . or at least its traditional form has been rejected.[6]

The doctrine of the Trinity is deliberately avoided in sizeable theological reflections because it is believed to be loaded with Western metaphysical categories. Gabriel M. Setiloane, an African theologian, hesitates to speak about the Holy Spirit simply because doing so is tantamount to endorsing what he alleges to be the Western metaphysically originated doctrine of the Trinity. Setiloane thus calls for articulating an African pneumatology that undermines the Trinitarian understanding of God.[7] Though the doctrine of the Trinity owes its origin and categories to the Latin and Greek thought-forms, undoubtedly, the Trinity is a biblical (rather than Western or Eastern) doctrine. As a biblical doctrine that expresses the communion of the Triune God with the Triune persons themselves and the cosmic community in Jesus Christ through the Spirit, pneumatology and the Trinity belong together. The two cannot be separated without violating the entire doctrine of God.

The doctrine of the Trinity also receives little attention in African Christianity because the Trinity is often thought to be too complicated for many African Christians to comprehend. In fact, too many African believers even think that the doctrine of the Trinity is obsolete. They allege that since the doctrine of the Trinity is incomprehensible, it is irrational to confess faith in the Triune God! As Cristopher Mwoleka laments,

> It is a pity that many people find it difficult to understand what this mystery is all about. Many Christians do not know what to do with it except that it must [be] believed. It is a dogma they cannot apply to their daily life.[8]

Introduction 3

As a doctrine that affirms three persons in one God, it is believed the Trinity is not only incompatible with African thought but also is meaningless to too many African Christians. J.N.K. Mugambi has suggested that the doctrine of the Trinity should be "re-interpreted in terms of traditional African monotheism." He has argued, "This is not syncretism because the objective of such re-interpretation is to clarify to African Christians the classical Christian doctrine of God, rather than distort it."[9] Mugambi has recommended that

> the notion of "person" in the Trinity should be discarded because in the African mind they are misleading, vague and confusing. . . . The best and most relevant way to understand the Trinity, we thought, is in terms of the *modes of being of God's manifestation to Man.*[10]

Sadly, the Trinitarian theology that occupies a central place in Christian faith and life is probably easier professed than interpreted by the clergy and laity alike. Too many Christians (including even some clergy) who accept and study the doctrine of the Trinity at theological institutions do not hesitate to admit that they do not understand the Trinity when challenged to explicate it by their members and non-Christians alike. Some of them quickly jump to conclusions, giving the exaggerated answer that the doctrine of the Trinity is a "mystery" beyond human thinking and interpretation. Even those who gather Spartan courage to explicate the Trinity simply reiterate its ancient Sabellian Trinitarian heresy. Some clergy would tell members of the church that all they need to know about the Christian faith is that Jesus is the savior of the world – as if Jesus being the savior of the world has nothing to do with the Triune God! Thus, a good number of African Christians have come to perceive the Trinity as a "fragmented" rather than a "defragmented" divine persons in communion. They tend to overemphasize, whether explicitly or implicitly, one of the members of the Trinitarian communion at the expense the others. Lutherans, for example, are so obsessed with the expression "Christ alone" (in other words, Christology) that they often forget not only that the person and works of Christ are by no means divorced from the other members of the Trinitarian communion, but also what the divine persons are up to as a communion.[11]

Though the doctrine of the Trinity has become a "no go area" and fragmented divine communion in the African context, one will be intrigued to discover that it is in neither Christ's nor the Spirit's name alone that any one of us has been baptized. Rather, it is in the entire Triune name – Father, Son, and Spirit – that the clergy invoke worship services and all Christians are baptized as members of the church and say prayers within and outside the Church. For many, the Trinitarian communion of God rooted and revealed in Christ and the Spirit is simply meant to accomplish such a liturgical function! Apart from this role, the doctrine of the Trinitarian communion of God has no other practical relevance. Consequently, the question of whether the Trinitarian communion of God has any transformative implications for all spheres of the Christian and public community life is often not raised. There is no doubt that the excellent attempt at reinterpreting the doctrine of the Trinity from the African worldview of human and divine community made by Okechukwu Ogbonnaya in his book *On Communitarian Divinity: An African*

4 Introduction

Interpretation of the Trinity has not explored the transformative significance of the doctrine for the African society.

To make matters worse, many African theological institutions where pastors and theologians receive spiritual, ministerial, and academic formation pay little or no attention to the doctrine of the communion of the Triune God. Even when they do, the theological curriculum is planned in such a way that the doctrine of the Trinity is usually the last item to be taught under the doctrine of God. The teaching of the doctrine of God usually starts with the proof of the existence of one God, then nature and attributes of God before handling the doctrine of the Trinity. Thus, the Trinity is then being treated as a doctrine that stems simply from abstract metaphysical speculation rather than salvation history, a marginal belief rather than a core and summary of the content of Christian revelation and faith. In other words, the teaching of the doctrine of the Trinity is usually detached from the economy of salvation without stressing the definite significance of God's perichoretic communion for real-life human and non-human community situations.

Therefore, the marginalization of the Trinitarian doctrine of God's perichoretic communion both in theory and practice in African theology has contributed in no diminutive way not only to misconstruing divine authority or power in patriarchal and monarchial terms[12] as familial, political, and ecclesial leaderships, but also to justifying oppressive hierarchy, which destabilizes the elegant African tradition of community. (Authority and power belong together; hence, to draw a clear demarcation between the two is hard. Socio-politically, authority is the exercise of legitimate power by those in authority to influence the behavior of humanity and creation toward a given collective *telos*. However, the exercise of authority by human rulers is often bound not only to lose its legitimacy, but also to degenerate into the abuse of its *telos* toward personal ends. As human tendency to abuse authority does not apply to God, "authority" and "power" are used interchangeably in this work with reference to God as the source and prototype of legitimate human authority and power.) This also undermines the egalitarian gift of the Triune God to humanity and creation, and by extension, the Nigerian national goal of building a "just and egalitarian society. . . . [A] land bright and full [of] opportunities" for all citizens.[13] The hierarchical stratification creates and perpetuates social inequality, injustice, and conflict in Nigerian and the African community as a whole. Those who suffer from these unjust structures always yearn for radical changes, which the gift of the perichoretic communion of God provides for, liberating them from these structural evils.

Leonardo Boff has suggested that the doctrine of the Trinity not only promotes the cause of those oppressed and struggling for liberation, egalitarian sharing, and communion, but also provides a solid foundation for a just and free society. He argues, "Faith in [the] Trinity will mean criticism of all social injustices and a source of inspiration for basic changes."[14] I will argue that it is not just the doctrine of the Trinity itself that liberates, but the prototypical gift of God's perichoretic communion granted to us in Word and Sacrament. This gift liberates and purifies the African tradition of community corrupted by systemic evils.

Additionally, the marginalization of the Trinitarian communion of God has left unchallenged the systemic issues that taint the practice of the African community.

The common effects of all these systemic issues are underdevelopment, severing human relationships, and depriving the weak and poor of the right to life and other basic needs. Above all, these systemic evils block Africans from fully accepting and living out justice, equity, and rule of law, which are the Triune God's incomparable requirement and gift for the building of a just and egalitarian community. I will return to this in Chapter 2. Given their adverse effects on the precious African tradition of community, the question is what definitive significance the new Trinitarian hermeneutics of God has for transforming the African tradition of community. Put differently, in what ways is the Trinitarian communion of God of unambiguous significance for shaping and re-forming the African concept of community?

Indeed, rediscovery of the significance of the new hermeneutics of God's perichoretic communion has multi-dimensional implications for restructuring of the African community. This is because in the face of all structural evils and their adverse distortion of the African tradition of community, my Trinitarian theological reflections cannot afford to be mere cerebral exercises. These systemic realities will no doubt shape the way we articulate our understanding of the Triune God. Undeniably, the doctrine of the Trinity is unfathomable to too many Christians, but the incomprehensibleness has to do with its abstraction from the systemic vices affecting the African people rather than the "Western-ness" of the Trinitarian categories, as many African theologians assume. Though reinterpreting the doctrine of the Trinity with African metaphysics will certainly make it comprehensible to African Christians, the best possible way to make the doctrine of the Trinity intelligible and relevant to them lies in salvaging the African tradition of community from its protracted systemic problems. The authentic African tradition of community is fully given and actualized in the gift of inclusive and reciprocal communion of the Triune God!

However, the new Trinitarian hermeneutics of God is not used in this book to mean a mere synthetic and speculative approach to the understanding of the Triune God that pieces together fragmented biblical witness to the divinity of the Son and the Spirit and their union with the Father into the doctrine of the Trinity. But it is an analytical reflection on the doctrine of the Triune God as a summary of biblical witness to God's Trinitarian communion constituted and revealed in Christ and the Spirit. This new hermeneutics of the Trinity has radical significance for impacting human and non-human relationships in church, society, and the whole of the global community.[15] I will come back to this issue in Chapters 4 and 5. This does not mean we are instrumentalizing the doctrine of the Trinity for transforming the African tradition of community, but rather, reaffirming the ongoing and eschatological in-breaking of the Triune God's gift of just, merciful, and egalitarian communion in the world via Word and Sacrament. Nonetheless, as a hermeneutics of the Triune God that is rooted in the divine economy of salvation, it has a direct bearing on what it takes for humanity to be in communion with God and with one another and the world, based on mutuality rather than pyramidal hierarchy. In the words of Catherine Mowry LaCugna, "The doctrine of the Trinity revolutionizes not only how we think of God and what it means to be human,

6 *Introduction*

it drastically transforms the political and social forms of life appropriate to God's economy."[16]

The new Trinitarian hermeneutics of God is a public discipline. It not only analyzes the ultimate truth about who God is and how God relates with creation, and us, but also investigates how God transforms us to relate to one another and the whole of creation. Thus, the mutual relation and interdependence of the distinct divine co-equal persons of the Triune God in their divine life *ad extra* (internal) and *ad intra* (external) is a critique and liberating gift for reconstructing the African practice of community. As a critique, the Trinitarian communion of God calls into question the "Big Man" syndrome, patriarchal domination, and ethnoreligious nepotism that mar the African tradition of community. As a liberating gift, God's perichoretic communion salvages the African treasured tradition of community from structural evils.

Indeed, the most promising development in contemporary theology is the rediscovery of the significance of the doctrine of the Trinity rooted in the economy of salvation. This rediscovery, which crucially impacts personal and interpersonal relationships, as we have seen on pp. 17–19. has largely remained unexplored in the contemporary African continent. The claim of this book is that the perichoretic communion of God is a liberating gift and not an ethical ideal. Martin Luther claims that God is the source and giver of every good gift. Certainly, one such great gift is the Triune perichoretic communion, which is given in Christ and distributed by the Spirit. Luther argues that Christ is not just an example; Christ is God's own gift,[17] a gift that is bestowed by the Spirit on humanity and the nonhuman world through the act of God's sheer abundant grace. Drawing on Luther's understanding of gift, we can say God's Trinitarian communion is a gift that critiques, frees, and empowers the African people. Thus, the original contribution of this work to theology is the articulation of a vibrant New Trinitarian hermeneutics of God for rethinking the African practice of community.

The key to making this contribution a reality is the explication and application of the new Trinitarian theology of God, which affirms three co-equal persons in God and their union with one another, humanity, and creation as perichoresis. The Trinitarian perichoresis, which means the Triune God's mutual life of relating to and liberating human and cosmic community, correlates,[18] critiques, and recasts the predominant African concept of community. I do not by this claim argue that God as perichoretic persons in communion is an ideal divine community that inspires Christians to live up to it in the church and society, but rather, the perichoretic communion of the Triune God constituted in Christ and gifted to them by the Spirit itself that salvages the African tradition of community. As we shall see in Chapter 5, the Triune transforms God mediates and shares with us God's own gift of perichoretic communion through the Sacrament of the Eucharist.

As a practical hermeneutics of the Triune God, the new hermeneutics of the Christian faith in the Triune God not only interprets God, but also shapes our relationships with God, our fellow humans, and the cosmic community. In other words, faith in the Triune God, which is imparted to us by the Spirit through Word and Sacrament, transforms our being and action as a church in real-world situations. As D. S. Cunningham writes, "Our faith in the triune God shapes us in profound ways – affecting what we believe, what we say, how we think, and how we live."[19] Thus the hermeneutic of the Triune God, unless it impacts the African community, is simply an abstract theological project. Hence, the authentic new hermeneutics of the Trinity must find expression in a mutually empowering service with the oppressed members of the African human and cosmic community. These oppressed members are the preferential concern of the Triune God's solidarity, justice, and mercy.

Purpose, significance, and procedure adopted

The purpose of this book is to recast the African tradition of community from the Trinitarian perspective. This does not mean we intend to either demystify the "mystery" of the Trinity or provide a perfect understanding of the Trinity. Rather, it aims to describe analytically the Trinitarian communion of God and to reclaim its radical transformative gift for critiquing and restructuring the African community. The outcome of this work will be not only to produce an authentic African understanding of community rooted in the inclusive and reciprocal gift of the Triune God, but also to make the doctrine of the Trinity lucid to a non-Western audience, the audience of which are the Triune God's vessel for spiritual and social transformation. This also leads to articulation of perichoretic theological education for theological institutions engaged in spiritual, clerical, and academic formation of church leaders. These leaders are the Triune God's earthly means of mediating the transformation in the church and society.

The significance of the work cannot be overemphasized. The work provides a practical Trinitarian analysis and proposals for reframing of the authentic African tradition of community. It is not a mere theoretical hermeneutics of the Trinity that distances itself from African contextual realities. We do not need a doctrine of the Trinity that is simply an obscure belief about God. Therefore, our hermeneutic of the doctrine of the Triune God is undertaken in a concrete way that impacts every aspect of the African life. When approached as a practical doctrine, the new Trinitarian theology of God bridges the gap between orthodoxy and orthopraxis, reflection and action, profane and sacred, religion and politics so that the authentic Trinitarian hermeneutics of God plays itself out in real-life situations. To speak rightly of God in Trinitarian terms is to speak of a God who is always involved in everyday life. To ask rightly what the new Trinitarian theology of God is up to in Africa is to affirm what the gift of the Trinitarian communion of the Triune God is up to in shaping and reshaping the faith and life of the people of Africa. The Triune God, who encounters us in Word and Sacrament, empowers us with grace to receive and embody the Trinitarian prototypical gift of equality, reciprocity, and non-hierarchy along with others in the church and society. But the Trinitarian communion of God cannot liberate Africa from systemic evils without the participation of Africans themselves, for, as Luther suggests, God does not work in us without us![20] Thus the hermeneutics of the Triune God is of crucial significance insofar as it empowers African Christians to impact every aspect of African public

8 Introduction

life. My creative contribution to the field of theology is to develop the perichoretic African theology of community rooted in the paradigmatic life of the Triune God's perichoretic communion.

There are three procedural levels at which the Trinitarian restructuring of the African tradition of community might occur. The first level is the analysis of the African tradition of community. At this level, I will describe and analyze the correlation between the African practice of community and the Trinitarian communion of God. Having done this, I unearth the systemic issues that distort and constrain the actual expression of the practice of community in Africa. In doing this, the book explores the historical background of these issues, their causes, and adverse effects on the African tradition of community, drawing on the social sciences and humanities.

The second level is unpacking of the new hermeneutics of the Trinity. At this stage, the work will describe and dissect the historical emergence and development of the doctrine of the Trinity. In doing this, mainline Trinitarian thinkers in the history of the church from the early church to modernity are individually described and analyzed. Having done this, the book describes and analyzes original contributors to the new Trinitarian reflections thematically (and not individually). The thematic approach is used because many scholars such as Ted Peters, Stanley J. Grenz, and Veli-Matti Kärkkäinen, among others, have already have done this individual approach to the study of contemporary Trinitarian theology.

The thematic approach has been adopted not only to avoid unnecessary duplication of their method, but also to complement it. This does not presuppose that the Triune God can be thematized, because the Triune God can certainly not be put into any theological system. Nevertheless, the Trinitarian reflection on the Triune God can be understood thematically without losing sight of the human limitations of that reflection! As Wolfhart Pannenberg rightly sees it, every intelligent reflection on the Triune God must begin and end with the confession of the inconceivability of God's majesty. Confessing the incomprehensibility of God's majesty, which no doubt transcends all human concepts, is no excuse at all for refraining from undertaking a critical reflection on God. Pannenberg insists, "Between this beginning and this end comes the attempt to give a rational account about God."[21] As the new Trinitarian theologies of the contemporary Trinitarian thinkers are quite dense and complicated, the thematic approach is very necessary in that it seeks to make the new Trinitarian theology of God more transparent and relevant for the African context.

The third level is where we articulate a Trinitarian communion of God as a paradigmatic gift for recasting the African tradition of community. This is the level where the transformation of that tradition becomes a reality or, in the words of Hans-Georg Gadamer, "a real fusing of horizons occurs."[22] This means that the last stage is where we participate actively with the Trinitarian God under the power of the Spirit in bringing about much-needed redemption in Africa. The third is the most decisive stage because it inspires not only a Trinitarian theological reconstruction,[23] but also, most importantly, participation of our faith that is active in love. Faith bestowed on us by the Triune God via Word and Sacrament

Introduction 9

liberates us from self-narcissism into radically living out the Trinitarian communion of God in the context of community. Confessing genuine faith in God as Trinity goes beyond merely paying lip service to the Triune God. The Trinitarian faith frees and empowers an integrated thorough living out of the Triune God's life in the concrete situations of our particular context. Genuine confession of faith in the Trinitarian God is accompanied by concrete spontaneous responses, which bring such Trinitarian faith to bear on the systemic evils that impede human and non-human well-being and development.

Without such tangible deeds springing spontaneously from our faith in the Triune God, it is just like the practice of confessing "Lord, Lord" (Matthew 7) without taking any corresponding action to do the Triune God's will – which is to build a just, merciful, peaceful, and egalitarian spiritual and temporal community. This means faith in the Triune God and its practice in a concrete situation belong together. Consequently, no amount of confessing that we "believe in God the Father, Son, and Holy Spirit" in worship can liberate the African corrupted practice of community in Africa. In fact, it might only make non-Christians (Muslims) nervous, as they believe that the doctrine of the Trinity is blasphemous anyway.

Thus, faith in God as perichoretic communion in the African context is a costly confession that generates a radical response to systemic vices, hampering the acceptance and radical embodying of God's gift of Trinitarian communion. As Dietrich Bonhoeffer puts it, "only those who believe are obedient . . . only those who are obedient believe."[24] Faith in the Triune God active in love and obedience finds expression in public life. It empowers the church as a corporate body and individuals to engage in reciprocal service along with the sinner, the poor, victims of injustice, and the degraded earth. This is the significance of the hermeneutic of the new Trinitarian theology that explicates the Triune God's perichoretic communion as a liberating gift. The goal of this book is to articulate an authentic African understanding of community drawing on this paradigmatic gift. Thus, it is designed to provide answers to the following questions:

1   What is the African tradition of community? What are the structural evils that impede total acceptance and living out of the gift of the African tradition of community, which is fully given and rooted in God's perichoretic communion?
2   What is the new hermeneutics of the Trinity? Why is the Triune God's gift of perichoretic communion significant for recasting the African tradition of community?
3   How does God's Trinitarian communion recast the African tradition of community from these systemic evils?

Scope and limitation of the book

This work is undertaken to recast the African understanding of community from the perspective of the new Trinitarian hermeneutics of God. In Chapter 1,

10   *Introduction*

I analytically describe the African tradition of community, which emphasizes not personal but communal relationships binding together the living as well as the living dead. The African concept of community is correlated with the Trinitarian communion in terms of relatedness, interdependence, and openness to the other. As this Chapter deals with the Trinitarian recasting of the African concept of community with specific reference to Nigeria, it contains a brief description of the evolution of Nigeria as a nation-state, which sets the background of the entire book. In Chapter 2, the book undertakes the critical description of the structural issues: the Big Man syndrome, patriarchal domination, and ethno-religious nepotism that are inimical to African society.

In Chapter 3, I analyze mainline Trinitarian thinkers from the fourth century to the early part of the modern era. Such historical analysis is necessary because it provides us with a sound historical basis on which the contemporary Trinitarian theology is built. We cannot fully comprehend the new hermeneutics of the Trinity and its significance for contemporary society and church without its historical background. We cannot know where we are today regarding the doctrine of the Trinity, let alone where we will be tomorrow without knowing where we were previously. This, however, does not mean that this is a comprehensive history of the emergence and development of the doctrine of the Trinity. The early Trinitarian controversies and ecumenical councils convened to settle them are beyond the scope of this book. Instead, this book is limited to select Western, Eastern, and African mainline Trinitarian thinkers in the past and today.

In Chapter 4, I undertake a systematic analysis of the various ideas of the contributors (Pannenberg, Moltmann, Zizioulas, LaCugna, and Boff) of the new hermeneutics of the Trinity with reference to the hermeneutical starting point, perichoretic relations, and the unity of the Triune God. I specifically describe whether or not the economy of salvation rather than abstract metaphysics is the reliable epistemological ground to start off any authentic Trinitarian hermeneutics. I also investigate whether or not mutual or pyramidal relations of the Trinitarian persons truly express the interpersonal perichoretic communion of the Triune God and whether or not the unity of such Trinitarian communion excludes or includes humanity and the whole of creation. The essence of the analytical description is to create a coherent theology of God's perichoretic communion for reconstructing the African community.

In Chapter 5, the book embarks on the Trinitarian recasting of the African tradition of community in Nigeria and, by extension, the whole of Africa. In other words, it reframes the African practice of community, in both a faith-based and secular sense (church and society) rooted in the paradigmatic gift of God's perichoretic reciprocity, equality, and freedom. This book neither charts a new course of understanding of Trinitarian theology nor constructs a new African Trinitarian theology, even though it does not rule out the possibility of providing new insights in this direction. Though the book theologically recasts the African tradition of community by drawing on the gift of God's perichoretic communion, it does not articulate an elaborate, concrete plan of action for effective practical implementation of this theological proposal in Africa. Drawing up such guidelines would require another book.

The African tradition of community: what is it?

The African tradition of community, which developed over time, is as old as the African community. The tradition is more than a group of African people living together in a specific location. It is about the nexus of relationships between the people that transcends earthly boundaries. As Ogbonnaya rightly sees it, in the African ontological framework, a community is not merely a physical network of relationships between physical persons, it is spiritual bond that binds people together across infinite spans of time and space in unbreakable relationships, which includes the living as well as the "living dead" – ancestors and spirits.[25] K.A. Dickson also affirms that

> The African sense of community requires the recognition of the presence of the ancestors as the rallying point of the group's solidarity and they, being the custodians of law and morality, may punish or reward in order to ensure the maintenance of the group's equilibrium.[26]

Neglecting or severing the communal relationship with the ancestors and other members of the community results not only in conflict with other human beings, but also in natural disasters which are a mark of disharmony in the community. Therefore, there must be an undisturbed harmonious relationship between God, the deities, the ancestors, and human beings if the community is to experience peace, prosperity, and the good life.

Consequently, in the African traditional communal worldview, sacred and secular aspects of life belong together in the communal life. The good of every communal activity and social institution is bound up with religion. John Mbiti maintains that "because traditional religions permeate all the departments of life, there is no formal distinction between the sacred and the secular, between the religious and the non-religious, between the spiritual and the material areas of life."[27] As God is an integral part of the concept of community, the role, responsibility, and relationship that a person has in the family and the community are seen as divinely ordered. As John Parrat claims,

> God himself is the ultimate source of life, and he is its fullness. The degree to which a person participates in the life of the community is determined by social rank, beginning from the invisible order . . . to the visible order of the king and queen mother, the heads of clan and families, and, finally the individual.[28]

Fulfilling one's role in the community is valued much more than personal self-development, and neglecting one's responsibility (as we will see on p. 28.) not

12   Introduction

only disrupts life in the community, but also affects the personality of a person, since the family and community, where one plays the role, determine one's identity. Thus, many people have to go out of their way to perform their role in the community – even to the detriment of their personal goals and plans to maintain their integrity and identity. Such unbreakable communal relationships and social responsibility, which have become a way of life binding people together and giving them a sense of identity, and continuity determine who the people are and the way they live. Without such a communal identity, people will ordinarily feel confused and lost.

The critical part or aspect of the African tradition of community is the relation between a person and the community. In African thought, Ogbonnaya claims people are not first and foremost individuals before they are related to the community; rather, they are primordially connected to the community before they are individuals.[29] He contends that the African sense of community, holding a person and community in balance, is an indestructible spiritual bond which neither death nor distance can destroy. The bond between person and the community is so fixed that their rights, duties, and responsibilities are not divorced from that of the community. The connection between a person and the community is so intimate that whatever affects a person affects the entire community, and vice versa. As Mbiti suggests,

> Whatever happens to the individual happens to the whole group, and whatever happens to the whole group happens to the individual. The individual can only say: 'I am, because we are; and since we are, therefore I am.' This is a cardinal point in the understanding of the African view of man.[30]

Some of the Western missionaries who brought the gospel to Africa dismissed virtually everything about African tradition as superstitious, uncultured, and barbaric, as we shall see later in the next section on p. 32–33. But the most compelling quality of the African tradition of community is its reflection of the communal character of the Triune God. Several examples abound. Just as no person of the Trinity can exist apart from the others, so a person in the community does not and cannot exist alone except in relation to the community. Just as one person of the Godhead is a person only through the others, a person in an African community is a person only through members of the community, and owes their existence to those today and in the past.

Similar to how the divine persons of the perichoretic Trinity are dependent on each other for their personal identity and divinity, a person in the African communal culture is entirely reliant on the community for their identity. A person does not have the freedom to determine their own identity; the community gives this freedom to them: "The community must therefore make, create or produce the individual[,] for the individual depends on the corporate group."[31] Communality is an essential part of an African's being and identity. There is no way a person cannot be communal in their interpersonal relation. Thus, freedom in African communal life is not *from* the other; rather, it is freedom *for* the other. To be a free person is

Introduction 13

not to pursue extreme personal liberty and privacy by avoiding the other, but to be in relationship with other members of the community. As F.A. Oborji accurately observes, traditional Africans place humanity (the individual and community) at the center of consideration. Oborji asserts that "for traditional Africans, humanity is first and foremost the community . . . individuals acquire their basic identity through [their relationships with other members of the community]."[32] Such communal interdependence, through which the people depend on each other for identity, care, support, and security, is valued over and above individualism and personal independence. This is much like the Triune God, where there is no individualism except mutual interdependence. Therefore, the life of a person is bound up with that of the community such that detaching oneself from the community means severing oneself from the foundation of one's being and security.[33] In the words of D.N. Hopkins, "to be me is to be a result of the existence of a conditional we."[34]

Therefore, to lose one's community is to lose one's own identity. According to Augustine Shutte, unlike in European thought, which views the self as something which lies "inside in a person," the self "in African thought is something which lies 'outside,' subsisting in relationship to what is other, the natural and social environment."[35] This openness to the other replicates the openness of the perichoretic communion of the Trinity to accept the whole of humanity and the world into the divine life. As the perichoretic divine persons are "centers of relationships" with one another and all of creation, so the person in African thought is the center of relationship with the community and natural environment. It is in relation to the physical and social environment that they live, move, and find happiness. Descartes' maxim "I think, therefore, I am" is reversed in the African context of community to mean "I am related, therefore, we are."[36] This, however, does not suggest that reason is inconsequential in one's interpersonal relationship with others, but that it is relationality and not human reason that ontologically defines a person. Put differently, a person is not conscious of himself or herself in isolation, but in the company of the group, who sharpen personal consciousness and appreciate one's existence. It is then that the individual can say "I am, therefore I think." Hence, personal expressions of wisdom do not have a copyright; they are properties of the community.

Therefore, as the being of the Triune God is communal, a person in the African sense is a communal being. As Kwame Gyekye suggests, in African thought, a person is "embedded in the context of social relationships and interdependence, and never as an isolated, atomic individual."[37] To belong to a community is not a matter of choice for a person, it is an inherent human character since one must not and cannot exist apart from other members of the community. As a divine person of the Trinity is constituted by their relationship with others, so only their relation to the other members of the community constitutes a person in the African worldview. A person is always implicated in an intricate web of social relationships at every level of the community. Sipho Mtetwa writes,

> One of the most remarkable and tangible dimensions of African spirituality relates to the unique notion of communality and collective solidarity that the

14 *Introduction*

African society exhibits in all spheres of life. There is a profound sense of interdependence, from the extended family to the entire community.[38]

As a result of this complex network of relationships, there is hardly such a thing as a personal problem in African community. Every personal problem has a communal dimension. For example, when there is a disagreement between a married couple, the problem is never left to the couple alone to resolve. It takes the intervention of the whole community to resolve the conflict. As Polycarp Ikuenobe claims,

> Marital problems usually call for and necessitate counseling and intervention by elders and family members. As a communal issue, the people who have to intervene and counsel the couple have a stake and social responsibility in ensuring the success of the relationship.[39]

He contends that such an African communal way of resolving marital problems differs from the Western practice of counseling, where the couple are often left alone to "sort it out" by themselves or the counseling therapist has nothing at stake except their payment. Similarly, when African people say, "we have been attacked," it means one member of their community was attacked, hence the whole of the community, and not just the victim. The whole community takes the responsibility for the misdeed. This does not imply that a person takes no responsibility for her misconduct; rather, she does not do so alone, that is, the community to which the person belongs is unavoidably implicated in the misdeed.

As such, even suffering is not just a personal problem. It is a communal issue, and a person does not suffer alone apart from other members of the community. When a person suffers, the whole community suffers along with the person so that the suffering becomes a shared burden, which every member of the community carries. Mbiti claims, "When he suffers, he does not suffer alone, but with the corporate group; when he rejoices, he rejoices not alone but with his kinsmen, his neighbours, and his relatives whether dead or living."[40] Ikuenobe also underscores such an idea of corporate solidarity in suffering when he writes,

> The problem of an individual becomes other people's or the community's problem, and usually, the community's problem. . . . The communal structures in African cultures help to reduce the stress of dealing with many life problems by oneself alone, and they also provide structures of social responsibilities, relationships, and expectations by constant reinforcement, chiding, ribbing or prodding. This is a sharp contrast from the practice or attitude in the West. . . . Because of its extreme individualism and privacy, when one has a problem, one keeps it to oneself.[41]

Ikuenobe further contends that such is not the case in African community. He claims, "The [African] communal way of life, and the social responsibility it engenders, indicates that family, friends and neighbors have to help one to cope

Introduction   15

with difficult and stressful aspects of one's life."[42] This expression of the African collective solidarity in suffering with a person correlates or reflects expression of the corporate solidarity by the Father and the Spirit – not just with the suffering of the Son on the cross, but also with resurrection of the Son from death. As the resurrection is the victory of the entire Triune God over sin, death, and the devil, and not that of the Son alone, so the victory or success of one person in the African organic community becomes the victory or joy of the entire community. As such, a person cannot single-handedly enjoy or celebrate success alone devoid of other living and living dead members of the community. E. A. Ruch and K. C. Anyanwu rightly put it,

> The whole African society, living and living-dead, is a living network of relations almost like that between the various parts of an organism. When one part of the body is sick the whole body is affected. When one member of a family or clan is honoured or successful, the whole group rejoices and shares in the glory, not only psychologically . . . but ontologically: each member of the group is really part of the honour.[43]

This shows the ontological and experiential interconnectedness of the people, sharing in common every aspect and experience of life. Therefore, to isolate oneself from this shared life of the community not only undermines the identity of a person, but also the collective good of the community.

In effect, the communal sharing of life, problems, property, power, and events among the members of the African community is a reflection of the communal sharing of life, monarchy, suffering, and resurrection among the divine persons of the Triune God. As such, it is not an overstatement to say that even the African understanding of the church, and above all the Christian faith, is shaped by such an African communal worldview. Unlike in the West, where the Christian religion is a personal faith, in Africa, Christianity is more than simply a private matter. It is both personal and communal faith. The dictum that defines the identity of a Christian in Africa is "I am who I am by faith alone because of who are we in Christ." Seen in this light, the church is more than just a functional community of separate members, where the word is preached and the sacraments are duly administered, it is an *obuntu*[44] community in relationships where the Christians faithfully find the true meaning and purpose of their relationships with God, one another, and all of God's creation. There is no one who is morally and spiritually autonomous; the people are mutually dependent on one another for moral and spiritual formation, nourishment, and empowerment. It is only in communal relationships and collaboration that the people discover the ultimate truth of what it means to be the concrete body of Christ in the world.

The interdependence, solidarity, and togetherness that the African tradition emphasizes promotes the communal understanding of evil and salvation. Evil and salvation have always had a communal dimension. Consequently, any evil that befalls one member of the community invariably affects every member of the community. Similarly, salvation is not simply a private, underserved divine favor,

16   *Introduction*

but communal grace that impacts the entire community. The communal insignia, which the church has assumed in Africa, is a powerful strength of African Christianity that may re-create a value of shared life (in the West) where extreme individualism has become the normative way of life.

Indeed, both the Trinitarian relationality and the African theory and practice of community are characterized by relationships, interdependence, and openness to the other. This correlation shows that the African practice of community corresponds somewhat to the perichoretic life of the Triune of God, and this may indicate that Africans do faintly bear the communal image of the Triune God. But unlike the Trinitarian relationality, which is characterized by reciprocity and equality, African practice of community is based on complementary role relationships, hierarchy, and ethnic and religious nepotism, which not only marginalize some members of the community, but also result in ethnic and religious violence. I will come back to these issues in the next chapter. By and large, freedom (*with* the other), which is central to Trinitarian relationality, is either missing or undermined in the African communal way of life, which overemphasizes the community at the expense of the individual. Even if there is freedom, it is merely a freedom *for* and not *with* the other.

Evolution of Nigeria as a nation-state

It is paramount to briefly describe the history of Nigeria, the context in which the book recasts the African concept of community. In the following section, I describe analytically the colonial and post-colonial history of Nigeria. While the bulk of the book has to do with the contemporary Nigerian secular and faith community, what is not included in this section is the pre-colonial history of Nigeria. The evolutionary formation of Nigeria as an independent geo-political nation-state occurs over a considerable period of time, dating back to the time of colonialism. Thus, it is significant to begin the account of the evolutionary emergence of Nigeria with the fundamental assumptions that undergirded the colonization and Christianization of Africa, and particularly Nigeria.

Some European scholars assumed at the turn of the nineteenth century that Africa had neither history nor development to exhibit to the world as a mark of its civilization. These European scholars claimed that the African peoples are natural human beings existing completely in a wild and untamed state. They lack any idea of God and law necessary for full realization of human volition and existence, and thus needed to be tamed and domesticated with European religion and civilization. Friedrich Hegel claimed this succinctly: "What we properly understand by Africa, is the Unhistorical, Undeveloped Spirit, still involved in the conditions of mere nature, and which had to be presented here only as on the threshold of the World's History."[45] Suggesting that Africans lack any category of Universality and sense of humanity, Hegel claimed that one must lay aside all thought of reverence and morality in order to comprehend them rightly. As people who lack the fully developed consciousness to distinguish between themselves as individuals and the universality of their essential being, Hegel claimed that the Africans are

Introduction 17

altogether devoid of the "Knowledge of an absolute Being, an Other and a Higher than [their] individual self."[46] Far from being seen as wrong, Hegel claimed that tyranny and cannibalism among Africans are considered to be quite customary and proper. Richard F. Burton also claimed that the African, as a lower human race, inferior to the European, is characterized by "childish passion." In the words of Burton, the African

> "is inferior to the active-minded and objective . . . Europeans, and to the . . . subjective and reflective Asiatic. He partakes largely of the worst characteristics of the lower Oriental types – stagnation of mind, indolence of body, moral deficiency, superstition, and childish passion.[47]

Such an exotic representation of Africa was instrumental in European colonization and Christianization. The scramble for Africa that culminated in the agreement of 1884 provided the political justification for British colonization, and by extension Christianization, of Nigeria. Patrick Brantlinger argues that "the British tended to see Africa as a center of evil, a part of the world possessed by a demonic 'darkness' or barbarism, represented above all by slavery and cannibalism, which it was their duty to exorcise."[48] He claims that missionaries such as David Livingstone believed that Africa was doomed forever to savagery and damnation without the European, who is the bearer of the "light" of civilization and true religion to this Dark Continent. It was because of these exotic perceptions of Africa that the British and other missionaries colonized and Christianized Nigeria. They created not only an artificial nation, as we shall see in the following paragraphs and in Chapter 4, but also introduced an exclusive understanding of Christianity. All of which had devastating consequences for the African practice of community. Having said this, we shall now turn to the evolution of Nigeria as a nation-state right from the colonial era.

Nigeria, the most populous black African country in the world, is located on the coast of Western Africa, sharing common borders with the Republics of Benin, Niger, Cameroon, and Chad. The emergence of Nigeria as a single political enclave began in 1861, when the British colonial government first annexed Lagos as a crown colony. Thereafter, under the inspiration of the Berlin Conference, held in 1884–5 for the partition of the African continent by the European imperial powers, Britain was able to conquer southwestern Nigeria in 1897 and northern Nigeria in 1903, marking the complete conquest of the entire "country." By 1906, Britain divided the whole of Nigeria into the Southern Protectorate and Northern Protectorate. The geo-political entity called "Nigeria" came into existence in its present form only when Sir Frederick Lugard, who became its first Governor General, amalgamated the two Protectorates in 1914. According to Michael Crowder, "Sixteen years earlier, Flora Shaw, who later married Lugard, first suggested in an article for *The Times* that the several British Protectorates on the Niger be known collectively as Nigeria."[49]

The amalgamation was a crucial landmark in the history of the country and partly responsible for its past and current socio-religious and political woes. As

18   *Introduction*

an artificial creation by the British colonial administration, the amalgamation brought together people of incompatible ethnic and religious diversity, as we will see later in Chapter 4, who have hardly tolerated and co-existed with one another as an indivisible nation. This is because most of the ethnic national communities brought together were sharply divided along linguistic, religious, geographical, and cultural lines and thus virtually hostile toward one other. As A. T. Mbachirin argues,

> The different groups brought together were not willing to live together for religious and socio-economic reasons. The various groups were at different stages of economic and political development. Thus it was protested and there were numerous secession threats before and after the independence.[50]

This division was aggravated by Lugard's decision to administer Northern and Southern Protectorates through an "indirect rule" as separate geo-political provinces even after the amalgamation.[51] Following the amalgamation and protest of Nigerian nationalists against what they considered to be "non-inclusion" by the colonial administrators in the running of the affairs of their own country,[52] the Nigerian Legislative Council was in 1922 established by the Sir Hugh Clifford Constitution. It had limited powers, but was based on the principle of direct democratic election into the Council. The membership of the Legislative Council elected only from Lagos and Calabar excluded the Northern Province. Later, in 1939, the Southern Province was divided into the Eastern and Western Provinces, and this administrative expansion not only brought the total number of the provinces to three, but also broadened African participation in the administration of their own nation. The three provinces, which were disproportionate (i.e., the North was larger than the West and the East combined), were renamed "Regions" in 1954 as part of the evolutionary process of reconstructing Nigeria into a federal state. While the Hausa-Fulani dominated the North, the Yoruba and Igbo dominated the West and the East, respectively. A more democratic government did not emerge after 1922 until the "Richards Constitution" of 1947, which, in addition to the Central Legislative Council for Nigeria, provided for Houses of Assembly in each of the three Regions and the House of Chiefs, specifically for the Northern Region. Though the Richards Constitution marked a turning point in Nigeria's journey toward self-government, it was drafted without the consultation of the people, and thus it was short-lived. As Alan Burns claims, "Although it had been intended that the 1947 Constitution should run for six years, it was replaced in 1951 by a new [Macpherson] constitution."[53]

The Macpherson Constitution, which was drafted with the due consultation of Nigerians, provided for a central House of Representatives. Consequently, political parties were formed to run for various elective positions at the regional and national levels. The three main parties that emerged were the National Council of Nigeria and the Cameroons (NCNC) in the East, the Action Group (AG) in the West, and the Northern People's Congress (NPC) in the North. But, like the Richards Constitution, the regional and ethnic character of the parties fueled the

Introduction 19

power tussle between the central and regional legislatures that eventually led to its demise. Following two crucial constitutional conferences held in London and Lagos between Nigerian leaders and the British government in 1953 and 1954, a new constitution was drafted and came into effect on October 1954. The new constitution established the Federation of Nigeria and created the Federal Territory of Lagos.[54] The impact of the 1954 constitution was that it brought an end to the Nigerian political leaders' struggle with the British government and got them preoccupied with the issues of daily administration, development, and negotiation of the unity of their own country. By 1957, the Eastern and Western Regions were granted internal self-governing status, and two years later, the Northern Region also followed suit.

The entirety of Nigeria was granted its long-fought-for independence on October 1, 1960, and Dr Azikiwe became the first indigenous Governor General. As a result, Nigeria became a member of the Commonwealth and the United Nations. The option of staying in or leaving Nigeria was also given to the regions then known as Northern and Southern Cameroon. While Southern Cameroon decided to join francophone Cameroon, Northern Cameroon chose to remain with Nigeria. A federal system of government based on parliamentary democracy was adopted on October 1, 1963, when Nigeria became a republic. Dr Azikiwe became its first President, while Sir Abubakar Tafawa Balewa became the Prime Minister. In January 1966, Nigeria experienced the tragic end of its first republic when a group of young army officers (many of whom were Igbos) overthrew the federal government in a bloody coup and assassinated the Prime Minister, Premiers of the Northern and Western Regions, and many senior army officers. The fact that none of the Igbo Premiers had been murdered except one Igbo senior army officer made the coup a purely Igbo affair and thus unpopular. Announcing the reasons for the coup to the nation, Major Chukwuma Nzeogwu accused the politicians of corruption, tribalism, and nepotism, saying,

> Our enemies are the political profiteers, swindlers, the men in high and low places that seek bribes and demand 10 percent, those that seek to keep the country permanently divided so that they can remain in office as Ministers and VIPs of waste, the tribalists, the nepotists.[55]

Major General Johnson Aguiyi-Ironsi, the only surviving senior army officer at the time, became the head of state. Surrounding himself with advisors from his ethnic group, the Igbo, Ironsi dissolved the Regional governments and imposed a unitary government on the whole of the country. But this decision not only met with severe resistance from the Northern politicians, who perceived the unitary system as a calculated stratagem by the Igbos to dominate them, but also resulted in the merciless massacre of hundreds of Igbos in the North.[56] The chaos that ensued made the country quite ungovernable for Ironsi. The entire country, including the military, became factionalized along ethnic and regional lines. In July 1966, a group of northern army officers staged a countercoup, in which Aguiyi-Ironsi was assassinated, and Lt. Col. (later Gen.) Yakubu Gowon rose to power as the head

20 Introduction

of the military government. In 1967, Gowon promulgated a decree splitting the existing four regions of Nigeria into 12 states, which allayed fears of the minority ethnic groups and gave them a sense of belonging to the nation. But the Military Governor of the Eastern Region at the time, Lt. Col. Odumegwu Ojukwu, refused to recognize either the position of Gowon as the Head of the Armed Forces or the division of his Eastern Region. As a result, three days after Gowon's creation of the 12 states, Ojukwu declared the Eastern Region to be a sovereign republic of Biafra. Though new discovery of oil in the Region made the secession even more popular and attractive to the Igbos, it launched the rest of the country into a dismal civil war with Biafra. The war, which began as a mere "police action" in June 1967, came to an end with the surrender of Biafra on January 15, 1970.

Gowon not only magnanimously proclaimed after the war that there was neither victor nor vanquished, but also reconciled and integrated the two warring factions into the united Nigeria. Proclaiming a "Second Development Plan" on October 1, 1970, designed to transform Nigeria into a just and egalitarian community, he wrote:

> A just and egalitarian society puts a premium on reducing inequalities in inter-personal incomes and promoting balanced development among the various communities. . . . It organizes its economic institutions in such a way that there is no oppression based on class, social status and ethnic group or state.[57]

But failing to deliver on the promise of handing over power to civil rule in 1974, Gowon was overthrown on July 29, 1975, in a bloodless coup. Brigadier (later General) Murtala Ramat Muhammed assumed power as the head of the new military government. Believed to be the best Nigerian head of state ever, Muhammed, among other, things further divided the existing 12 states into 19 states, but more importantly, he audaciously fought corruption and inefficiency in public service. He also drew up the plans to move the Federal Capital Territory from Lagos to Abuja. However, without executing his plan to return power to civil government, he was murdered in a failed coup d'état in January of 1976. Lt. General Olusegun Obasanjo became the head of the government. Adhering faithfully to the plan of his predecessor to hand over the government to the civilian regime, Obasanjo successfully conducted elections in 1979. Alhaji Shehu Shagari, who ran for the presidency under the umbrella of the National Party of Nigeria (NPN), won the presidential election, defeating his close rival, Chief Obafemi Awolowo, who vied under the banner of the Unity Party of Nigeria (UPN).[58]

Shagari was re-elected in August of 1983, but owing to the massive fraud that marred the election, and above all, corruption that characterized his government, he was overthrown in December of 1983 in a military coup and Major General Muhammadu Buhari took over the mantle of the leadership of the country. To fight indiscipline, corruption, and lack of environmental sanitation among Nigerians, Buhari declared what was called a "War Against Indiscipline" (WAI), in which many were arrested and imprisoned. He also promulgated Decree No. 5, which gagged the press from publishing "false" information that would tarnish the image of the government.[59] In the wake of the growing unpopularity of his regime, in August of 1985, Buhari was deposed in yet another coup, which elevated Major General Ibrahim Babangida to power. Babangida increased the numbers of the states from 19 to 30 and in 1991 moved the national capital from Lagos to Abuja. After much procrastination of the deadline of transition to civil rule, he reluctantly allowed a presidential election to be held on June 12, 1993. Though national and international observers believed that the election was the freest and fairest ever and was apparently won by Chief M.K.O. Abiola, a Yoruba business tycoon, Babangida, against all odds, annulled the result.[60] As the evil a person does lives after them, the political turmoil caused by the annulment eventually led to his abrupt exit from office.

General Sani Abacha, who became the President, forced (at gunpoint) the appointed head of the Interim National Government, Ernest Shonekan, out of office after three months. As the most vicious leader Nigeria ever had, apart from institutionalizing corruption, Abacha was an embodiment of military tyranny and impunity. As Toyin Falola accurately contends,

> Abacha had shown himself as the country's most brutal leader to date – he jailed or killed his opponents, flagrantly violated human rights, and disregarded domestic and international opinion. The country became a rogue state, condemned by nearly every other country on earth for Abacha's political excess and the irrationality of [its] military rulers.[61]

This accounts for why Abacha's sudden, untimely death in June of 1998, which brought General Abdulsalam Abubakar to power, was widely celebrated by most Nigerians across the country. Upon assumption of office, Abubakar swiftly released political detainees (one of whom was Obasanjo, who later became the first democratically elected civilian President after 19 years of military dictatorship), unrolled a fresh plan of transition to democratic rule, and lifted the ban on politics. Political parties were formed, and in February of 1999, a presidential election was conducted. General Obasanjo, the flag bearer of the People's Democratic Party (PDP), was declared the winner and was sworn in on May 29, 1999, to rule the nation in accordance with the provisions of the new constitution drafted that month. After serving for two terms, Obasanjo handed over power to Umaru Yar'Adua, who sadly died from kidney disease on May 5, 2010, before completing his first term of office.

His Vice President, Goodluck Jonathan, was sworn in as the new president and commander-in-chief of the armed forces of the country. Jonathan, who served only for one term, was defeated in his bid for re-election in the March 28, 2015, poll. He became the first sitting Nigerian president in the history of Nigeria not only to lose an election, but also to concede defeat. According to the *Reuters* news service, Jonathan said, "Nobody's ambition is worth the blood of any Nigerian."[62] Muhammadu Buhari, who was the winner of the election, was sworn in to succeed Jonathan on May 29, 2015, to run the affairs of the country for the next four years.

Ever since 1999, Nigeria has had a presidential system of government with three distinct but related arms: the Executive, the Legislative, and the Judicial.

22 *Introduction*

Post-independence Nigeria is today a federation of 36 states, including the Federal Capital Territory (FCT), Abuja.

Stated briefly, the exotic stereotype of Africa as a primitive and idolatrous continent, which stood in need of the European civilization and Christian conversion in the nineteenth century, is what led to the eventual colonization and Christianization of Nigeria. The lasting legacy of British colonialism is the artificial creation of Nigeria as a nation-state. Amalgamating diverse ethnic and religious communities into one nation, British colonialism has created a country that is virtually unsustainable politically and religiously. This is evident by the military coups and counter coups, and the protracted ethnic and religious conflicts, which have continued to threaten the stability of the country. What further exacerbates such national instability is the colonial introduction of an extreme modern form of individualism, which is in many ways foreign to the African communal way of life. This modern European individualistic life, which leads to self-centeredness and greed, still expresses itself in the present religious and political institutions, where the public treasury intended for the common good is massively looted for personal enrichment. We will come back to this issue in Chapter 4. In other words, the selfish and exploitative character of the colonizer-colonized relationship, which characterized the colonial administration, has continued to manifest itself in the form of the "Big Man" syndrome even in the current African political and ecclesiastical leadership. This by no means implies that British colonialism is entirely responsible for the post-colonial political, religious, and social woes of Nigeria. But rather, the foundation for such discord and egoism, which was laid by colonialism during the colonial period, is persistently being sustained through colonial legacies with the complicity of Nigerian public leaders.

The impact of colonialism, which is subtle, takes varied forms and guises, affecting not only Africans' institutions, but also human imagination and perception. The colonial portrayal of the African mind as unreflective regarding transcendent reality is what impacts the attitude of many African Christian theologians that the conception of the Trinitarian God is too abstract and complicated. African scholars, who argue that the doctrine of the Trinity is quite metaphysical and thus incomprehensible to Africans, continue to share in and express the colonial assumption of the unreflective cognition of the African people in matters of ultimate reality. But as we shall see in Chapter 3, the God the Africans perceived in nature and worshipped through various divinities prior to the advent of Christianity is the same God of the Bible, who reveals Godself in Christ through the Spirit to them in Word and Sacraments. Thus, deconstructing the colonial assumption which impacts the African perception of the doctrine of the Triune God is critical for reclaiming the authentic African perception of the Triune God, which resonates, critiques, and reconstructs the African concept of community. It is against this political, religious, and social backdrop of Nigeria and the colonial African perception of the doctrine of the Triune God that we find it compelling to analyze the new hermeneutics of the Trinity for recasting the African tradition of community.

Notes

1 Hermeneutics is the method of understanding and interpreting specifically the doctrine of the Trinity as rooted and revealed in the economy of salvation.

2 As we will elaborate later in Chapter 4, the word "perichoretic" is derived from "perichoresis," which refers to the mutual indwelling of the divine persons of the Triune God not only in themselves alone, but also in humanity and creation.

3 The words "concept," "tradition," "idea," and "notion" are used interchangeably to refer to the African community in this book.

4 K. A. Dickson, *Aspects of Religion and Life in Africa* (Accra: Ghana Academic of Arts and Science, 1977), 4.

5 Kwame Gyekye, "Person and Community in African Thought," in *The African Philosophy Reader*, ed. Lesiba J. Teffo and Abraham P. J. Roux (London: Routledge, 1998), 317–34.

6 Mika Vähäkangas, "African Approaches to the Trinity," in *African Theology Today*, ed. Emmanuel Kantogole (Scranton, PA: University of Scranton Press, 2002), 69.

7 Gabriel M. Setiloane, "Where Are We in African Theology," in *African Theology En Route: Papers from the Pan-African Conference of Third World Theologians, December 17–23, 1977, Accra, Ghana*, ed. Kofi Appiah-Kubi and Sergio Torres (Maryknoll, NY: Orbis Books, 1979), 64–5.

8 Cristopher Mwoleka, "Trinity and Communion," *African Ecclesiastical Review* 17, no. 4 (1975): 203.

9 J. N. Kanyua Mugambi, *The African Heritage and Contemporary Christianity* (Nairobi: Longman, 1989), 77. I think there is nothing wrong with re-interpreting the doctrine of the Trinity with African categories, but to recast the Trinity in terms of African monotheism is erroneous. There is no such thing as "African monotheism," and even if there were, it would not be incompatible with the doctrine of the Trinity. Second, it amounts to modalism and denial of the basis of Christian salvation in Christ through the Spirit.

10 Ibid., 75. Emphasis in the original.

11 This is also true of Pentecostals. They are in many respects so concerned with the person and work of the Spirit that they forget that the person and work of the Spirit are bound up with the other members of the Trinity.

12 There is a very common adage in Hausa (which is the *lingua franca* of northern Nigeria) that says "shugabanci Allah ne ke bayaswa; bin na gaba bin Allah ne." This means "it is God who gives leadership and following your leader corresponds to following God." Northern Nigeria is a predominantly Islamic geo-political zone with massive concentrations of monarchial traditional rulers in both urban and rural areas. Since, in principle, Christians and Muslims alike believe in one God, the implication of this is that any leadership position one attains – be it familial, political, or religious – not only derives its powers from God, which demands others must bow as they bow before God, but also that just as God is one, there is always one ruler who shares his authority with no one. Such a God-like ruler wields absolute power. Thus, whoever is in a position of leadership, even in the family, becomes a boss and owner (of everything) who works for their own personal interests rather than the common good of the society. I will come back to this issue in Chapter 4.

13 Stephen O. Adenle and Raymond Uwameiye, "Issues in Utilization of Equalization of Educational Opportunities: Implication for Peace Education in Nigeria," *International Journal of Academic Research in Progressive Education and Development* 1, no. 4 (2012): 347–8.

14 Leonardo Boff, *Trinity and Society*, trans. Paul Burns (Eugene, OR: Wipf & Stock Publishers, 1988), 13.

15 The book does not propose here to synthesize a contemporary understanding of the Trinity with African traditional understanding of God or to develop an African

24 *Introduction*

understanding of the Trinity. For an African understanding of the Trinity see among others, Charge Nyamiti, "The Trinity from African Ancestral Perspective," *African Christian Studies* 12 (1996) 38–74; A. Okechukwu Ogbonnaya, *On Communitarian Divinity: An African Interpretation of the Trinity* (New York, NY: Paragon House, 1994); James Henry Owino Kombo, *The Doctrine of God in African Christian Thought: The Holy Trinity, Theological Hermeneutics, and the African Intellectual Culture* (Leiden; Boston, MA: Brill, 2007).

16 Catherine Mowry LaCugna, *God for Us: The Trinity and Christian Life* (San Francisco, CA: HarperSanFrancisco, 1991), 16.

17 Martin Luther, "Lectures on Galatians 1535, Chapters 5–6," in *Luther's Works*, ed. Jaroslav Pelikan and Walter A. Hansen, vol. 27 (Saint Louis, MO: Concordia Publishing House, 1964), 34–5.

18 By "correlate," I do not mean that the African tradition of community is identical or fits perfectly (corresponded) with perichoretic communion of God, but rather that it has a striking semblance with God's perichoretic communion, and hence it bears a vestige of that communion.

19 David S. Cunningham, *These Three Are One: The Practice of Trinitarian Theology* (Malden, MA: Blackwell Publishers, 1998), ix.

20 Martin Luther, "The Bondage of the Will," in *Luther's Works*, ed. Philip S. Watson and Hulmut Lehmann, vol. 33 (Philadelphia, PA: Fortress Press, 1972), 243.

21 Wolfhart Pannenberg, *Systematic Theology*, trans. Geoffrey W. Bromiley, vol. 1 (Grand Rapids, MI: Eerdmans, 1991), 337.

22 Hans-Georg Gadamer, *Truth and Method*, trans. Weinsheimer Joel and Donald G. Marshall, 2nd ed. (New York, NY: Continuum, 2004), 306.

23 Though the third stage might sound semi-Pelagian to those who have not attended closely to Luther's rich dialectical theology, the Triune God does not desire to act in us to transform the tripartite structural evils that undercut the tangible, full realization of the African traditional of community in Africa consistent with God's perichoretic of communion without us.

24 Dietrich Bonhoeffer, *A Testament to Freedom: The Essential Writings of Dietrich Bonhoeffer*, ed. Geffrey B. Kelly and F. Burton Nelson (San Francisco, CA: HarperSanFrancisco, 1995), 311.

25 Ogbonnaya, *On Communitarian Divinity*, 8.

26 Kwesi A. Dickson, *Theology in Africa* (London: Longman & Todd Ltd, 1984), 70.

27 John S. Mbiti, *African Religions & Philosophy* (New York, NY: Praeger, 1969), 2.

28 John Parrat, *Reinventing Christianity: African Theology Today* (Grand Rapids: MI: Eerdmans, 1995), 92.

29 Ogbonnaya, *On Communitarian Divinity*, 10–11.

30 Mbiti, *African Religions & Philosophy*, 141.

31 Ibid.

32 Francis Anekwe Oborji, "Building Relationship in Mixed African Communities," http://sedosmission.org/old/eng/oborji_3.htm (accessed October 14, 2014).

33 Mbiti, *African Religions & Philosophy*, 2.

34 Dwight N. Hopkins, *Being Human: Race, Culture, and Religion* (Minneapolis, MN: Fortress Press, 2005), 83.

35 Augustine Shutte, *Philosophy for Africa* (Rodenbosch: University of Cape Town Press, 1993), 47.

36 Hopkins, *Being Human: Race, Culture, and Religion*, 74.

37 Gyekye, "Person and Community in African Thought," 320.

38 S. Mtetwa, "African Spirituality in the Context of Modernity," *Bulletin for Contextual Theology in Southern Africa & Africa* 3 (1996): 24.

39 Polycarp Ikuenobe, *Philosophical Perspectives on Communalism and Morality in African Traditions* (Lanham, MD: Lexington Books, 2006), 301.

40 Mbiti, *African Religions & Philosophy*, 141.

41 Ikuenobe, *Philosophical Perspectives on Communalism and Morality in African Traditions*, 294.
42 Ibid.
43 E. A. Ruch and K. C. Anyanwu, *African Philosophy: An Introduction to the Main Philosophical Trends in Contemporary Africa* (Rome: Catholic Book Agency, 1984), 143.
44 Obuntu is an African concept that means a person is who they are only in relationships to the other members of the community.
45 Georg Wilhelm Friedrich Hegel, *The Philosophy of History*, trans. John Sibree (New York, NY: Dover Publications, 1956), 99.
46 Ibid., 93.
47 Richard F. Burton, *The Lake Regions of Central Africa*, vol. 2 (New York, NY: Horizon Press, 1961), 326.
48 Patrick Brantlinger, "Victorians and Africans: The Genealogy of the Myth of the Dark Continent," *Chicago Journals* 12, no. 1 (Autumn 1985): 175.
49 Michael Crowder, *The Story of Nigeria* (London: Faber, 1978), 11. Emphasis in the original.
50 Abraham Terumbur Mbachirin, "The Responses of the Church in Nigeria to Socio-Economic, Political and Religiousproblems in Nigeria: A Case Study of the Christian Association of Nigeria (C.A.N.)" (Ph.D Diss., Baylor Univeristy, 2006), 31.
51 Indirect rule was the colonial system of administration in which local chiefs were empowered to rule their subjects under the supervision of the British colonial officials. Indirect rule recorded a huge success in the north, where there was already in existence a centralized system administration and well-organized system of taxation, but it was a total failure in the south, due to the absence of a centralized administrative system. The warrant chiefs appointed in the south by the British, with powers to judge, supervise forced labor and collect taxes, were notorious, exploitative, corrupt, and oppressive in the discharge of their duties. See Elizabeth Isichei, *A History of Nigeria* (London: Longman, 1983), 382–3.
52 The prominent Nigerian nationalists who committed their time, energy, resources, and lives to fight for Nigerian's independence from the colonial government were Herbert Macaulay, often referred to as "the father of Nigerian nationalism," Dr Nnamdi Azikiwe, and Chief Obafemi Awolowo.
53 Alan Burns, *History of Nigeria* (New York, NY: Barnes & Noble, 1972), 251.
54 Ibid., 252.
55 As cited in Isichei, *A History of Nigeria*, 471.
56 Crowder, *The Story of Nigeria*, 269.
57 As cited in Isichei, *A History of Nigeria*, 474.
58 Ibid., 477–9.
59 Chris Ogbondah and Emmanuel U. Onyedike, "Origins and Interpretation of Nigerian Press Laws," *Africa Media Review* 5 (1991): 61.
60 Toyin Falola, *Violence in Nigeria: The Crisis of Religious Politics and Secular Ideologies* (Rochester, NY: University of Rochester Press, 1998), 65.
61 Ibid., 66.
62 Edward. Cropley, "Nigeria's Jonathan Urges Peace After Election Defeat," *Reuters*, 2015, www.reuters.com/article/2015/03/31/us-nigeria-election-jonathan-idUSKBN0M R2S820150331 (accessed June 18, 2015).

Bibliography

Adenle, Stephen O., and Raymond Uwameiye. "Issues in Utilization of Equalization of Educational Opportunities: Implication for Peace Education in Nigeria." *International Journal of Academic Research in Progressive Education and Development* 1, no. 4 (2012): 347–56.

26 Introduction

Boff, Leonardo. *Trinity and Society*. Translated by Paul Burns. Eugene, OR: Wipf & Stock Publishers, 1988.

Bonhoeffer, Dietrich. *A Testament to Freedom: The Essential Writings of Dietrich Bonhoeffer*. Edited by Geffrey B. Kelly and F. Burton Nelson. San Francisco, CA: HarperSanFrancisco, 1995.

Brantlinger, Patrick. "Victorians and Africans: The Genealogy of the Myth of the Dark Continent." *Chicago Journals* 12, no. 1 (Autumn 1985): 166–203.

Burns, Alan. *History of Nigeria*. New York, NY: Barnes & Noble, 1972.

Burton, Richard F. *The Lake Regions of Central Africa*. Vol. 2. New York, NY: Horizon Press, 1961.

Cropley, Edward. "Nigeria's Jonathan Urges Peace After Election Defeat." *Reuters*, 2015. www.reuters.com/article/2015/03/31/us-nigeria-election-jonathan-idUSKBN0MR2S8 20150331 (accessed June 18, 2015).

Crowder, Michael. *The Story of Nigeria*. London: Faber, 1978.

Cunningham, David S. *These Three Are One: The Practice of Trinitarian Theology*. Malden, MA: Blackwell Publishers, 1998.

Dickson, Kwesi A. *Aspects of Religion and Life in Africa*. Accra: Ghana Academic of Arts and Science, 1977.

———. *Theology in Africa*. London: Longman &Todd Ltd, 1984.

Falola, Toyin. *Violence in Nigeria: The Crisis of Religious Politics and Secular Ideologies*. Rochester, NY: University of Rochester Press, 1998.

Gadamer, Hans-Georg. *Truth and Method*. Translated by Weinsheimer Joel and Donald G. Marshall. 2nd ed. New York, NY: Continuum, 2004.

Gyekye, Kwame. "Person and Community in African Thought." In *The African Philosophy Reader*, edited by Lesiba J. Teffo and Abraham P. J. Roux. London: Routledge, 1998.

Hegel, Georg Wilhelm Friedrich. *The Philosophy of History*. Translated by John Sibree. New York, NY: Dover Publications, 1956.

Hopkins, Dwight N. *Being Human: Race, Culture, and Religion*. Minneapolis, MN: Fortress Press, 2005.

Ikuenobe, Polycarp. *Philosophical Perspectives on Communalism and Morality in African Traditions*. Lanham, MD: Lexington Books, 2006.

Isichei, Elizabeth. *A History of Nigeria*. London: Longman, 1983.

Kombo, James Henry Owino. *The Doctrine of God in African Christian Thought: The Holy Trinity, Theological Hermeneutics, and the African Intellectual Culture*. Leiden; Boston, MA: Brill, 2007.

LaCugna, Catherine Mowry. *God for Us: The Trinity and Christian Life*. San Francisco, CA: HarperSanFrancisco, 1991.

Luther, Martin. "The Bondage of the Will." In *Luther's Works*, edited by Philip S. Watson and Hulmut Lehmann. Vol. 33. Philadelphia, PA: Fortress Press, 1972.

———. "Lectures on Galatians 1535, Chapters 5–6." In *Luther's Works*, edited by Jaroslav Pelikan and Walter A. Hansen. Vol. 27. Saint Louis: Concordia Publishing House, 1964.

Mbachirin, Abraham Terumbur. "The Responses of the Church in Nigeria to Socio-Economic, Political and Religiousproblems in Nigeria: A Case Study of the Christian Association of Nigeria (C.A.N.)." Ph.D Diss., Baylor Univeristy, 2006.

Mbiti, John S. *African Religions & Philosophy*. New York, NY: Praeger, 1969.

Mtetwa, Sipho. "African Spirituality in the Context of Modernity." *Bulletin for Contextual Theology in Southern Africa & Africa* 3 (June 2, 1996): 21–5.

Mugambi, J. N. Kanyua. *The African Heritage and Contemporary Christianity*. Nairobi: Longman, 1989.

Mwoleka, Cristopher. "Trinity and Communion." *African Ecclesiastical Review* 17, no. 4 (1975): 203–6.

Nyamiti, Charge. "The Trinity from African Ancestral Perspective." *African Christian Studies* 12 (1996): 38–74.

Oborji, Francis Anekwe. "Building Relationship in Mixed African Communities." http://sedosmission.org/old/eng/oborji_3.htm (accessed October 14, 2014).

Ogbondah, Chris, and E. U. Onyedike. "Origins and Interpretation of Nigerian Press Laws." *Africa Media Review* 5 (1991): 59–70.

Ogbonnaya, A. Okechukwu. *On Communitarian Divinity: An African Interpretation of the Trinity*. New York, NY: Paragon House, 1994.

Pannenberg, Wolfhart. *Systematic Theology*. Translated by Geoffrey W. Bromiley. Vol. 1. Grand Rapids, MI: Eerdmans, 1991.

Parrat, John. *Reinventing Christianity: African Theology Today*. Grand Rapids, MI: Eerdmans, 1995.

Ruch, E. A., and K. C. Anyanwu. *African Philosophy: An Introduction to the Main Philosophical Trends in Contemporary Africa*. Rome: Catholic Book Agency, 1984.

Setiloane, Gabriel M. "Where Are We in African Theology." In *African Theology En Route: Papers from the Pan-African Conference of Third World Theologians, December 17–23, 1977, Accra, Ghana*, edited by Kofi Appiah-Kubi and Sergio Torres. Maryknoll, NY: Orbis Books, 1979.

Shutte, Augustine. *Philosophy for Africa*. Rodenbosch: University of Cape Town Press, 1993.

Vähäkangas, Mika. "African Approaches to the Trinity." In *African Theology Today*, edited by Emmanuel Kantogole. Scranton, PA: University of Scranton Press, 2002.

2 Major African communal structural evils

In the preceding chapter, I described the African tradition of community and its correlation with the relationality of the Persons of the Triune God. I have argued that the African spirit of community, which emphasizes interdependence, solidarity, and shared life, is to some extent a reflection of the perichoretic communion of the Triune God. The reflection, no matter how faintly, suggests eloquently that the tradition of community bears in it the image of the Triune God. The tradition is far from being uncivilized and barbaric. There are, however, African systemic issues in this cherished African tradition of community that inhibit full reception and embodiment of the Triune God's gifting of perichoretic communion. One has no option but to be critical of these African systemic contextual problems, as Veli-Matti Kärkkäinen challenges non-Western Trinitarian scholars to do.

According to Kärkkäinen, the fundamental weakness of new non-Western contextual Trinitarian theologies is the absence of a "self-critical ethos." Kärkkäinen charges that these contextual theologies are always critical of the Christian tradition. They often regard it as oppressive, destructive, or irrelevant to their contexts, but are never critical of their own environment, culture, thought patterns, or religious heritage. After studying contextual Trinitarian theologies, Kärkkäinen writes, "I do not see the kind of *critical analysis of the limitations and problems of their own contexts* that I see in their often one-sided critique of [the Christian] tradition."[1] Though Kärkkäinen's criticism is somewhat exaggerated, it is legitimate and cogent; hence, it has to be taken seriously. This is because developing a new contextual Trinitarian understanding of God must produce critical attitudes toward one's own contextual problems that prohibit and/or inhibit the Triune God's gift of perichoretic communion. Therefore, in this chapter, I will analytically describe those contextual structural problems with specific reference to the Nigerian church and society. These systemic problems are the destructive patriarchal complex, the Big Man syndrome, and ethnic and religious nepotism.

Destructive patriarchal complex

Though there is a resemblance between the African sense of community and Trinitarian relationality, the former is based on a hierarchal patriarchal complex, promoting complementary roles that block full reception of real Trinitarian reciprocity. One of the greatest defects of African theology (and, by extension, philosophy) is its failure to criticize the patriarchal complex that is ingrained in African community. As seen in the analysis in Chapter 1, Mbiti, the father of contemporary African theology, along with other African theologians, has romanticized the African tradition of community without calling into question the patriarchal domination inherent in it. An authentic African Christian theology that undertakes the faithful Trinitarian hermeneutics of the Triune God needs to challenge the African patriarchal complex. Patriarchal ideology is the traditional unjust gender system, which not only subordinates women to men in domestic life, but also treats women as second-class citizens in society. It is an instrument that men employ to exercise control over women by preventing them full access to the necessary economic and political resources that accord them equal rights and powers as men have. According to G. A. Makama, men exercise this control by excluding:

> women from access to necessary economically productive resources and by restricting women's sexuality. Men exercise their control in receiving personal service work from women, in not having to do housework or rear children, in having access to women's bodies for sex, and in feeling powerful and being powerful.[2]

The patriarchal complex objectifies women, arbitrarily treating them as tools to be simply used for sex and procreation of the human species. As a harmful social construct, patriarchy not only renders women perpetually dependent on men for economic sustenance, but also entrenches continued male supremacy, creating the psychological impression in women that apart from men, they cannot do anything. Such a patriarchal complex is so ingrained and deeply rooted in African cultures that challenging it today is often construed as destroying African tradition itself. As Daniella Coetzee argues, "Thus, to challenge patriarchy, to dispute the idea that it is men who should be dominant figures in the family and society, is to be seen not as fighting against male privilege, but as attempting to destroy African tradition."[3]

This harmful African patriarchal tradition promotes unwarranted gender inequality that aids and abets the oppression and marginalization of women at all levels of the Nigerian society.[4] According to Dr J. S. Omotola,

> The Nigerian society has become patriarchal, where traditional male values are institutionalized not only in the family, but also in the economic, social and religious dimensions. The implication is that the state is perpetually rigged against women, with a devastating legacy of inequalities between genders.[5]

The family is the basic unit of patriarchal exploitation of women in Africa. There exists in the family a rigid superior-inferior relationship between the man and the woman which engenders a pattern of disparity between sexes, demanding

30 *Major African communal structural evils*

complementary gender role expectations. For example, the woman is required to bear the children, perform household chores, cook, clean, and cater to her husband and children, while the man is expected to provide food and finance for the running of the family. As the "property" of the man in many African cultures, the woman is culturally required to submit unquestionably and obey her husband, who is sanctified as the boss of the family. Thus, after the death of a husband in some cultures, not only is the ownership of the woman passed onto his brother, but also she is denied any right to inherit property of the husband.

Unfortunately, the patriarchal complex continues to rear its ugly head in contemporary Nigerian society despite responses by government and civil society to address such gender injustice. Oni Samuel and Dr Joshua Segun claim that despite the introduction of democratic governance, "gender inequalities, discriminations and stereotypes continue to exist in all spheres of the Nigerian polity, preventing women from developing and exercising their full human capabilities and to play a powerful role in sustainable democracy."[6]

Studies in Nigeria have revealed that all forms of political and economic marginalization and deprivation have been meted out against women.[7] The deeply entrenched and institutionalized patriarchal complex in the Nigerian society partly accounts for such marginalization and oppression of women. Politically, women are not only underrepresented in government, but also victims of repressive public policies and political violence. A.A. Abayomi and T.O. Kolawole write,

> Because females are not well represented in Nigerian politics, gender-sensitive laws and policies are not a priority either at the state or national level. This has contributed to the non-realization of women's political rights and has contributed greatly to the perpetuation of violence against women.[8]

Economically, women have been discriminated against in securing employment in the economy, access to land, credit facilities, and other financial resources; hence, they have become victims of poverty. For this reason, a greater number of Nigerian women engage in petty trading, street hawking, and peasant farming. Makama contends that the economic discrimination that Nigerian women experience

> limit[s] their opportunities to develop their full potential on the basis of equality with men. They are far from enjoying equal rights in the labour market, due mainly to their domestic burden, low level of educational attainment, poverty, biases against women's employment in certain branches of the economy.[9]

Socio-culturally, women have been subjected to harmful cultural practices like female genital mutilation, forced marriage, and domestic violence without the perpetrators brought to justice. Such patriarchal ideology, according to which male and female social roles are defined in a way that claims to complement each other, only perpetuates the domination of one part of the community over the other. This socially and culturally structured gender inequality between men and women constrains most of the members of the community from actualizing their full human identity since they cannot excel beyond the position assigned to them in their complementary roles. A prominent feminist African theologian, M.A. Oduyoye, argues, "In practice, complementarity allows the man to choose what he wants to be and to do then demands that the woman fill in the blanks. It is the woman, invariably, who complements the man."[10] As a result, women, who are created in the image of the Triune God, are deprived from fully receiving and developing the gift of God's perichoretic communion.

The reasons for this lingering patriarchal complex in Nigeria range from the traditional to the religious to the colonial. According to the African patriarchal traditions as handed down through the ages, men are superior to their women counterparts, who are not only expected to submit to men without objection in the family, but, most tragically, are not allowed to do anything without the approval of their husbands. Men have the final say in matters of utmost importance in the family. As inconsequential members of the family, women are often excluded from decision-making regarding crucial issues affecting the well-being of the entire family. Abayomi and Kolawole argue,

> Customary Practices across Nigeria generally hold that the man is the head of the house and has the absolute control in the decision making process of the home. That is, a patriarchal society reinforces a norm that views men as leaders and women as followers.[11]

This sort of male hegemony over women is exacerbated by the patriarchal tradition of payment of bride price, a practice which many believe seals the deal that finalizes the ownership of the woman as the property of her husband and his relatives. Such a practice permits the man to do as he pleases with the woman and her personal property with or without her consent!

The introductions of Christianity and Islam have not significantly impacted the patriarchal tradition. Most adherents of the two religions strongly believe that patriarchy is divinely ordained, and have in many ways continued to endorse the wielding of such authoritarian power by men. For example, apart from teaching that a man is the head of the family, Christian preaching on family is often an exhortation that demands a wife be submissive and the husband be loving, as though being loving precludes the husband from being submissive to his wife and vice versa. Omotola contends that the traditional belief which subordinates women to men in Nigeria is reinforced by Islamic and Christian religions,

> both of which preached that women should be submissive to their husbands, the heads of the family. For this reason, the society tends to measure a woman's devotedness to God partially in terms of her loyalty and submission to her husband.[12]

32   *Major African communal structural evils*

It is thus believed that patriarchy is divinely sanctioned. Dr Chimaraoke O. Izugbara writes,

> The core of Christian narratives of sexuality is the belief that heterosexuality and patriarchy are divinely instituted. Christian identity thus consists in embodying patterns of control, domination, and submission that put men and women in an unequal relational status.[13]

Such male hegemonic control is underscored by a Hausa saying that claims *mace batada addini, addinin mace mai gidan tane*, literally meaning "a woman has no religion; the religion of a woman is her husband." In other words, a woman has no God; the God of a woman is her husband. It is through fearing and serving her husband that a woman fears and serves God and thus inherits God's kingdom. This explains why it is virtually unacceptable for any woman to exercise any form of control over her husband and his wealth in the family. As it is only the man who has the power and right to divorce by tradition and religion, any woman who dares to exercise such control risks being divorced and thus excluded from the society. As such, fear of divorce and exclusion has forced many Christian women to live in married relationships that are abusive, as a way of "bearing the cross," in other words, the burden of marital vows.

Colonialism, which was itself male dominated, did very little to liberate African women from the bondage of patriarchy. Though colonialism did not create patriarchy in Africa, it undoubtedly exacerbated it. Walter Rodney argues, "The colonialists in Africa occasionally paid lip-service to women's education and emancipation, but objectively there was deterioration in the status of women owing to colonial rule."[14] British colonial rule in Nigeria involved not only the imposition of a new system of government, but also the imposition of new socio-economic order, which ushered in new economic systems, gender relations, and social norms drawn from both European and indigenous African cultures. This hybrid social system had adverse effects on women as it reinforced indigenous patriarchal ideology and introduced new forms of sexism rooted in a capitalist system of production. In pre-colonial African communities, though women were not equal with men, they were more than mere housewives, merely procreating and rearing children; they played an active complementary role in the socio-economic and political life of their various communities. But the advent of colonial rule wrought havoc on the traditional complementary role system and aggravated the gender disparity between men and women in Nigeria. As Samuel and Segun argue, "The creation of patriarchal government by colonial administration, its gender policies and economic interests reinforced and generalized patriarchal values and perpetuated gender inequality in the country."[15]

Maria Rojas argues that the introduction of cash crop production in Nigeria for international market under the dictates of the colonial administrators and missionaries brought a new conception of patriarchy that altered the social and economic status of women in the country. Rojas writes,

> Males began to dominate the cultivation of cash crops for the international market and confined women to the growing of food crops[,] which received

lower returns. By focusing on men, the cash crop farmers, bureaucratic efforts to improve agriculture further encouraged the separation of economic roles of men and women that had previously complemented each other.[16]

This disrupted the traditional modes of production and the division of labor according to gender, depriving women of the customary privileges of contribution to the economic well-being of their families. The new colonial socio-economic order of patriarchy coupled with the new burden of heavy taxation introduced by the colonial government relegated women to the lowest ladder of the socio-economic stratum of the society, the marginalization of which resulted in women – especially Igbo women – staging public protests against colonial policies during the colonial period.

In brief, the patriarchal complex is socially conditioned, but is most importantly perpetuated by tradition, religious beliefs, and colonial legacies in Africa. The destructive consequence is that it dehumanizes and marginalizes women, denying them equal rights and full access to the public resources, power, employment, and quality of life that can aid them to actualize their God-given potentials as human beings made in God's image. Therefore, the Trinitarian communion of God constituted in Christ and gifted by the Spirit is a critique of the patriarchal complex that stratifies relationships that privilege certain sectors of humanity. That complex hinders, blocks, and even contradicts the gift of the Triune God's perichoretic communion coming to earth via Word and Sacrament.

The "Big Man" syndrome

In this section, I will describe the "Big Man" syndrome as a new field of Trinitarian criticism of the African idea of community in Africa, especially Nigeria. I will specifically explore the characteristics and effects of the syndrome in the Nigerian society and the church, and show that the Big Man syndrome is a distortion of the African spirit of community, as well as the perichoretic gift of the Triune God for a just and egalitarian human society and for the church in the world.

The Big Man syndrome in the Nigerian society

The highly celebrated African tradition of community has been marred not just in the Nigerian society, but also in the entire continent of Africa by a "Big Man" syndrome. The prevalence of the syndrome is in many ways the modern public expression of the patriarchal complex. Characterizing the Big Man in Africa as the person who "uses the resources of the state to feed a cult of personality that defines him as incorruptible, all-knowing, physically strong," Blaine Harden contends, "[H]is cult equates his personal well-being with the well-being of the state. His rule has one overriding goal: to perpetuate his reign as the Big Man."[17]

Harden argues that the Big Man employs several corrupt means to use the public resources of the state to promote his well-being and that of his cronies, both within and outside of his government. First, the Big Man awards overpriced contracts only to foreign companies that give him, his family, and friends large kickbacks.

34 *Major African communal structural evils*

Second, he populates the public service with people from his ethnic nationality. Third, he executes most of his government projects in his home region. Fourth, Harden claims, the Big Man "manipulates price and import control to weaken profitable businesses and leave them vulnerable to takeover at bargain prices by his business associates."[18] To perpetuate his rule, Harden argues that the Big Man not only dissolves his cabinet without warning, gags the press, rigs elections in his favor, enfeebles the judiciary, and stifles the academy from being critical of his government, but he also persecutes those political enemies he cannot buy off by questioning their patriotism, and arresting, detaining, torturing, or killing them using the apparatus of the state.[19]

These indices of the Big Man syndrome are glaringly exhibited and institutionalized in the Nigerian social and political systems. According to Femi Aribisala,

> Bigmanism is a chronic national malaise in Nigeria. It is a disease whereby members of a highly visible segment of society are paraded as higher breeds beyond the pale of the law. These big-men flout all conventions and they break all the rules.[20]

Bigmanism is a key to capturing power over public resources and the exercising of sole control over them. Once these Big Men grab such power, often through illegitimate means, they not only are disinclined to relinquish it, but also do everything humanly possible to maintain it, including by unlawful means. "[These] power holders," as Joshua Segun and Oni Samuel argue, "having obtained power by unlawful means, strive to maintain it with a high degree of lawlessness. Their gluttonous quest for boundless riches have [poisoned] their minds to stay put in power indefinitely."[21] As the syndrome is ingrained in the Nigerian private and public life, whoever assumes a position of leadership sees himself as a Big Man conferred with unilateral power not only to control every public resource under his jurisdiction, but also to manage such resources for his personal interests rather than the common good of the society. As Professor Timothy Palmer describes the Big Man in Nigeria,

> A "big man" is one who uses all the resources of the state or the institution to perpetuate his own rule and glory. . . . The big man is one who puts his own well-being above that of his subjects.[22]

Palmer claims that the Big Man pattern of behavior, which hinders the development and well-being of the people, is common in every aspect of the society including the church. The Big Men are often "worshipped," perhaps even more than God, because of the exclusive monopoly that they exercise over state power and resources. This is evidenced in the practice of sycophancy and undue homage, which too many people pay to these Big Men, seeking personal gain rather than what is in the interest of the community. Resisting them seems impossible, thus, they are able to do whatever they please. According to a prominent lawyer and human rights activist, Gani Fawehinmi,

The problem with Nigerians is that they worship authority too much; they worship officialdom too much; they worship people in power too much and that is why the people in power cheat them and that is why they lord things over them.[23]

Hence, Nigerian society, which is profoundly infected by the Big Man syndrome, bleeds from the appalling consequences of the Big Man leadership, which wields absolute power at every tier of government.

Therefore, the first deadly consequence of the Big Man syndrome on the well-being and development of Nigeria is massive bribery and corruption. Corruption as an abuse of public office for personal gain is a "virtue" and a way of life for Nigerians, and most importantly, for public office holders. Peter Cunliffe-Jones has argued, "*In Nigeria*, there is widespread resentment of corruption and the state of the economy. There is anger. But, after decades of living with corruption and its effects, people are now habituated to it."[24] To refuse to be bribed and corrupt is in many ways seen as abnormal. Thus, those who refuse to be bribed are viewed as deviants, while Big Men who acquire wealth and power through bribery and corruption are celebrated in both the church and the society as "saints."

Those who dare to fight bribery and corruption often do so at the peril of their job and life.[25] The law enforcement agents who are responsible for curbing bribery and corruption are themselves corrupt. Thus, bribery and corruption in the form of extortion, looting, mismanagement, and diversion of public funds by public officers has become a daily phenomenon. As Nigerian Big Men/Women are themselves corrupt, they often ignore or turn blind eyes to the corruption of their political cronies in their cabinets as a lucrative way of compensating them for political support. No wonder that corruption has eaten so deeply into the fabric of Nigeria's public life that the nation was ranked 144th among 177 most corrupt countries of the world in 2013.[26] Even the establishment of anticorruption commissions such as the Economic and Financial Crimes Commission (EFCC) and Independent Corrupt Practices and the Other Related Offences Commission (ICPC) has not stopped this cancer of corruption from spreading in the country. The punishment meted out against the corrupt Big Men is not punitive enough to serve as a deterrent to potential looters of the public treasury.[27] Though there are many corrupt public officials who have been arrested and prosecuted for theft of billions of dollars, between 2003 and 2011 only four of them have been convicted, with little or no prison time. Sadly, some of the Big Men convicted have been granted state pardon.[28]

The effect of these pervasive corrupt practices is that the strict legal distinction between legitimate and illegitimate means of acquiring wealth, power, and position has been abolished. Ridiculously, illegitimate means of acquiring these lawful resources have become most acceptable. The vociferous Roman Catholic Bishop M. H. Kukah points out that the case of corruption in Nigeria is the worst: "To respond to the peculiar nature of our situation, the abnormal has now become the normal."[29] Seeking wealth, employment, and public position through unlawful means has become normal, for seeking them through lawful means is often

36 *Major African communal structural evils*

frustrated by the powers that be. This has forced even law-abiding citizens to embrace illegal means of obtaining these legitimate resources. Specifically, corruption has denied many women the right to employment and admission to higher institutions of learning. Stories abound of poor women who have every qualification for certain jobs in the civil service, but do not have the money to bribe the public officials to secure employment and admission, and as a result have had to provide sexual favors in return for such legal entitlements.

The second consequence of the Big Man syndrome is injustice. As a result of the Big Man disease, public resources are unequally distributed to favor the privileged few at the expense of the poor and the most vulnerable. The poor struggle to make ends meet daily under the shackle of poverty and its attendant consequences – crime and insecurity. One of the worst injustices is the startling revelation that the Nigerian lawmakers are the highest-paid legislators in the world. According to *The Economist*, Nigerian legislators take an annual salary of about $189,000 – more than their counterparts in other countries such as Britain and the United States (who make $105,400 and $174,000, respectively).[30] This amount is 116 times more than Nigeria's per capita Gross Domestic Product (GDP). As a result, the gulf between the haves and the have-nots has been widened and aggravated by the unfair distribution of the so-called "national cake." O.F. Odumosu has suggested accurately, "The political leaders have been largely corrupt, inclined toward non-democratic practices and such capricious redistribution of the nation's wealth in manners that promoted poverty among many and opulence among a small privileged class."[31] It has been estimated that over $600 billion dollars of public funds has been stolen between independence in 1960 and 1999,[32] an amount which would have transformed Nigeria into the El Dorado of Africa.

The third impact of the Big Man syndrome is massive poverty in the midst of abundance. The distributive injustice perpetrated by the Big Man syndrome has created an endemic poverty in Nigeria in spite of the country's enormous material resources. Though Nigeria is the sixth largest oil exporter in the world, a recent World Bank report suggests that 100 million out of its 150 million residents live in abject poverty. According to the World Bank Country Director for Nigeria, Marie-Francoise Marie-Nelly, "One billion two hundred thousand people live in destitution [globally] out of which 100 million are Nigerians."[33] Though the government has tried to alleviate such poverty through the National Poverty Eradication Programme (NAPEP), it has not considerably impacted the poor. Mass poverty still abounds.

The worst-affected people are women. Seventy percent of poor Nigerians are women.[34] Some of them, out of desperation to elevate themselves and their families from poverty, have fallen prey to human trafficking. The number of Nigerian young women who have become victims of trafficking over the past 15 years amounts to between 40,000 and 50,000.[35] They have been trafficked as prostitutes to various countries in Western Europe under the false promise of good job offers. Shalini Nadaswaran has suggested that

> Once they arrive at their destination, these women are raped, beaten and humiliated into submission, ensuring they never try to escape. Their vulnerability

Major African communal structural evils   37

is compounded by the fact that their passports and papers are taken away and kept by their traffickers, sealing their fate to a life of slavery.[36]

Fourth, the Big Man syndrome has partly contributed to the current insecurity problem threatening life and property in the country. Distributive injustice perpetrated by the Big Man syndrome has deprived the poor and the underprivileged of opportunities to access the common good. Hence, the growing numbers of unemployed youths have not only been attracted to violent crimes, but also have become ready-made labor for desperate, power-hungry, and discontented politicians who hire them as thugs and assassins of their perceived or real political enemies. "These youths are lured and armed by 'second-term politicians' who want to retain power no matter the cost [and who arm] with guns. After these elections, none of these guns were recovered from these new merchants of death."[37] Gunmen who have not yet been apprehended have killed politicians such as Bola Ige, Alfred Rewane, Dikibo Dina, Marshall Harry, and Funsho Williams in recent times with the connivance of the Big Men/Women in government, hiring them as assassins.

Consequently, insecurity has assumed unprecedented dimensions in Nigeria since the inception of the democratic era beginning in 1999. As we shall discuss later, Boko Haram, an Islamist insurgent group, constitutes a serious security threat to life and property, and has killed over 11,000 people since the insurgency erupted in 2009. Further, the outbreak of the "Ombatse" ethnic militia violence in Nasarawa state of Nigeria has killed over 69 policemen, not to mention the lingering ethno-religious conflict in Plateau state. Kidnapping dens have also sprung up, becoming a lucrative business in the southwest, notoriously kidnapping clergy, politicians, and business tycoons, sparing not even women and children. This is not to mention the ongoing destruction of life and property of farmers across the country by Fulani herdsmen with the complicity of the present administration. The Nigerian security forces saddled with the responsibility to contain insecurity are corrupt and ill-equipped, despite the lion's share of the national budget often allocated to defense and police.[38] The normal response of the government to major threats of security is to set up a committee of inquiry, which makes recommendations that the government never cares to respect or implement, resulting in no substantial improvement of the situation. Therefore, the real perpetrators and sponsors of such insecurity are often not brought to justice, as if the law has no power over them.

The fifth consequence of the Big Man syndrome is dictatorship. The democratic system of government that Nigerians hoped would restore human dignity, equality, and freedom (and thereby improve their lives) is a mirage. Too many Nigerian political leaders are simply civilian dictators who masquerade themselves as vanguards of democracy. These Big Men hardly tolerate free and fair elections, which they perceive as a threat to their power and influence. For them, an election is free and fair only if they or their "anointed" candidates win the election. As "godfathers" who have an exclusive monopoly on the state's resources and power, it is these civilian dictators and not the votes of the electorate that determine who should win an election, which often is characterized by rigging, harassment of

38 *Major African communal structural evils*

political opponents, and all forms of electoral irregularities. Dr A. M. Katsina has observed that "in all corners of the country the phenomena of 'Godfathers[,]' rigging and vote buying [are] actually substituted for the exercise of popular will and choice in electing public officials."[39]

This creates an unjust situation where losers are often declared winners, while genuine winners are declared losers. Even when these genuine winners seek redress in a court of law, they are seldom granted justice. State-managed electoral tribunals arguing for the genuine winners often are dismissed for lack of evidence. This leaves the Nigerian electorate frustrated, disenfranchised, and disgruntled with the entire democratic system of government. "As a result of this politics of exclusion," Katsina argues, "a deeper psychological and social inequality is fostered among the citizenry[,] part of the implication of which today is the total loss of confidence in the democratic experiment, and great disenchantment among most citizens with the government."[40]

Since these political leaders do not have to get the popular mandate of the people in a free and fair election to get elected or re-elected, they do whatever they please in office without respect for the rule of law, serving themselves rather than the people. The constitutional immunity conferred on the political leaders while in office, intended to guarantee their security of tenure, makes such abuse of power even more appalling. Their immunity has been perceived by too many as allowing plunder of government funds for personal benefit without fear of prosecution, and by extension, without fear of God.

Last but having the most devastative impact is that the Big Man syndrome results in the abuse of the rule of law in Nigeria. Though the rule of law is unambiguously embedded in the constitution, the Big Men saddled with the duty to make, interpret, and enforce the law are virtually lawless. They have blatantly suspended, subverted, ignored, or even violated the rule of law with impunity, in favor of the rich and the powerful while the poor and less privileged are harassed daily in the name of enforcing the law. All three arms of the government are guilty of this appalling misconduct.[41] In the short years it has been a democratic country, Nigeria's executive arm has disobeyed with impunity the judgments of the courts of the land.[42] What exacerbates this executive lawlessness is the "immunity clause" enshrined in Section 308 of the 1999 constitution. This clause protects elected executive political leaders from any civil or criminal proceedings instituted against their persons during their term in office. The legislative branch of the government that is vested with the power for checking executive lawlessness through impeachment and legislation is ineffective and corrupt. Its investigatory committees have successfully probed many cases of executive abuses of office, but the measures that they have recommended to eliminate these abuses have been either neglected or abandoned:

> [T]he investigations undertaken by various committees of the central legislature were often meant to arm twist government ministries or agencies into giving money to members of the assembly. Lack of sincerity has, in most

cases, affected the extent to which the various committees of the house could provide effective check[s] against abuse of executive power.[43]

The police force is complicit in the abuse of rule of law. The police force that is saddled with responsibility for maintaining the law is guilty of breaking the law with impunity. Dr E.C. Onyeozili claims that "the police are [a] constituent part of police ineffectiveness."[44] Police corruption in Nigeria has destroyed the noble mission of the police. Rather than protecting citizens' life and property, they instead appear to escalate crime rates. Onyeozili claims that police corruption takes "various forms: extortion from motorists at illegally mounted road blocks, [and] collection of monetary gratification (bribery) in order to alter justice in favor of the highest bidder."[45] While some police officers commit premeditated crime by arming criminals with guns, others engage themselves in armed robbery and kidnapping. Onyeozili reports a case where the police's Biggest Man, that is, the Inspector General of Police (IG) laundered bribe and police service money, including N1.4 billion paid to the police for security during the 2003 general elections. When the head of the police force is lawless, it is difficult to expect anything else of the rank and file.

A liberal political democracy, which Nigerians expected would deliver a better life in line with the African spirit of community, has been extinguished by the Big Man syndrome, determining unilaterally who should rule and who should be ruled, who should be rich and who should be poor, who should be privileged and who should be marginalized. The type of democracy that is practiced in Nigeria is nothing but what Bakili Muluzi has described as void democracy: "Democracy without food, clothing, healthy and educational facilities is void. People do not eat 'democracy.' A hungry and poor man cannot appreciate democracy."[46] There is gross loss of public trust in democratic institutions and the emergence of a social pyramid where the Big Men at the top oppress the small men and women at the bottom. Therefore, the trouble with Nigerian society is the Big Man disease that infects secular leadership. As Chinua Achebe rightly sees it,

> The trouble with Nigeria is, simply and squarely, a failure of leadership. . . . Nigeria's problem is the unwillingness or inability of its leaders to rise to the responsibility, to the challenge of personal example which is the hallmark of true leadership.[47]

The Big Man syndrome in the Nigerian church

The "Big Man" syndrome, which is the characteristic feature of Nigerian political leadership, also infiltrates Nigerian church leadership. This is evident by the way these churches are swift at deserting the cruciform life of servant leadership that Christ Himself exemplified for a life of leadership based on power and glory. Hence, the cross, which is a symbol of the Triune God's self-humiliation and

40 *Major African communal structural evils*

powerlessness in Christ and the Spirit, is reserved only to be worn by exalted leaders of the church, such as the bishops, as a symbol of power and authority. This distortion of the cross, which is the formation of pyramidal structures of leadership, has alienated clergy from the laity in some churches. As such, the churches are clergy-centered; the laity has little or nothing to say in running the affairs of the churches. The clergy claim to know it all, dominating the leadership and worship life of the churches! Dr Chika Asogwa and Damian Amana argue, "Under such a hierarchical, clerical and an institutional arrangement of the church, the people of God shy away from their participative function in the building up of the kingdom of God."[48] Rather than the church being a communion of saints, it has now become a communion of the clergy. A Nigerian professor of sociology at Bethel University, Dr Samuel Zalanga, claims:

> Protestant African Christianity is just like pre-reformation Christianity in terms of its structure and how it treats the laity – very hierarchical. Protestants at one point attacked the Catholic Church on the question of hierarchy but they are as hierarchical, if not more, compared to Catholic Church in this respect.[49]

As spiritual Big Men, some Nigerian church leaders assign to themselves almost absolute and autocratic power in managing the human and material resources of their churches and in making crucial decisions affecting their churches without approval of their councils.[50] For such Big Men of the church, leadership is not a privilege to serve and promote the well-being of their members, but a life-and-death position that they must hold at all cost for personal benefit. As such, some of them are ready to blackmail, kill, or destroy those they perceive as enemies threatening their power.

Though hierarchy in the church is intended for maintaining order in the smooth running of the church, it has turned out to be a huge financial burden on the members. Equating themselves with political leaders, some Big Men in the hierarchy of the church demand that whatever salary and condition of service these political leaders enjoy should be granted to them, regardless of whether or not their churches are financially stable enough to afford it. Some of them live an ostentatious lifestyle at the expense of poor members, who do not even have enough to eat and yet are required to contribute toward the support of the church. But such contributions, which are often made in the name of God and for the propagation of God's mission in the world, translate into personal aggrandizement and pride of church leaders. The extravagant way of life of these leaders is much akin to the life of medieval popes:

> The lifestyle of many Pentecostal ministers who have private jets is the functional equivalent of the life of the Renaissance Popes. Christianity among the great majority of denominations in Nigeria and Africa has become domesticated and bourgeois-ified. Its egalitarian principles have been siphoned out of it.[51]

Major African communal structural evils 41

Apart from putting pressure on the members to donate to support their flamboyant lifestyle in the name of God, these church leaders also sell whatever spiritual gifts they claim to possess to gullible members for personal enrichment. Characterizing these church leaders as "pope-like pastors," journalist O. G. Osamwonyi charges,

> Some pastors in Nigeria, for economic gains, readily brandish mutated doctrines of indulgence, like deliverance consultation fees, [and] pay as you hear prophesy. Some pray over Ribena [juice concentrate] and sell it as the blood of Jesus. Others market olive oil as the power of God.[52]

Osamwonyi argues that the acid test of power of leadership for these pastors is not the extent to which they empower their members; rather, these pastors think it is the degree to which the members idolize them and they control the members. Their exercise of power is one-sided, often top-down. Instead of exercising power with the people, they exercise power *over* them. Threat of sanctions or curses is an effective tool in the hands of these leaders in wielding control over their members.

As Big Men obsessed with unbridled love for power, glory, and money, Nigerian church leadership has failed to contain the pervasive Big Man syndrome responsible for ubiquitous government corruption and injustice in the country. Too many church leaders are uncritical buddies of the corrupt and unjust Big Men in government on whom they often depend for financial support. This is evident in the way many churches welcome these corrupt leaders into their fellowship without remorse while excluding other genuine members:

> The church has often been silent to the corruption perpetuated by the political class and has accommodated criminal bankers that have impoverished millions of depositors and shareholders. The church has become a radio that broadcasts the ideas and principles of the privileged class to its congregation rather than a television that exposes the injustices of the oppressor.[53]

Thus, rather than openly and honestly rebuking these big Nigerian political leaders for corruption and oppression of the poor, these church leaders are bold at proclaiming to these public villains sweet messages that appease rather than disturb their guilty conscience. They often preach such sugarcoated prophetic messages that keep these crooks in their churches as invaluable assets. These unjust and corrupt leaders who dispossess the poor and the most vulnerable are treated with exceptional respect as indispensable gifts to the church, rather than as crooks. Femi Aribisala puts it more bluntly:

> Thieves and robbers are Satan's gifts to the churches. Visit the mega-churches in Nigeria and you will discover the people seating in the front-row are the big-time thieves who have robbed the country blind. . . . The messages preached are carefully-crafted so they are not offended and remain comfortable in their thievery.[54]

42 *Major African communal structural evils*

Not only are some of the church leaders unashamed to "wine and dine" with the oppressive powers, but they also accept the "brown envelope" with large donations from them without remorse. As such, they do not believe it is unethical to welcome corrupt leaders into their fellowship. This intimate alliance of the church leaders with the powers-that-be has enslaved their prophetic conscience of justice, and thus betrayed their divine authority to publicly rebuke oppressors of the weak and powerless members. The prophetic voice of these church leaders who feed at the tables of Big Men in government has been compromised. As Dr M .D. Nyiawung rightly argues,

> The church that feeds at the tables of the rich and only brings crumbs to the poor cannot produce convincing prophetic witness for the public. . . . By appeasing oppressors with pampering messages, the church neutralises its prophetic witness, rendering it obsolete.[55]

Some churches still appeal to Holy Scriptures to perpetuate men's monopoly on leadership positions within the ecclesial hierarchy, to the exclusion of women. Thus, women, who form the numerical and financial mainstay of churches in Nigeria, are sadly excluded from ordination, which denies them the right to occupy any church leadership position on the basis of ritual impurity. As Philip Jenkins rightly sees it, in the Global South, "concerns about ritual impurity often form the grounds, explicit or implicit, on which women are excluded from ordination."[56] The church is incomplete without women. Dr Teresa Okure contends, "Women are the Church and the Church is Women."[57] Therefore, any church that marginalizes women marginalizes itself. Conversely, any church that empowers women empowers itself.

The Big Man syndrome as manifested in the Nigerian society and church can be attributed partly to the legacy of colonial rule, even though the exercise of epistemic authoritarian powers by elders is alleged to be part of the legacies of the African community.[58] Except for the centralized Islamic theocratic states of northern Nigeria, such as the Sokoto Caliphate where emirs were highly autocratic, the pre-colonial Nigerian and African communities were largely democratic, if not in the modern liberal sense. There was little to no existence of the Big Man syndrome. Even if there were Big Man malaise, it was effectively contained. Apart from practicing a participatory form of government, as evidenced in the existence of a collective mode of decision-making in African community, there were checks and balances put in place in the traditional system of government which prevented leaders of the community from degenerating into Big Men who abuse power and common wealth for personal enrichment. Ruch and Anyanwu contend,

> The traditional consensus democracy is generally affirmed, not only as being a form of consultative debate which enabled the equal participation of all adult males in the decision making of the tribe, but also a system full of checks and balances which ensured that nobody could abuse power or grab it for his own benefit.[59]

Major African communal structural evils   43

Along the same lines, Segun and Samuel argue,

> Rulers of pre-colonial African society were made accountable to the people through various mechanisms put in place to check their excesses. The African political model did not provide or make provision for absolutism or tyranny. All societies provided elaborate and explicit rules of behaviour for their rulers.[60]

For example, whenever any *Alaafin*, the Yoruba king of the old Oyo kingdom of Western Nigeria, became despotic in ruling the people, Oyemessi, the council of kingmakers, presented him with an empty calabash. This symbolized not only that the people and land have rejected him as their king, but also required him to commit suicide. Thus, in African society, power and wealth were virtually granted or acquired not for self-service, but for the benefit of the entire community. Whoever acquired wealth and power was to hold them in trust for the community:

> There exists in the African traditions, a conception of *wealth* as being *at the service of the community* rather than for the benefit of the individuals. No individuals ought to be able to exploit his fellow human beings on the grounds of that he is richer than they. Capitalism has never truly held sway in the traditional African community.[61]

Acquiring power and wealth for personal enhancement, and most importantly, for the domination of the other, is almost foreign to Africa and thus contradicts its spirit of community. Though this appears to be a romanticized notion of the traditional African community, the point is that the Big Man syndrome with the motive to amass wealth and power for domination of the other as seen in contemporary African community has its antecedents in the colonial legacy of liberal individualism and authoritarian rule.

According to Rodney, the notion of liberal European individualism as introduced in Africa by colonialism was more destructive in African society than it was in European capitalist society. He contends that in Europe, individualism led to entrepreneurship and adventurism that empowered Europe to conquer the rest of the world. In Africa, however, individualism intensified the exploitation of African labor and "colonialism destroyed social solidarity and promoted the worst form of alienated individualism without social responsibility."[62] This libertarian colonial individualistic capitalism produced big owners of property and industry and improved middle classes in Europe, but in Nigeria and Africa as a whole, it robbed the African people of their property and created miserable classes of people. This was accomplished through slavery, forced labor, over-taxation, and exploitative trade between Africa and Europe. The impact of this spirit of extreme form of European capitalistic individualism, which spreads like a crown fire in contemporary Africa, is very scandalous:

> The effects of capitalism are already being felt in our families. Individualism in society is increasing [in Africa]. Even families in rural areas like to operate

44 *Major African communal structural evils*

in isolation. . . . The (conjugal) family is becoming more independent. . . . The communal system is breaking down.[63]

Colonial rule was all about wielding of absolute control over Africa and its human and material resources for the development of European capitalist industries, to the detriment of African society. The exploitative and asymmetric character of this relationship impacted the Big Man leadership style of post-colonial Africa. The colonial ruler's oppressive use of power, which was the apex of autocratic rule over African people and their resources for the benefit of Europe, also paved the way for a handful post-colonial Nigerian Big Men to exercise autocratic power over state resources for personal enrichment. Dr J.A. Alemazung writes,

> The ruling structure, which was based on the control by a few, through oppression and the use of force, laid a basis for patron-client rulership after colonialism. Neo-patrimonial leadership as practiced in many African countries is an extension of the kind of autocratic and alien tyrant rule that the colonial masters had initiated.[64]

European colonialism bequeathed to African countries the legacy of democracy, but this rule overthrew the traditional African democratic system of government and replaced it with a vicious form of despotism. E.O. Iheukwumere and C.A. Iheukwumere contend that what colonial rule bequeathed to African countries was the legacy of tyrannical rule and plunder, and sowed the seeds for the vicious cycle of corruption that currently plagues the continent:

> Using the pretext of bringing Christianity and civilization to the "natives," European colonizers instead brought barbarism and unspeakable savagery to the Africans. Through brute force and greed, the colonizers ushered in slave labor, divested the African of the ownership of his or her land and the resources therein,[65]

Some Christian missionaries were, for instance, implicated in the selfish exploitation and underdevelopment of Africa. Colonialism was interpreted as the extension of the Christian liberation ordained by God. The missionaries believed that the motive of colonialism was very much the same as that of Christianity. As Jan Boer sees it, colonialism in northern Nigeria was an imperial rule rooted in the divine mandate to bring spiritual, cultural, economic, and political liberation to Africans suffering under satanic forces of oppression, ignorance, and disease by sharing with them the blessings of the Christ-inspired civilization of the West.[66] Christianity was thus seen as a necessary foundation for establishing the much-needed virtues for social and commercial intercourse in Nigeria, and Christian evangelization was the key to the integration of the country into the global capitalist economy.[67] Drawing on the theology that the "Bible and the plough" should

Major African communal structural evils 45

go together, the missionaries encouraged the British capitalists to invest in the country. Dr Levi I. Izuakor argues that "the missionaries were not only interested in proselytisation; they were not averse to uninterrupted British commercial preponderance in [Nigeria]."[68] The missionaries not only recruited Nigerians into the kingdom of God through preaching the gospel, but also initiated them into an exploitative capitalist economic system by promoting the production of cash crops. The missionaries promoted farm practices to improve economic well-being of the people, but their good efforts were co-opted by the commercial interest of the British colonial administration.

European colonial powers executed such exploitation and dehumanization of Africa with both complicity and the connivance of Christianity. The theological hermeneutics of the Christian God as a triumphant God who conquers and rules the world and humanity by power and in glory inspired the complicity of Christian religion. Moltmann argues that the collaboration of Western Christianity with an instrumentalized science and technology is responsible for conquering and exploiting the world:

> From science and technology, Europe acquired that instrumentalizing knowledge which enabled it to use the resources of the colonized world to build up a world civilization. . . . The triumphal march of science and technology conferred on Christianity the status of being the religion of the triumphant god.[69]

Moltmann claims that the Christian messianic hope that informs the European ideology to dominate global human and material resources for self-enrichment not only gave birth to the new modern world, but also created a polarity between *modernity* and *sub-modernity*. Though the emergence of the modern world brought impressive progress and development for Europe, it produced underdevelopment and misery in African countries, which is the price Africans paid for European political domination and economic gain.

The new Trinitarian hermeneutics of God has the potential to repudiate the Big Man syndrome as exhibited in Africa, whether Africans themselves caused it or it was bequeathed to them by colonialism. God's gift of Trinitarian communion rooted in Christ and the Spirit does not promote domination of the world and humanity by superior military might and political coercion. Rather, it empowers the liberation of humanity through the gospel, justice, and love. Any hermeneutics of a Christian God that aids and abets the domination of some parts of humanity for the sake of the other parts and the subjugation of the world for personal profit is at odds with the new Trinitarian hermeneutics of the Christian God rooted in Christ and the Spirit as a just and liberating God. It is unthinkable that such a Triune God, who is always on the side of those at the margins, can and will approve oppression of the most vulnerable people who exist at the margins of the world and society. Therefore, the Big Man syndrome, whether inflicted from within or without Africa, is the antithesis of the just and liberating character of the Triune God and thus unacceptable.

46 *Major African communal structural evils*

Ethnic and religious nepotism

The final Trinitarian critique of the systemic problems that distort the African spirit of community in Nigeria is of ethnic and religious nepotism. Here I will examine ethnic and religious forms of nepotism, which blossom into ethno-religious conflict in Nigeria. I will specifically explore their causes and damaging impacts, which undermine the character of African community in Nigeria.

Ethnic nepotism: a cancer in the flesh

Nigeria is an ethnically diverse nation-state. It consists of a plethora of minor and major ethnic nationalities, the major ones of which are the Hausa, Igbo, and Yoruba. Nigeria is home to over 400 different ethnic communities. This ethnic heterogeneity creates an atmosphere potentially conducive to ethnic nepotism. Ethnic nepotism is the putting of one's own ethnic interests over against the interests of the other ethnic groups and of the nation as a whole. As a nation that is virtually contaminated by the vice of ethnic nepotism, Nigerians see themselves first and foremost as members of these ethnic groups before they see themselves as Nigerians, and thus are more loyal to their ethnic groups than to the nation. This is evidenced in the existence of the different ethnic associations and militias in Nigeria where members meet regularly to discuss their own ethnic interests, and remind themselves of the loyalty that they owe to their ethnic groups. Because ethnic allegiance has become pervasive,

> In Nigerian society today, many prefer identification with their ethnic group rather than with the nation or even state. . . . That Nigerians still exhibit a strong allegiance to ethnic group . . . has consequently encouraged primordial sentiments among Nigerian people.[70]

In Nigeria, ethnic nepotism takes different forms, ranging from the major ethnic groups sharing power and national resources among themselves, to the systematic exclusion of minority ethnic groups, to the imposition of ethnic hegemony over minorities through the control of land and traditional leadership positions, which often legitimately belong to the minorities. These major ethnic groups believe they are divinely anointed to rule over the minorities. S. O. Eboh contends that

> in Nigeria, [the dominant] ethnic groups believe that God created them to *rule* and *exploit* others. Systematically they suck the *economic life-blood* of the minority ethnic groups. They are not ashamed that they are *born to rule* and *dominate* others.[71]

The result of this is inter-ethnic hostility among ethnic groups in search of power and dominance. The perverse desire of these so-called "major" ethnic groups to dominate the others and to reduce them to second-class citizens inevitably leads to ethnic mistrust and anger:

> Such [a] domineering presence and control of . . . the "national cake" has always irked the other ethnic groups who are in the minority. These minority

groups feel left out in the scheme of things in Nigeria, a situation that has now bred distrust, fear and [a] sense of hopelessness[.][72]

What exacerbates ethnic nepotism is politicization and institutionalization of ethnic identity, which has now become a normative yardstick for national presidential and parliamentary elections and for political appointments and promotions. Hence, certain exalted political offices are often reserved for the dominant ethnic groups. E. E. Anugwon argues, "The ethnic factor, however, did not diminish with the advent of independence; rather, it became a yardstick for measuring contribution to the national development effort and especially for allocating and distributing power and national resources."[73] This has enthroned the political culture of selecting national leaders not on the basis of merit, competence, and wealth of experience, but on the basis of one's ethnic identity and region.

As a game of numbers and a winner-takes-all culture, Nigerian politics usually favors the dominant ethnic groups ruling the nation at the expense of the minority ethnic groups. The struggle for power among these so-called dominant ethnic groups, who consider it to be their birthright to rule no matter what, led to the post-election violence of 2011, which claimed many lives and properties. E. G. Irobi claims, "Since independence, the situation in Nigeria has been fraught with ethnic politics whereby the elite from different ethnic groups schemed to attract as many federal resources to their regions as possible, neglecting issues that could have united the country."[74] Ethnic politics has produced corrupt leaders who always put their ethnic interest before the interest of the nation. Apart from ethnic identity being a tool used for powering sharing, ethnic origin is also an instrument for determining the location of industries, the suitability for employment, and other development projects. David Lamb succinctly sums up the dilemma of manipulating ethnicity in Africa:

> African leaders deplore ethnocentrism. They call it the cancer that threatens to eat out the very fabric of the nation. Yet almost every African politician practices it, most African presidents are more ethnic chief than national statesman, and it remains perhaps the most potent force in day-to-day African life. It is a factor in political struggles and distribution of resources. It often determines who gets jobs, who gets promoted, who gets accepted to a university, because by its very definition ethnicity implies sharing among members of the extended family, making sure that your own are looked after first. To give a job to a fellow ethnic member is not nepotism, it is an obligation. For a political leader to choose his closest advisers and bodyguards from the ranks of his own ethnic group is not patronage, it is a good common sense. It ensures security, continuity, and authority.[75]

Beside the Big Man question and its consequences, which perennially provide a socio-economically and politically climate favorable for ethnic nepotism to persist in Nigeria, ethnic nepotism itself was the product of colonialism. The undemocratic amalgamation of disparate pre-colonial ethnic nationalities into one nation by the British colonial administration sowed the seed of ethnic discord in Nigeria.

48 *Major African communal structural evils*

The helplessness of diverse ethnic groups to negotiate their amalgamation into a nation-state is at the root of ethnic wrangling and agitations and of ethnic hues and cries of marginalization and nepotism in Nigeria.[76] Their forceful amalgamation has done more harm than good to the ethnic unity of Nigeria. Before the advent of colonial rule, Nigerian ethnic nationalities had little interaction among themselves and hardly discriminated against each other on the basis of ethnic identity, except perhaps in terms of intermarriage. Therefore, there was virtually no inter-ethnic antagonism. But with imposition of colonial rule, ethnic nepotism was introduced and institutionalized in Nigeria:

> Nowhere in the history of pre-colonial independent Nigeria can anyone point to the massacre of Ibos by Hausas or any incident which suggests that people up to the 19th century were fighting each other because of ethnic origin. . . . What came to be called tribalism at the beginning of the new epoch of political independence in Nigeria was itself a product of colonialism so as to be exploited.[77]

The British colonial administrators used the tactic of "divide and rule," separated the various ethnic groups from each other, and thus prevented them from uniting against the colonial government. For example, the division of Nigeria into three regions (see Chapter 1), each dominated by one of the three major ethnic groups, created ethnic consciousness, politics, competition and animosity, which became a stumbling block to the development of a genuine national consciousness. The regional division also marginalized the minorities and subsumed them into the dominant ethnic nationalities. Dr Tunga Lergo argues,

> Over time, national narrative and political discourse took on an increasingly regional format, undercutting the influence of minority ethnic groups. They were almost forgotten in the equation. . . . Regional minorities, by political expediency and economic self interests, were forced to line up behind their respective regional majority.[78]

Ethnic inequality is now a stark reality that one cannot afford to deny in spite of the formation of the Federal Character Commission and creation of more states to address the issue! Many ethnic nationalities are not only perpetually oppressed and excluded from participating in running the affairs of their own country, but also are treated as aliens in their ancestral land. The frequent recurrence of ethnic conflicts in the country abounds. This includes Tiv-Jukun, Chamba-Kuteb, Hausa-Yoruba, Birom-Fulani, Hausa/Fulani-Igbo ethnic conflicts, and even the civil war (1967–70). As a "cancer in the flesh" of African community, ethnic nepotism poses a lethal threat to national integration and unity. The sharp division of Nigerians along ethnic lines shows that Nigeria is a mere name designating a geo-political location rather than a united people.

The church, which in many ways is the product of the society, is not immune from ethnic nepotism. As in the wider society, ethnic identity has been politicized in the church. Power-thirsty clergy and members use it as a weapon in campaigning for church leadership. The spirit of the church as a united communion hardly prevails in the election of church leaders. In the politics of the church, the blood of ethnic connection often takes precedence over the water of baptism, the essential sacramental symbol of the unity of the church. As Bishop Albert Obiefuna expresses it,

> When it comes to the crunch, it is not the Christian concept of the church as a family that prevails, but rather the adage *blood is thicker than water*. And by water here one can presumably include the waters of Baptism.[79]

Even when one is Christian, it appears one's allegiance to the blood of one's ethnic group is more important than the water of baptism. This has brought about ethnic division and strife in the church. For example, the Lutheran Church of Christ in Nigeria (LCCN) has witnessed ethnic strife, which has split the church along ethnic lines since its inception in 1913. Describing this ethnic animosity as "chronic," Dr M. P. Filibus argues that ethnic tensions in the church have coalesced around issues of leadership and allocation of resources. Filibus says that some members of the church have used ethic identity as a tool for not only achieving personal ambition, which they have failed to obtain by merit, but also for evading consequences of personal responsibility.[80] Rather than using ethnic diversity for building up the church, it has been used to set it apart. Filibus writes,

> Successive tribal and ethnic feuds have led the LCCN to live in a state of disunity, rather than unity. Chronic tribal and ethnic disagreements have bred misunderstanding, suspicion and mistrust among the various tribes of its members. Different tribes seem to feel threatened by others.[81]

Such ethnic sentiment at times creates obstacles for local churches to accept pastors from different ethnic groups, and this jeopardizes the unity of the church of the Triune God. The church of the Triune God is a multi-ethnic community of faith, but the Nigerian church is far from being such. Some Nigerian churches exist as closely-knit ethnic communities, and those that are urban and multi-ethnic are bedeviled by internal ethnic tensions. The existence of the church along ethnic lines is part of the legacy left behind by the missionaries. As A. T. Mbachirin contends, "Missionaries did not help the ethnic problem in Nigeria. The problem was mainly with their method of planting churches. They preferred to plant churches along ethnic lines."[82]

Though the noble intension was to translate the Bible into the local language of a particular ethnic group and indigenize the gospel, Mbachirin argues that the consequence of such a mission strategy was the establishment of the churches that became identical with their ethnic group. But the new Trinitarian interpretation of God leads us to oppose ethnic nepotism in whatever forms it manifests itself in the society and church. As we shall see in Chapter 5, it is a betrayal of the beauty of the unity in diversity of the Triune God who created and set free every ethnic community from the sin of ethnic nepotism to live out such beauty in church and society.

50 *Major African communal structural evils*

Religious nepotism: an antithesis of true religion

Religious nepotism is expressed through undue preferential treatment that members of one religious group or those in authority give their own religion and its members over members of other religions. This not only means preference of one's own religious beliefs and practices over against that of other religions, but also includes preference of one's own religious members over adherents of other religious groups for employment, promotion, awarding contracts, voting, and the allocation of any public resources. Religious nepotism is inspired by the belief that whoever does not profess our religion is either against us or does not belong to us and thus is not welcome. The relationship between religions is often viewed in terms of "believers" and "unbelievers," "the faithful" and "the infidels," "us" and "them," and "the saved' and "the lost." Those who perceive themselves as the "saved" firmly believe that those who they labeled as the "lost" must be either converted or killed in the name of God. The perpetrators of such religious perspectives deploy every necessary resource at their disposal, including brute force, to accomplish their mission. Saliu Aruna describes well this fanatical religious nepotism:

> To them the belief in a religion other than theirs runs foul of the injunctions handed down by God through a messenger or prophet as the case may be. The fanatics see other "believers" as those who have gone astray and who need some sermon or preaching to make them fall in line with their doctrine, which to them is always the best and most reliable basis for redemption on the judgment day. . . . They believe rather wrongly that those who do not share their mode of worship or the doctrine of their religion were better dead than alive.[83]

As a multi-religious society,[84] there is perhaps no country in the world where such a "holier than thou" mentality is more manifested than Nigeria. Here there are two dominant monotheistic religions – Islam and Christianity – that command the absolute loyalty of most Nigerians. Both claim to be the exclusive means of salvation. Each denounces the other as false, while each insists on being the true religion:

> Both religions claim monopoly of religious truths as well as the absolute prerogative to eternity in heaven. This religious cliché is contemptuously imbued in the public preaching of both religious groups, as religious sermons are often laden with messages signifying the monopoly of salvation and truth.[85]

The making of such controversial absolute truth claims is the fundamental character of every religion in a multi-religious society, claims S. Awoniyi. Each religion, he argues, believes that its own "religion is special, and in fact, the best and the only one that gives assurance of ultimate salvation to man."[86] While Awoniyi's generic argument is flawed, there is no doubt that the making of conflicting absolute truth claims by the dominant religions in Nigeria has become the norm of everyday religious affairs there.

Major African communal structural evils   51

For example, many Nigerian Christians draw on scriptural passages such as "there is salvation in no one else, for there is no other name under heaven given among men by which we must be saved" (Ac 4:12) and "He who believes in him is not condemned; he who does not believe is condemned already, because he has not believed in the name of the only Son of God," (Joh. 3:18), and a host of others, to openly preach that all non-Christians are doomed to perish unless they accept Christ as their personal Lord and savior. Also, many Muslims appeal to Quranic verses such as "Surely the true religion with God is Islam" (Quran 3:19) and "O my sons, God has chosen the religion for you; so die not unless you are Muslims" (Quran 2:132), in order to publicly proclaim that Islam is the only means of salvation, hence the only right religion. All non-Muslims are thereby lost and it is, therefore, the divine duty of Muslims to subdue and convert them to Islam. The former influential religious bigot Grand Khadi, Abubakar Gumi, was untiring in making this sort of exclusive claim about Islam:

> Indeed, if I do not usually take Christians seriously in this country in matters of faith, it is because there is hardly any platform for discussing our differences. They have simply lost the original essence of their religion. Surely "the only religion in the sight of God," as the Holy Qur'an has emphasized, "is the religion of Islam."[87]

As the only divinely approved religion, according to Gumi, Islam would ultimately triumph over Christianity. He believed that no force against Islam could prevail. Islam has come to stay no matter what. A Christian would never become the president of Nigeria. Should this happen, Nigeria would split.

The underlying motive of the proponents of religious nepotism is not fear of God and love of the neighbor, but rather, the exercise of power and control over the adherents of their own religion. Religious and political leaders alike use this religious ideology for personal gain. Religious leaders capitalize on this exclusive religious ideology to keep their followers and non-followers permanently subjugated to their religious hegemony in the name of God.

Politicians also use it for seizing and maintaining their grip on state political power and resources. To gain this political acceptability, these politicians publicly patronize their own religion to the exclusion of others, in spite of the constitutional provision that explicitly prohibits such preferential religious patronage. In predominantly Islamic northern states, Muslim politicians openly use public funds to finance Sallah celebrations, Muslim pilgrimage welfare boards, and the teaching of Islamic religion in public schools without extending the same support to Christians. Muslim politicians' preferential patronage of Islam is also true of Christian politicians in some dominant Christian states. Therefore, Falola is right to argue, "Religion is used by the power-hungry as a stepping-stone to power and political legitimacy. Since the mid-seventies, politicians have urged their followers to vote along religious lines – Muslims are told to vote for Muslims, and Christians for Christians."[88] To reciprocate this support, these hypocritical politicians while in office give leaders of their own religions

52 *Major African communal structural evils*

positions in government and other privileges, but deny the same opportunity to other religious leaders:

> In most states, the dominant religion denies the other religious groups access to certain privileges like land for locating worship houses or air time for transmitting religious messages. This attitude translates into political and economic preferentialism towards the favoured religious group(s), while marginalising the others.[89]

What Nigeria is witnessing today is the increasing "religionization" of politics and politicization of religion. The consequence of this is very daunting. The two religions do not perceive each other as friends, but enemies; each suspects the other and accuses the other of domination. One competes with the other over "winning converts" and controlling every socio-economic and political sphere of national life: "Both major Nigerian religions tend to see one another as rivals fighting for control of converts and of the state itself."[90] One religion condemns the other for distorting its religion, even despising and ridiculing the beliefs and way of life of the other. The pervasive stereotyping of religious adherents also compounds the mockery of opposing faiths. For instance, Muslims, especially those from the northern part of Nigeria, are in the habit of referring to all non-Muslims as *Arna* or *Kafir*, Arabic words for "heathen," or unbelievers, while it is fashionable for Christians to refer to all Muslims as terrorists and violence-mongers.[91]

The contradictory religious truth claims, ways of life, and mission of the two religions have metamorphosed into a catalogue of religious conflicts, which Nigeria has experienced in recent times.[92] The ongoing deadly religious violence is carried out by the Islamist group Boko Haram, which means that "Western education is forbidden." The deadly attacks unleashed by Boko Haram in Nigeria in an attempt to forcibly Islamize the north, and if possible, the entire country, are informed by the idea of harmful religious exclusivism coupled with political motives. The insurgents fight mainly against Christians – infidels, the government, and Western education. They destroy schools and churches in the north, claiming they are fighting for God. Sheik Abubakar Imam Shekau, the leader of the group, who had threatened to overthrow President Goodluck Jonathan's government at the time, said:

> If death is your worldly gain, for us, it is eternal victory to die working for Allah. Our joy is to die in Jihad for Allah against infidels like you. . . . We are not afraid because we are not doing man's work but Allah's work. And we will see who will carry the day.[93]

Shekau vowed that his group would not only destroy Christians and Christianity in Nigeria, but would also kill all Muslims, assisting the arrest and harassment of its members. All the efforts of the former President, Goodluck E. Jonathan, to contain the religious violence have yielded little or no success. Boko Haram appears to be unaffected, even waxing stronger, continuing with deadly attacks

Major African communal structural evils 53

while bragging the government will not be able to bring order and justice. Jonathan, for example, acknowledged that members of Boko Haram had infiltrated his administration, but has update failed to fish them out. Consequently, Boko Haram has continued to carry out attacks on Christians, churches, government institutions, and even Muslims in the northeast, in spite of the security task force put in place by the government:

> The church bombings, along with the recent spate of kidnappings [over 250 Chibok school girls] and other high-profile civilian attacks, appear to be part of a deliberate effort to . . . discredit and delegitimize the national government by exposing the weakness of its security apparatus and justice mechanisms and, potentially, to ignite a religious war.[94]

The impact of religious conflict on Nigeria is incalculable. Apart from wanton destruction of life and property worth millions of dollars, it has brought untold hardship to Nigerians. It has been estimated that about 1.5 million people have been displaced by the ongoing Islamic terrorism.[95] These internally displaced persons, many of whom are women and children, lack shelter, food, and medical care. The religious conflict has discouraged both domestic and foreign investment and aggravated the country's unemployment problem. Moreover, the African spirit of community that used to hold the people together in unity has been broken. The spirit of discord, mistrust, hatred, and fear has been rekindled. Nigerians have never been polarized along religious lines like this before. The spirit of the Christian communion has been broken following the constant religious violence that is being meted out against it. Sadly, in this brokenness and hopelessness, some Christians have resorted to employing violence to defend their faith, life, and property whenever they are attacked. They have abandoned the Sermon on the Mount, which promotes a culture of non-violence, while drawing inspiration from the Mosaic injunction that permits violent retaliation in search of peace:

> Before [now], many Christians had hoped that calm, prayer, and fasting would suffice, but they [have today begun] to speak of the [L]aw of Moses – eye for an eye. They [have] voiced determination to physically defend their lives, houses, families, and property. This mood has not abated, and the use of violence is now regarded by Christians as a legitimate defense.[96]

Several factors have been identified as causes for religious nepotism and conflict. Part of the underlying cause is the Big Man issue, and blatant inability on the part of the government to objectively investigate, arrest, prosecute, and bring to justice those responsible for perpetrating religious bigotry and violence. Too often the Government sets up a commission of inquiry to identify the remote and immediate causes of religious conflict, but the matter ends after the commission submits its report only for another panel to be set up when a new religious conflict breaks out. The report of the World Council of Churches and the Royal Aal al-Bayt Institute for Islamic Thought on the inter-religious tensions and crisis in

54 *Major African communal structural evils*

Nigeria suggests that the government's ineffectiveness is evidenced from "[t]he lack of willingness or ability to punish those directly or indirectly responsible for incidents of violence especially when these are powerful personalities in society (the 'Big man'/'Little man' syndrome: the little man gets punished, the big man[has impunity] is unscathed)."[97]

There is also the unguarded practice of religion anywhere and anytime by most Nigerians, to the brazen disregard of the law and the rights of other people. This is evidenced in the blockage of public roads during worship, using loud offensive public address systems during and after worship, and the uttering of provocative public statements by one religion against the other. Such lawless practice of religion has stimulated and will continue to stimulate religious animosity in Nigeria. To make matters worse, the constitutional human rights of the individual to freedom of thought, conscience, and religion, which allows the individual to renounce or change his or her religious belief at will, have been systematically eroded. Those who exercise this constitutional right in Nigeria risk being disowned, persecuted, and even killed by their immediate family members and members of their own faith community. For example, when my mother, who was a Muslim at the time, became engaged to my father, everyone else in her family and faith community disowned her on the grounds that my Christian father was an unbeliever, and when she became a Christian, condemned her to hellfire. Thus, being a member of one religion or another is more a matter of coercion rather than choice. Such forced imposition of religion on others often degenerates into religious intolerance and violence.

Religious nepotism, especially in northern Nigeria, is also part of the legacy bequeathed by colonialism. The colonial government openly supported and protected Islam against the threat of Christian proselytization of Muslims by banning missionaries from entering the north, let alone to evangelize. E.P.T. Crampton reports that the colonial administrators did not permit missionary enterprise in the predominant Muslim areas of the north because it would violate their policy of non-interference in Islamic religion and threaten the authority of northern emirs, thus impeding their much-prized indirect rule.[98] Christian missionaries were permitted only to evangelize among the "pagan" ethnic minorities of the north. Muslim leaders took advantage of this protection to conquer and dominate many of these non-Muslim minority ethnic groups, which they had failed to conquer by force prior to colonial rule. Muslim emirs, in collaboration with the British colonial administrators, also capitalized on the policy of exclusion to deny missionaries the land to build churches, freedom of worship, and circulation of Christian literature. Such preferential patronage, which the British colonial government accorded Islam, allowed Muslims to consolidate their superiority over Christianity and non-Muslims. Muslim leaders and politicians today erroneously or deliberately have embraced that act of exclusion and domination as the normative method of relating with Christians today, long after their colonial masters had gone.

It goes without saying that religious nepotism is the antithesis of true religion, which is about a God who shows no partiality in dealing with humanity, whether they are believers or unbelievers, "for he makes his sun rise on the evil and on the good, and sends rain on the just and on the unjust" (Mat. 5:44–5). The acid test of a true religion is not determined by its unique superiority to other faiths in terms of its absolute doctrine, which excludes non-members from its own fold. Rather, what determines it is an inclusive God, who unqualifiedly liberates and welcomes all humans to Godself so that they may welcome unconditionally one another into their faith and civic community. When God is there for anyone, regardless of who they are and what they believe, one would expect nothing else than this from any true religion and ethnic group. Humanity is first and foremost the creation of God before being members of any religious and ethnic group. What determines humanness is not our human allegiance to religious faith and ethnic affiliation, but to God, who set us free in Christ and the Spirit to embrace without discrimination every human being created in the image of God. Therefore, there is one mission of God for every religion, and that mission is not to subdue and dominate the other by brute force, but rather, to participate with God in liberating humanity and the world through the gospel of forgiveness, justice, and love from the demonic and human powers and shackles of domination and oppression into the inclusive kingdom of freedom.

Summary and conclusion

What I have critically analyzed in this chapter is three main systemic problems that distort the African practice of community. The first is patriarchal malaise. The malaise of patriarchy that stratifies men and women into unequal members of the community is noxiously entrenched in the African traditional communal cultures. As a structural injustice, the patriarchal syndrome empowers men to exercise near absolute control over the body and labor of women for sex and domestic chores, which excludes women from assuming public leadership positions in the society and church. As a result, women have been socially, economically, and political marginalized and oppressed. Too many of them exist at the fringes of the society, with their God-given potential remaining virtually undeveloped and unharnessed. The advent of Christianity has not drastically impacted the patriarchal syndrome. Christianity as preached and practiced in Nigeria has often reinforced rather than challenged it. The absolute submission of a woman to man is perceived as the measure of her devotedness to God in Nigeria, which is reinforced when the doctrine of God is understood and proclaimed as monarchial rather than Trinitarian. Colonialism has also made the patriarchal complex even worse. It disrupted the traditional complementary gender role system and exacerbated the gender imbalance between men and women.

The gift of the Triune God's perichoretic communion calls into question whatever perpetrates the patriarchal complex in the Nigerian church and society. The communion of the Triune God offers a paradigm for a more reciprocal form of rule. As an eschatological in-breaking of God's gender-inclusive rule into the present world, the patriarchal structural exploitation of women's bodies and labor for the selfish end of men is non-Trinitarian and thus idolatrous. Such patriarchal

56 *Major African communal structural evils*

exploitation is informed by patriarchal rule rather than by the new Trinitarian hermeneutics of God.

As for the second major structural problem, which is the Big Man syndrome, I have demonstrated that it has enormous devastative consequences on the African community. Apart from obliterating the spirit of the community, which requires that whoever acquires power and property should use them for the common good of the community, the Big Man malaise has bred corruption, injustice, and abject poverty amid abundance, insecurity, despotism, and breakdown of rule of law in the Nigerian society. This syndrome has resulted in the emergence of an oppressive pyramidal hierarchy in the church that alienates the clergy from the laity, abandonment of the servant model style of leadership for a model based on power and glory, exclusion of women from leadership, and stifling of the critical prophetic public ministry of the church. Bigmanism is relatively alien to traditional African community, which had a traditional system of checks and balances that prevented its leaders from becoming oppressive Big Men. The Big Man syndrome is largely the offshoot of colonial rulers who were authoritarian and oppressive in ruling Nigeria and its material resources for the economic enrichment of the colonial administration. Like the colonial masters, too many post-colonial Nigerian leaders who took over the mantle of leadership from the colonial rulers have consciously or unconsciously adopted colonial rulers' tyrannical style of leadership as a norm of for ruling the country's abundant human and natural resources for personal enhancement.

Sadly, Christianity was complicit in the colonial oppression and brutalization of Nigeria that destroyed the African spirit of community. It provided a theological hermeneutics of God that justified colonialism, and worked so hard through its missionaries to conquer souls not just for Christ, but also for the British colonial government.

As a just and merciful perichoresis in communion, the Triune God provides grounds for criticizing and rejecting the Big Man syndrome. God's rule of justice and mercy empowers Christians to faithfully challenge monarchical Big Persons who rule humanity and the world by power and force. The Triune God as constituted and revealed in Christ and the Spirit can repudiate the persistence, emulation, and perpetration of the colonial tyranny of the Big Man rule by African Big Men in the church and society.

The final systemic problem is ethnic and religious nepotism. Such ethnic sentiment stems from the inordinate pride and confidence that people have in their own ethnic identity. As institutionalized ethnic nepotism, ethnic identity is also used for government employment, political appointment, and the sharing of other public resources, often to the exclusion the minority ethnic groups and non-indigenes. This manipulation and institutionalization of ethnic nepotism in Nigeria is the root cause of the recurring ethnic communal rivalries and violence. The story of ethnic nepotism is true also of the church. Religious nepotism is endemic in Nigerian public and private affairs, with people, especially those in power, favoring the members of their own religion for employment, awarding contracts and allocation of public resources. I have claimed that such religious nepotism is rooted in the

Major African communal structural evils 57

absolute doctrine of religious exclusivism. As a result, the two religions of Christianity and Islam perceive each other as rivals, competing for converts, supremacy, and influence. These conflicting truth claims, coupled with manipulation of religion by religious and political leaders for personal interests, are responsible for the past and ongoing religious violence in Nigeria. Boko Haram's protracted terrorism is the grossest expression of fanatical religious nepotism. The Northern colonial legacy of openly preferring Islam to Christianity laid the foundation for religious nepotism, culminating in inter-faith tensions and conflicts today. However, the unwillingness on the part of the government to bring perpetrators of religious nepotism to justice has continued to exacerbate the persistence of a religious atmosphere conducive to religious nepotism. On the whole, the root cause of the tripartite systemic evils is human sin, for which the Triune God died.

The Triune God who welcomes every human regardless of his or her ethnic and religious identity deconstructs any ethnic and religious ideology that inspires religious and ethnic nepotism. The Triune God's gift of welcoming communion critiques ethnic and religious forms of nepotism that destroy the African spirit of community under the pretext of promoting ethnic and religious uniqueness and superiority. As the Triune God is the creator of every human being, any preferential treatment of one section of humanity on the basis of ethnic and religious affiliation at the expense of the others is unjust. Ethnic and religious diversity is God's own gift and thus is destroyed when people's rights to exist as distinct ethnic and religious communities are trampled upon for personal development. In the next chapter, I will explore how the paradigmatic gift of the Triune God's just and egalitarian communion can transform the African tradition of community.

Notes

1 Veli-Matti Kärkkäinen, *The Trinity: Global Perspectives* (Louisville, KY: Westminster John Knox Press, 2007), 398.
2 Godiya Allanana Makama, "Patriachy and Gender Inequality in Nigeria: The Way Forward," *European Scientific Journal* 19, no. 17 (2013): 118.
3 Daniella Coetzee, "South African Education and the Ideology of Patriarchy," *South Africa Journal of Education* 21, no. 4 (2001): 300.
4 The patriarchal complex is not something that is peculiar to Nigeria. It is an ideological complex that cuts across Africa and, by extension, the world over. However, its devastating impact is probably felt more in African societies than any part of the world.
5 J. Shola Omotola, "What Is This Gender Talk All About After All? Gender, Power and Politics in Contemporary in Nigeria," *African Study Monographs* 28, no. 1 (2007): 39.
6 Oni Samuel and Joshua Segun, "Gender Relations in Nigeria's Democratic Governance," *Journal of Politics & Governance* 1, no. 2/3 (2012): 5.
7 Omotola, "What Is This Gender Talk All About After All? Gender, Power and Politics in Contemporary in Nigeria," 37.
8 Adebayo Anthony Abayomi and Taiwo Olabode Kolawole, "Domestic Violence and Death: Women as Endangered Gender in Nigeria," *American Journal of Sociological Research* 3, no. 3 (2013): 57.
9 Makama, "Patriachy and Gender Inequality in Nigeria: The Way Forward," 122.
10 Mercy Amba Oduyoye, *Daughters of Anowa: African Women and Patriarchy* (Maryknoll, NY: Orbis Books, 1995), 177.

58 *Major African communal structural evils*

11 Kolawole, "Domestic Violence and Death: Women as Endangered Gender in Nigeria," 57.
12 Omotola, "What Is This Gender Talk All About After All? Gender, Power and Politics in Contemporary in Nigeria," 38.
13 Chimaraoke Otutubikey Izugbara, "Patriarchal Ideology and Discourses of Sexuality in Nigeria," *Africa Regional Sexuality Resource Centre* no. 2 (2004): 15–16.
14 Walter Rodney, *How Europe Underdeveloped Africa* (London: Bogle-L'Ouverture Publications, 1972), 247.
15 Samuel and Segun, "Gender Relations in Nigeria's Democratic Governance," 6.
16 Maria Rojas, "Women in Colonial Nigeria," 1990, www.postcolonialweb.org/nigeria/colonwom.html (accessed October 19, 2014).
17 Blaine Harden, *Africa: Dispatches from a Fragile Continent* (New York, NY: W. W. Norton & Company, 1990), 218.
18 Ibid., 217–18.
19 Ibid., 218.
20 Femi Aribisala, "Bigmanism in Nigeria," *Vanguard*, 2013, www.vanguardngr.com/2013/10/bigmanism-nigeria/ (accessed January 2014).
21 Joshua Segun and Oni Samuel, "Democracy and Accountability in Pre-Colonial Africa: Lessons for Contemporary African States," *JFE Journal of the Humanities and Social Studies (IJOHUSS)* n.v. (2013): 49.
22 Timothy P. Palmer, "Martin Luther's Theology of the Cross in the Nigerian Context," *TCNN Research Bulletin* no. 48 (2007): 4.
23 As cited in Pius Oyeniran Abioje, "Liberation Theology Vis-a-Vis Nigeria's Socio-Political and Economic Development," *Journal of Cultural and Religious Studies* 6, no. 1 (2008): 8–9.
24 Peter Cunliffe-Jones, *My Nigeria: Five Decades of Independence* (New York, NY: Palgrave Macmillan, 2010), 162. Italics in the original.
25 "Ribadu Speaks on Dismissal, Demotion Reversed from Police," *Vanguard*, 2013, www.vanguardngr.com/2013/10/got-police-dismissal-demotion-reversed-ribadu/ (accessed October 22, 2014).
26 "2013 World Corruption Index: Nigeria Ranks 144 Among 177 Countries," *Vanguard*, 2013, www.vanguardngr.com/2013/12/afghanistan-n-korea-somalia-top-world-graft-index/ (accessed October 22, 2014).
27 "Director Jailed 2yrs for Stealing N33bn Pension Fund Freed on N250, 000 Fine," *Premium Times*, 2013, www.premiumtimesng.com/news/117599-director-jailed-2yrs-for-stealing-n33bn-pension-fund-freed-on-n250000-fine.html (accessed October 22, 2014).
28 Human Rights Watch, *Corruption on Trial? The Record of Nigeria's Economic and Financial Crimes Commission* (New York, NY: Human Rights Watch, 2011), 22; Olanrewaju Suraju, "Presidential Pardon for Diepreye Alamiyesegha: Abuse of Power and Morality," *Sahara Reporters*, 2013, http://saharareporters.com/2013/03/18/presidential-pardon-diepreye-alamieyesegha-abuse-power-and-morality-olanrewaju-suraju (accessed October 22, 2014).
29 Mathew H. Kukah, "The Cost of Democracy," *Newswatch*, 2010, 49.
30 Alaba Johnson, "Economist Magazine: Nigerians Legislators World Highest Paid," *Naija Pundit*, 2013, www.naijapundit.com/news/economist-magazine-nigerian-legislators-world-s-highest-paid (accessed October 22, 2014).
31 Olakunle F. Odumosu, "Social Costs of Poverty: The Case of Crime in Nigeria," *Journal of Social Development in Africa* 14, no. 2 (1992): 72–3.
32 Omololu Ogunma, "Nigeria: U.S. $600 Billion Stolen by Nigerian Elite Since Independence," *This Day*, 2013, http://allafrica.com/stories/201306190182.html (accessed October 22, 2014).
33 Everest Amaefule, "100 Million Nigerians Live Destitution-World Bank," *Punch*, www.punchng.com/news/100-million-nigerians-live-in-destitution-world-bank (accessed October 22, 2014).

Major African communal structural evils 59

34 Adunola Adepoju, "Feminisation of Poverty in Nigerian Cities: Insights from Focus Group Discussions and Participatory Poverty [1] Assessment," *African Population Studies Supplement* 19, no. 2 (2004): 141.

35 Jœrgen Carling, "Migration, Human Smuggling and Trafficking from Nigeria to Europe," *IOM International Organization for Migration* no. 23 (2006): 45.

36 Shalini Nadaswaran, "Neo-Liberal Nigeria and Sex Trafficking in Nigerian Women's Writings," *2011 International Conference on Humanities, Society and Culture IPERD* 20 (2011): 273.

37 Eme Okechukwu Innocent and Anthony Onyishi, "The Challenges of Insecurity in Nigeria: A Thematic Exposition," *Interdisciplinary Journal of Contemporary Research in Business* 3, no. 8 (2011): 174–5.

38 Ibid. About $4 billion was allocated to defense and police.

39 Aliyu Mukhtar Katsina, "Nigeria's Security Challenges and the Crisis of Development: Towards a New Framework for Analysis," *International Journal of Developing Societies* 1, no. 3 (2012): 114.

40 Ibid.

41 For more discussion see Ibrahim Bitrus, "Disturbing Unjust Peace in Nigeria Through the Church and Legal Reforrms: The Contribution of Luther's Critical Public Theology," in *On Secular Goverment: Lutheran Perspectives on Contemporary Legal Issues*, ed. R. W. Duty and M. A. Failinger (Grand Rapids, MI: W. B. Eerdmans Publishing Co., 2016).

42 Rafiu Adeyanju Lawal-Rabana, "The Nigerian Bar Association and the Protection of Rule of Law in Nigeria," www.ibanet.org/barassociations/bar_associations_Zagreb_conference_materials.aspx (accessed December 13, 2013).

43 Mojeed Olujinmi A. Alabi and Joseph 'Yinka Fashagba, "The Legislature and Anti-Corruption Crusade Under the Fourth Republic of Nigeria: Constitutional Imperatives and Practical Realities," *International Journal of Politics and Good Governance* 1, no. 1.2 (2010): 31–2.

44 Emmanuel C. Onyeozili, "Obstacles to Effective Policing in Nigeria," *African Journal of Criminology and Justice Studies* 1, no. 1 (2005): 45.

45 Ibid., 42.

46 As cited in Clement Majawa, "The Church's Role in Defining Genuine Democracy in Africa," in *African Theology Today*, ed. Emmanuel Katongole (Scranton, PA: University of Scranton Press, 2002), 101.

47 Chinua Achebe, *The Trouble with Nigeria* (Enugu, Nigeria: Fourth Dimension Publishers, 1983), 76.

48 Chika Asogwa and Damian Amana, "Communication: A Challenge to the Nigerian Church," *Asian Culture and History* 4, no. 1 (2012): 94.

49 Samuel Zalanga, "In the Name of God . . . the Commoditization of Faith: The Need for African Liberation Theology," *Baobab – Africa People & Economy Magazine*, n.d., www.baobabafricaonline.com/faith_as_commodity.htm (accessed October 24, 2014).

50 Fred Itua, "Assemblies of God Church Crisis Deepens." *The Sun*, 2014. http://sunnewsonline.com/new/?p=63933 (accessed October 24, 2014).

51 Zalanga, "In the Name of God . . . the Commoditization of Faith: The Need for African Liberation Theology."

52 Omozuwa Gabriel Osamwonyi, "How Pope-Like Pastors Control People," *Daily Post*, August 3, 2014, http://dailypost.ng/2014/08/03/omozuwa-gabriel-osamwonyi-pope-like-pastors-control-people/ (accessed August 5, 2014).

53 Ahmed Olayinka Sule, "The Nigerian Church Leadership and Social Justice," *Arise Nigeria*, 2011, www.arisenigeria.org/peoples-news/198-the-nigerian-church-leadership-and-social-justice (accessed October 24, 2014).

54 Femi Aribisala, "Money Laundering in the Churches," *Vanguard*, 2012, www.vanguardngr.com/2012/10/money-laundering-in-the-churches/ (accessed October 25, 2014).

55 Mbengu D. Nyiawung, "The Prophetic Witness of the Church as an Appropriate Mode of Public Discourse in African Societies," *HTS Theological Studies* 66, no. 1 (2010): 5.

60 *Major African communal structural evils*

56 Philip Jenkins, *The New Faces of Christianity: Believing the Bible in the Global South* (Oxford: Oxford Univeristy Press, 2006), 162.

57 Teresa Okure, "Women Building the Church in Africa: A Focus on Nigerian Catholic Women," *ANVIL* 8, no. 4 (2001): 274.

58 Kwasi Wiredu, *Philosophy and an African Culture* (Cambridge, UK: Cambridge University Press, 1980), 3–5. In the African communal cultures, Kwasi Wiredu charges that African elders, who are respected as repositories of knowledge of the community, are epistemologically authoritarians. This authoritarianism, he contends, unjustifiably overrides the exercise of the individual's creativity, will, and autonomy. But Ikuenobe thinks that Wiredu's criticism is unfounded. He argues that epistemic authoritarianism is often exercised for the good of the individual and the entire African community. In that sense, Ikuenobe thinks that overriding the will of the individual is justifiable. He writes, "A community, in this paternalistic, rational, authoritarian model, may decide for some intersubjectively justifiable epistemic reasons, that the harmful effects of 'light drugs' (marijuana in the USA, for instance) on society are such that they warrant the society to disallow their use. The society may disallow their use against the will of those who refuse to accept or are not aware of the reasons, but believe that the drugs are good for them and insist on using them. Does this involve the unjustified overriding an individual's will?" Polycarp Ikuenobe, *Philosophical Perspectives on Communalism and Morality in African Traditions* (Lanham, MD: Lexington Books, 2006), 181–2.

59 E. A. Ruch and K. C. Anyanwu, *African Philosophy: An Introduction to the Main Philosophical Trends in Contemporary Africa* (Rome: Catholic Book Agency, 1984), 305.

60 Segun and Samuel, "Democracy and Accountability in Pre-Colonial Africa: Lessons for Contemporary African States," 46.

61 Ruch and Anyanwu, *African Philosophy*, 324.

62 Rodney, *How Europe Underdeveloped Africa*, 280.

63 As cited in James E. Lassiter, "African Culture and Personality: Bad Social Science, Effective Social Activism, or a Call to Reinvent Ethnology?" *African Studies Quarterly* 3, no. 3 (2000): 9.

64 Joy Asongazoh Alemazung, "Post-Colonial Colonialism: An Analysis of International Factors and Actors Marring African Socio-Economic Andpolitical Development," *The Journal of Pan African Studies* 3, no. 10 (2010): 67.

65 Emmanuel O. Iheukwumere and Chukwuemeka A. Iheukwumere, "Colonial Rapacity and Political Corruption: Roots of African Underdevelopment and Misery," *Journal of International and Comparative Law* 3, no. 4 (2003): 7.

66 Jan H. Boer, *Christianity and Islam Under Colonialism in Northern Nigeria* (Jos: Institute of Church and Society, 1988), 7.

67 Allan D. Galloway, "Missionary Impact on Nigeria," in *Nigeria 1960: A Special Independence Issue of Nigeria Magazine October*, ed. Michael Crowder (Lagos: Federal Ministry of Information, 1960), 64.

68 Levi I. Izuakor, "Introduction: Colonialism and Exploitation?" in *Britain and Nigeria: Exploitation or Development?* ed. Toyin Falola (London: Zed Books Ltd, 1987), 52.

69 Jürgen Moltmann, *God for a Secular Society: The Public Relevance of Theology* (Minneapolis, MN: Fortress Press, 1999), 8.

70 Bashiru Salawu and A. O. Hassan, "Ethnic Politics and Its Implications for the Survival of Democracy in Nigeria," *Journal of Public Administration and Policy Research* 3, no. 2 (2011): 31.

71 Simeon Onyewueke Eboh, "Ethnicity and Domicity in the Church and State in Nigeria," in *Ethnicity and Christian Leadership in West African Sub-Region*, ed. Ferdinand Nwaigbo, Jude Asanbe, Camillus Umoh, Onyema Anozie, Thaddeus Guzuma, John Gangwari, Innocent Ejeh, Austin Echema, and Emmanuel Nwaoru (Port Harcourt: CIWA Publications, 2004), 270.

72 Joseph C. Ebegbulem, "Ethnic Politics and Conflicts in Nigeria: Theoretical Perspective," *Khazar Journal of Humanities and Social Science* 14, no. 3 (2012): 80.

Major African communal structural evils 61

73 Edlyne E. Anugwon, "Ethnic Conflict and Democracy in Nigeria: The Marginalisation Question," *Journal of Social Development in Africa* 15, no. 1 (2000): 61.
74 Emmy Godwin Irobi, "Ethnic Conflict Management in Africa: A Comparative Case Study of Nigeria and South Africa," www.beyondintractability.org/casestudy/irobi-ethnic (accessed October 31, 2014).
75 David Lamb, *The Africans* (New York, NY: Vintage Books, 1984), 9.
76 Jacob Oluwole Odeyemi, "A Political History of Nigeria and the Crisis of Ethnicity in Nation-Building," *International Journal of Developing Societies* 3, no. 1 (2014): 9.
77 Rodney, *How Europe Underdeveloped Africa*, 250.
78 Tunga Lergo, "Deconstructing Ethnic Politics: The Emergence of a Fourth Force in Nigerian Political Discourse," *International Journal of Humanities and Social Science* 1, no. 15 (2011): 89.
79 As cited in Joseph Healey and Sybertz Donald, *Towards an African Narrative Theology* (Maryknoll, NY: Orbis Books, 1996), 148–9. Italics in the original.
80 Musa P. Filibus, "An Exploratory Study of the History, Nature and Management Model of Conflict Within a Local Congregation with Theological Implications for Pastoral Ministry: LCCN No. 1, Cathedral Numan, Adamawa State, Nigeria, as a Case Study" (Ph.D. Dissertation, Luther Seminary, 1998), 208.
81 Ibid., 206.
82 Abraham Terumbur Mbachirin, "The Responses of the Church in Nigeria to Socio-Economic, Political and Religiousproblems in Nigeria: A Case Study of the Christian Association of Nigeria (C.A.N.)" (Ph.D Diss., Baylor Univeristy, 2006), 44.
83 As cited in Toyin Falola, *Violence in Nigeria: The Crisis of Religious Politics and Secular Ideologies* (Rochester, NY: University of Rochester Press, 1998), 17.
84 It is inaccurate to describe Nigeria as a pluralistic religious society if religious pluralism means that all religions are equal and true ways of salvation. I prefer to use the term "multi-religious" society when speaking of the religious status of Nigeria to stress the exclusiveness of each of the different religions.
85 Isaac Terwase Sampson, "Religious Violence in Nigeria: Causal Diagnoses and Strategic Recommendations to the State and Religious Communities," *African Journal on Conflict Resolution* 12, no. 1 (2012): 120.
86 S. Awoniyi, "A Discourse on Religious Conflict and Tolerance in Multi-Faith Nigeria," *European Scientific Journal* 9, no. 20 (2013): 127.
87 Sheikh Abubakar Gumi and Tsiga Ismaila Abubakar, *Where I Stand* (Ibadan: Spectrum Books, 1992), 192.
88 Falola, *Violence in Nigeria*, 2.
89 Sampson, "Religious Violence in Nigeria: Causal Diagnoses and Strategic Recommendations to the State and Religious Communities," 123.
90 Falola, *Violence in Nigeria*, 37.
91 Sampson, "Religious Violence in Nigeria: Causal Diagnoses and Strategic Recommendations to the State and Religious Communities," 121. Emphasis added.
92 For a comprehensive catalogue of these religious conflicts, see Awoniyi, "A Discourse on Religious Conflict and Tolerance in Multi-Faith Nigeria," 130–5.
93 Emaka Mamah and Sam Eyoboka, "Boko Haram Threatens Jonathan," *Vanguard*, 2012, www.vanguardngr.com/2012/04/boko-haram-threatens-jonathan/ (accessed November 4, 2014).
94 Lauren Ploch Blanchard, "Nigeria's Boko Haram: Frequently Asked Questions," in *Congressional Research Service* (2014), 4. At the time of this writing, Boko Haram invaded the village of my mother in-law in our state, Adamawa, burning the house of the pastor and killing several people. They are now refugees in their own motherland.
95 Ibrahim Abdul'aziz and Chika Oduah, "Nigeria Camps Struggle with Aid for the Displaced," *The Tribune*, 2014, www.sanluisobispo.com/2014/11/28/3371872/nigeria-camps-struggle-with-aid.html (accessed November 28, 2014).
96 Falola, *Violence in Nigeria*, 185.

62 *Major African communal structural evils*

97 World Council of Churches, *In the Name of God: Report on the Inter-Religious Tensions and Crisis in Nigeria* (Geneva, Switzerland: The World Council of Churches, 2012), www.idmarch.org/document/World+Interfaith+Harmony+Week/2gAp-show/In+the+Name+of+God++REPORT+ON+THE+INTER-RELIGIOUS+TENSIONS+AND+CRISIS (accessed November 15, 2014).

98 Edmund Patrick Thurman Crampton, *Christianity in Northern Nigeria* (Zaria: Gaskiya Corp., 1975), 46–71.

Bibliography

"2013 World Corruption Index: Nigeria Ranks 144 Among 177 Countries." *Vanguard.* 2013. www.vanguardngr.com/2013/12/afghanistan-n-korea-somalia-top-world-graft-index/ (accessed October 22, 2014).

Abdul'aziz, Ibrahim, and Chika Oduah. "Nigeria Camps Struggle with Aid for the Displaced." *The Tribune*, 2014. www.sanluisobispo.com/2014/11/28/3371872/nigeria-camps-struggle-with-aid.html (accessed November 28, 2014).

Abioje, Pius Oyeniran. "Liberation Theology Vis-a-Vis Nigeria's Socio-Political and Economic Development." *Journal of Cultural and Religious Studies* 6, no. 1 (2008): 1–15.

Achebe, Chinua. *The Trouble with Nigeria*. Enugu, Nigeria: Fourth Dimension Publishers, 1983.

Adepoju, Adunola. "Feminisation of Poverty in Nigerian Cities: Insights from Focus Group Discussions and Participatory Poverty [1] Assessment." *African Population Studies Supplement* 19, no. 2 (2004): 141–54.

Alabi, Mojeed Olujinmi A., and Joseph 'Yinka Fashagba. "The Legislature and Anti-Corruption Crusade Under the Fourth Republic of Nigeria: Constitutional Imperatives and Practical Realities." *International Journal of Politics and Good Governance* 1, no. 1.2 (2010): 1–39.

Alemazung, Joy Asongazoh. "Post-Colonial Colonialism: An Analysis of International Factors and Actors Marring African Socio-Economic and Political Development." *The Journal of Pan African Studies* 3, no. 10 (2010): 62–84.

Amaefule, Everest. "100 Million Nigerians Live Destitution-World Bank." *Punch*. www.punchng.com/news/100-million-nigerians-live-in-destitution-world-bank (accessed October 22, 2014).

Anugwon, Edlyne E. "Ethnic Conflict and Democracy in Nigeria: The Marginalisation Question." *Journal of Social Development in Africa* 15, no. 1 (2000): 61–78.

Aribisala, Femi. "Bigmanism in Nigeria." *Vanguard*. 2013. www.vanguardngr.com/2013/10/bigmanism-nigeria/ (accessed January 2014).

———. "Money Laundering in the Churches." *Vanguard*. 2012. www.vanguardngr.com/2012/10/money-laundering-in-the-churches/ (accessed October 25, 2014).

Asogwa, Chika, and Damian Amana. "Communication: A Challenge to the Nigerian Church." *Asian Culture and History* 4, no. 1 (2012): 90–9.

Awoniyi, S. "A Discourse on Religious Conflict and Tolerance in Multi-Faith Nigeria." *European Scientific Journal* 9, no. 20 (2013): 124–43.

Bitrus, Ibrahim. "Disturbing Unjust Peace in Nigeria through the Church and Legal Reforrms: The Contribution of Luther's Critical Public Theology." In *On Secular Government: Lutheran Perspectives on Contemporary Legal Issues*, edited by Ronald W. Duty and M. A. Failinger. Grand Rapids, MI: W. B. Eerdmans Publishing Co., 2016.

Blanchard, Lauren Ploch. "Nigeria's Boko Haram: Frequently Asked Questions." In *Congressional Research Service*, 2014.

Boer, Jan H. *Christianity and Islam Under Colonialism in Northern Nigeria*. Jos: Institute of Church and Society, 1988.

Carling, Jœrgen. "Migration, Human Smuggling and Trafficking from Nigeria to Europe." *IOM International Organization for Migration* no. 23 (2006): 1–72.

Churches, World Council. *In the Name of God: Report on the Inter-Religious Tensions and Crisis in Nigeria*. Geneva, Switzerland: The World Council of Churches, 2012. www.idmarch.org/document/World+Interfaith+Harmony+Week/2gAp-show/In+the+Name+of+God++REPORT+ON+THE+INTER-RELIGIOUS+TENSIONS+AND+CRISIS (accessed Novermber 15, 2014).

Crampton, Edmund Patrick Thurman. *Christianity in Northern Nigeria*. Zaria: Gaskiya Corp., 1975.

Cunliffe-Jones, Peter. *My Nigeria: Five Decades of Independence*. New York, NY: Palgrave Macmillan, 2010.

Daniella, Coetzee. "South African Education and the Ideology of Patriarchy." *South Africa Journal of Education* 21, no. 4 (2001): 300–4.

"Director Jailed 2yrs for Stealing N33bn Pension Fund Freed on N250, 000 Fine." *Premium Times*, 2013. www.premiumtimesng.com/news/117599-director-jailed-2yrs-for-stealing-n33bn-pension-fund-freed-on-n250000-fine.html (accessed October 22, 2014).

Ebegbulem, Joseph C. "Ethnic Politics and Conflicts in Nigeria: Theoretical Perspective." *Khazar Journal of Humanities and Social Science* 14, no. 3 (2012): 76–91.

Eboh, Simeon Onyewueke. "Ethnicity and Domicility in the Church and State in Nigeria." In *Ethnicity and Christian Leadership in West African Sub-Region*, edited by Ferdinand Nwaigbo, Jude Asanbe, Camillus Umoh, Onyema Anozie, Thaddeus Guzuma, John Gangwari, Innocent Ejeh, Austin Echema, and Emmanuel Nwaoru. Port Harcourt: CIWA Publications, 2004.

Falola, Toyin. *Violence in Nigeria: The Crisis of Religious Politics and Secular Ideologies*. Rochester, NY: University of Rochester Press, 1998.

Filibus, Musa P. "An Exploratory Study of the History, Nature and Management Model of Conflict Within a Local Congregation with Theological Implications for Pastoral Ministry: LCCN No. 1, Cathedral Numan, Adamawa State, Nigeria, as a Case Study." Ph.D. Dissertation, Luther Seminary, 1998.

Galloway, Allan D. "Missionary Impact on Nigeria." In *Nigeria 1960: A Special Independence Issue of Nigeria Magazine October*, edited by Michael Crowder. Lagos: Federal Ministry of Information, 1960.

Gumi, Sheikh Abubakar, and Tsiga Ismaila Abubakar. *Where I Stand*. Ibadan: Spectrum Books, 1992.

Harden, Blaine. *Africa: Dispatches from a Fragile Continent*. New York, NY: W. W. Norton & Company, 1990.

Healey, Joseph, and Sybertz Donald. *Towards an African Narrative Theology*. Maryknoll, NY: Orbis Books, 1996.

Human Rights Watch. *Corruption on Trial? The Record of Nigeria's Economic and Financial Crimes Commission*. New York, NY: Human Rights Watch, 2011.

Iheukwumere, Emmanuel O., and Chukwuemeka A. Iheukwumere. "Colonial Rapacity and Political Corruption: Roots of African Underdevelopment and Misery." *Journal of International and Comparative Law* 3, no. 4 (2003): 1–61.

Ikuenobe, Polycarp. *Philosophical Perspectives on Communalism and Morality in African Traditions*. Lanham, MD: Lexington Books, 2006.

Innocent, Eme Okechukwu, and Anthony Onyishi. "The Challenges of Insecurity in Nigeria: A Thematic Exposition." *Interdisciplinary Journal of Contemporary Research in Business* 3, no. 8 (2011): 172–85.

64 Major African communal structural evils

Irobi, Emmy Godwin. "Ethnic Conflict Management in Africa: A Comparative Case Study of Nigeria and South Africa." 2005. www.beyondintractability.org/casestudy/irobi-ethnic (accessed October 31, 2014).

Itua, Fred. "Assemblies of God Church Crisis Deepens." *The Sun*, 2014. http://sunnewsonline.com/new/?p=63933 (accessed October 24, 2014).

Izuakor, Levi I. "Introduction: Colonialism and Exploitation?" In *Britain and Nigeria: Exploitation or Development?* edited by Toyin Falola. London: Zed Books Ltd, 1987.

Izugbara, C. Otutubikey. "Patriarchal Ideology and Discourses of Sexuality in Nigeria." *Africa Regional Sexuality Resource Centre* no. 2 (2004): 1–34.

Jenkins, Philip. *The New Faces of Christianity: Believing the Bible in the Global South*. Oxford: Oxford University Press, 2006.

Johnson, Alaba. "Economist Magazine: Nigerians Legislators World Highest Paid." *Naija Pundit*, 2013. www.naijapundit.com/news/economist-magazine-nigerian-legislators-world-s-highest-paid (accessed October 22, 2014).

Kärkkäinen, Veli-Matti. *The Trinity: Global Perspectives*. Louisville, KY: Westminster John Knox Press, 2007.

Katsina, Aliyu Mukhtar. "Nigeria's Security Challenges and the Crisis of Development: Towards a New Framework for Analysis." *International Journal of Developing Societies* 1, no. 3 (2012): 107–16.

Kolawole, Adebayo Anthony Abayomi and Taiwo Olabode. "Domestic Violence and Death: Women as Endangered Gender in Nigeria." *American Journal of Sociological Research* 3, no. 3 (2013): 53–60.

Kukah, Mathew H. "The Cost of Democracy." *Newswatch*, 2010.

Lamb, David. *The Africans*. New York, NY: Vintage Books, 1984.

Lassiter, James E. "African Culture and Personality: Bad Social Science, Effective Social Activism, or a Call to Reinvent Ethnology?" *African Studies Quarterly* 3, no. 3 (2000): 1–21.

Lawal-Rabana, Rafiu Adeyanju. "The Nigerian Bar Association and the Protection of Rule of Law in Nigeria." 2007. www.ibanet.org/barassociations/bar_associations_Zagreb_conference_materials.aspx (accessed December 13, 2013).

Lergo, Tunga. "Deconstructing Ethnic Politics: The Emergence of a Fourth Force in Nigerian Political Discourse." *International Journal of Humanities and Social Science* 1, no. 15 (2011): 87–94.

Majawa, Clement. "The Church's Role in Defining Genuine Democracy in Africa." In *African Theology Today*, edited by Emmanuel Katongole. Scranton, PA: University of Scranton Press, 2002.

Makama, Godiya Allanana. "Patriarchy and Gender Inequality in Nigeria: The Way Forward." *European Scientific Journal* 19, no. 17 (2013): 115–44.

Mamah, Emaka, and Sam Eyoboka. "Boko Haram Threatens Jonathan." *Vanguard*. 2012. www.vanguardngr.com/2012/04/boko-haram-threatens-jonathan/ (accessed November 4, 2014).

Mbachirin, Abraham Terumbur. "The Responses of the Church in Nigeria to Socio-Economic, Political and Religious problems in Nigeria: A Case Study of the Christian Association of Nigeria (C.A.N.)." Ph.D Diss., Baylor Univeristy, 2006.

Moltmann, Jürgen. *God for a Secular Society: The Public Relevance of Theology*. Minneapolis, MN: Fortress Press, 1999.

Nadaswaran, Shalini. "Neo-Liberal Nigeria and Sex Trafficking in Nigerian Women's Writings." *2011 International Conference on Humanities, Society and Culture IPERD* 20 (2011): 271–6.

Nyiawung, Mbengu D. "The Prophetic Witness of the Church as an Appropriate Mode of Public Discourse in African Societies." *HTS Theological Studies* 66, no. 1 (2010): 1–8.

Odeyemi, Jacob Oluwole. "A Political History of Nigeria and the Crisis of Ethnicity in Nation-Building." *International Journal of Developing Societies* 3, no. 1 (2014): 87–95.

Odumosu, Olakunle F. "Social Costs of Poverty: The Case of Crime in Nigeria." *Journal of Social Development in Africa* 14, no. 2 (1992): 71–85.

Oduyoye, Mercy Amba. *Daughters of Anowa: African Women and Patriarchy*. Maryknoll, NY: Orbis Books, 1995.

Ogunma, Omololu. "Nigeria: U.S. \$600 Billion Stolen by Nigerian Elite Since Independence." *This Day*, 2013. http://allafrica.com/stories/201306190182.html (accessed October 22, 2014).

Okure, Teresa. "Women Building the Church in Africa: A Focus on Nigerian Catholic Women." *ANVIL* 8, no. 4 (2001): 269–75.

Omotola, J. Shola O. "What Is This Gender Talk All About After All? Gender, Power and Politics in Contemporary in Nigeria." *African Study Monographs* 28, no. 1 (2007): 34–46.

Onyeozili, Emmanuel C. "Obstacles to Effective Policing in Nigeria." *African Journal of Criminology and Justice Studies* 1, no. 1 (2005): 32–54.

Osamwonyi, Omozuwa Gabriel. "How Pope-Like Pastors Control People." *Daily Post*, August 3, 2014. http://dailypost.ng/2014/08/03/omozuwa-gabriel-osamwonyi-pope-like-pastors-control-people/ (accessed August 5, 2014).

Palmer, Timothy P. "Martin Luther's Theology of the Cross in the Nigerian Context." *TCNN Research Bulletin* no. 48 (2007): 4–12.

"Ribadu Speaks on Dismissal, Demotion Reversed from Police." *Vanguard*, 2013. www.vanguardngr.com/2013/10/got-police-dismissal-demotion-reversed-ribadu/ (accessed October 22, 2014).

Rodney, Walter. *How Europe Underdeveloped Africa*. London: Bogle-L'Ouverture Publications, 1972.

Rojas, Maria. "Women in Colonial Nigeria." 1990. www.postcolonialweb.org/nigeria/colonwom.html (accessed October 19, 2014).

Ruch, E. A., and K. C. Anyanwu. *African Philosophy: An Introduction to the Main Philosophical Trends in Contemporary Africa*. Rome: Catholic Book Agency, 1984.

Salawu, Bashiru, and A. O. Hassan. "Ethnic Politics and Its Implications for the Survival of Democracy in Nigeria." *Journal of Public Administration and Policy Research* 3, no. 2 (2011): 28–33.

Sampson, Isaac Terwase. "Religious Violence in Nigeria: Causal Diagnoses and Strategic Recommendations to the State and Religious Communities." *African Journal on Conflict Resolution* 12, no. 1 (2012): 103–33.

Samuel, Oni, and Joshua Segun. "Gender Relations in Nigeria's Democratic Governance." *Journal of Politics & Governance* 1, no. 2/3 (2012): 4–15.

Segun, Joshua, and Oni Samuel. "Democracy and Accountability in Pre-Colonial Africa: Lessons for Contemporary African States." *JFE Journal of the Humanities and Social Studies (IJOHUSS)* n.v. (2013): 41–54.

Sule, Ahmed Olayinka. "The Nigerian Church Leadership and Social Justice." *Arise Nigeria*. 2011. www.arisenigeria.org/peoples-news/198-the-nigerian-church-leadership-and-social-justice (accessed October 24, 2014).

Suraju, Olanrewaju. "Presidential Pardon for Diepreye Alamiyesegha: Abuse of Power and Morality." *Sahara Reporters*, 2013. http://saharareporters.com/2013/03/18/presidential-pardon-diepreye-alamiyesegha-abuse-power-and-morality-olanrewaju-suraju (accessed October 22, 2014).

Wiredu, Kwasi. *Philosophy and an African Culture*. Cambridge, UK: Cambridge University Press, 1980.

Zalanga, Samuel. "In the Name of God . . . The Commoditization of Faith: The Need for African Liberation Theology." *Baobab – Africa People & Economy Magazine*, n.d. www.baobabafricaonline.com/faith_as_commodity.htm (accessed October 24, 2014).

3 The "amazing history" of the Trinity

The task of recasting the African community from the perspective of the new Trinitarian theology of God cannot effectively be accomplished apart from the astonishing history of the doctrine of the Trinity. "The doctrine of the Triune God has had an amazing history,"[1] which we cannot afford to ignore. E.J. Fortman argues that the doctrine, which is not explicitly found in the Bible, emerged from "three centuries of gradual assimilation of the Biblical witness to God."[2] However, in this chapter, I will show that the classical doctrine of the Trinity developed as a result of the synthetic and speculative reflections on the scrappy elements of the biblical witness to God. I will further show that the new Trinitarian theology emerged from a critical and intelligent analysis of the entire compendium of that scriptural witness to God's self-revelation in Christ.

The new Trinitarian theology did not emerge from reflection on the basic concepts that bind people together in human society, concepts which are then projected onto the Trinity. If this were the case, the doctrine would cease to be a summary of biblical witness to the Triune God and become a mere concoction of human imagination. The new Trinitarian understanding of God arises from reflection on the scriptural witness to the Triune God's communion as constituted and revealed in Christ and distributed by the Spirit in response to issues affecting human relationships in the world. As there is no way from humanity to God, we cannot draw human relationships in the context of society to comprehend and shape our understanding of the Triune God. But because there is always a way from God to humanity, we can draw on who God is in God's revelation to analyze and shape human relationships.

The amazing history of the doctrine of the Trinity that I will explore here is a specific investigative history of the doctrine. In this chapter, I will analyze the historical emergence and development of the classical doctrine of the Trinity as the indispensable precursor to the new Trinitarian theology of God. I will pay particular attention to the hermeneutical question of the relation between the three-ness and oneness of the Triune God as it concerns God's relational character in Godself and in the economy of creation and redemption. I will specifically look at Western, Eastern, and African mainline contributors to the formation and interpretation of the Trinity from the fourth century to the early modern period through the contemporary African contributors to the doctrine, and I will unpack the hermeneutical starting points, philosophical presuppositions, and contextual theological concerns which informed these respective Trinitarian hermeneutics of God.

In the first section, I will analyze early mainline Eastern Trinitarian thinkers. These are Athanasius and the Cappadocian or Greek Fathers: Basil the Great, Gregory of Nyssa, and Gregory of Nazianzus. In the second section, I will investigate four mainline Western Trinitarian thinkers: Irenaeus, Tertullian, St Augustine, and Thomas Aquinas. In the third section, I will explore the eclipse of the synthetic classical doctrine of the Trinity in the Western modern period and the emergence of a new analytical hermeneutical approach to the doctrine in contemporary theology. Here, I will examine Friedrich Schleiermacher as the main representative figure for the former, while for the latter, I will explore Karl Barth and Karl Rahner as major representatives. In the fourth section, I undertake the analytical description of three contemporary African Trinitarian thinkers: A. Okechukwu Ogbonnaya, James Henry Owino Kombo, and Agbonkhianmeghe E. Orobator.

Mainline Eastern Trinitarian thinkers

In this section, I will investigate the history of the doctrine of the Trinity in the fourth and fifth centuries, one of the most decisive periods in the emergence of the Trinitarian doctrine. The significance of these periods is two-fold. First, the fourth and fifth centuries were formative stages in which the Trinity received the traditional form that it still commands today. Second, these were critical times during which the Trinitarian controversy started by Arius and the Arians was eventually settled, thus paving the way for subsequent fruitful conversations about the Trinity. Specifically, I will explore the four mainline Eastern Trinitarian thinkers of these centuries: Athanasius, Basil the Great, Gregory of Nyssa, and Gregory of Nazianzus, the last three often referred to as the Cappadocian Fathers.

Athanasius: indivisible Trinity

Athanasius' ideas of the mutual understanding of the Father-Son relationship and the co-divinity of the Spirit in the Godhead are the two key components of his Trinitarian thought. Athanasius was one of the most prominent early Eastern and African theologians, whose Trinitarian ideas were very significant for the emergence of the Eastern doctrine of the Trinity. As a stalwart defender of the Nicene Creed, which affirmed that the Son is of the same substance *(homoousios)* with the Father, at a critical time of the Arian heresy, Athanasius expressed without hesitation a faith in the Triune God. Athanasius wrote, "We confess God to be one through the Triad, and . . . entertain a belief of the One Godhead in a Triad . . . for there is but one form of Godhead."[3] The one Godhead, according to him, is revealed in the Son, who is the perfect visual expression of the Father, meaning whoever sees the Son sees the Father. As the epistemological quintessence of the Father, to know the Son means to know the Father, whose being is identical with the Son. As he wrote,

The *"amazing history"* of the Trinity   69

For the Son is in the Father, as it is allowed us to know, because the whole Being of the Son is proper to the Father's essence, as radiance from light, and stream from fountain; so that who sees the Son, sees what is proper to the Father, and knows that the Son's Being, because from the Father, is therefore in the Father.[4]

Refuting the Arians, who describe Christ as a creature made from nothing, claiming Christ is "called Son by grace," and "not from the Father, but he as others was made God by participation," Athanasius argued that the Son is not only co-eternal with the Father, but also his eternal offspring. He is eternally begotten, not made, from the Father's substance. Athanasius insists that the Father-Son relationship in the Godhead is mutual, meaning the Father would not be Father without the Son. The reciprocal implication of this claim in the new Trinitarian hermeneutics will be explored in Chapter 4. For Athanasius, it is unimaginable that there was a time when God was a Father without a Son: "Therefore 'Father' is proper to the 'Son'; and not 'creature,' but 'Son' is proper to the 'Father.'"[5] Unlike human fatherhood and sonship, which are changeable, divine Fatherhood and Sonship are immutable. As the Father is always the Father and will never become the Son, so the Son is always the Son and will never become the Father. The two are distinct, but indivisible.

As the Father and the Son are always inseparable, to be a Father is to be in a begetting relationship with the Son, a relationship that binds them together and distinguishes them from each other.[6] Athanasius argued that the *ousia* of God the Father is relational in that it involves sharing of His being with the Son. Athanasius denied the Arians' idea that the generation of the Son is either by necessity or by will on the part of the Father and thus precludes sharing the Father's essence. As the Father is generative by nature, Athanasius claimed that the generation of the Son is also by nature apart from any will and necessity, for no one "imposes this necessity on Him" and is thus truly "Father of the Son by nature and not by will."[7] God's *ousia* is neither diminished nor divided by sharing his being with the Son.[8] However, whether this means that the Son is begotten "without the pleasure of the Father and not with the Father's will," Athanasius said,

No, verily; but the Son is [begotten] with the pleasure of the Father, and, as He says Himself, "The Father loves the Son, and shows Him all things" . . . as His own Subsistence is by His pleasure, so also the Son, being proper to His Essence, is not without His pleasure.[9]

In other words, the generation is out of the Father's sheer delight and love for the Son. Therefore, the relationship between the Father and the Son is that of reciprocal love and good pleasure. As Athanasius expressed it,

For by that good pleasure wherewith the Son is the object of the Father's pleasure, is the Father the object of the Son's love, pleasure, and honour . . .

70   *The "amazing history" of the Trinity*

that the Father has love and good pleasure towards the Son, and the Son has love and good pleasure towards the Father.[10]

Athanasius, therefore, affirmed without reservation the consubstantiality of the Father and the Son when he wrote that the Son's "divinity is the same as His Father's . . . and thus there is one God."[11] He also suggested, "Since they are both one in Essence and Divinity, it follows that whatever can be affirmed of the Father, may as truly and properly be affirmed of the Son, except only the relation of Paternity."[12] Whoever contemplates the Son contemplates that which is proper to the Father's essence because the Godhead of the Father is the being of the Son. Athanasius maintained that the Word is divine and not created, as opposed to Arius, who taught that the Son is a creature because there was a time when the Son was not. Athanasius argued that if the Son is simply a creature, then he wouldn't have accomplished our salvation, for the Son, who is divine, became human that we might be made divine!

As for the Spirit, Athanasius insisted that the Spirit is co-divine with the Father and the Son, though he never called the Holy Spirit "God." Athanasius' Trinitarian pneumatology arises as a reaction to the Tropici, who denied the deity of the Spirit, regarding the Spirit merely as a creature, a super angel and, at best, one of the "ministering spirits."[13] As a member of the eternal and indivisible Godhead that is a Triad, Athanasius argued that the Spirit is truly divine and thus consubstantial with the Father and Son. The Spirit, who issues from God, not only bestows sanctification and life to the church, but also is linked to the Son's work of creation and incarnation. He insisted that there is no way the Holy Spirit can deify humanity unless the Holy Spirit is divine! The Spirit is inseparable from the Son and the Father and shares an identical substance with them.[14] The Father and the Son, who are always inseparable, also have in their embrace the Spirit, who is intimately connected to them.

The affirmation of the co-divinity of the Spirit in the Godhead eventually leads Athanasius to the perception of the Trinity as the Triad of eternal divine persons of the one indivisible Godhead. Thus, whenever one of them is mentioned, the two others are duly implicated. Though the Father, Son, and Spirit are distinguished from each other by the peculiar personal properties of *agennesia* (unoriginated), *genesis* (generated) and *ekporeusis* (proceeded), Athanasius insisted they share one and the same essence and activity. As the Trinity is one indivisible substance, Athanasius claimed that the three divine persons work together undividedly such that the Father accomplishes everything through the Word in the Holy Spirit. In other words, whatever the Father does, whether in creation or redemption, God does through the Word in the Spirit.[15] Implied in this claim is the fact that the three persons are distinct without separation and united without confusion in their action in the economy of salvation.

In affirming the consubstantiality of the Son and the Father and by extending it to the Holy Spirit, Athanasius has succeeded in producing "a well-rounded doctrine of the Trinity," Fortman claims.[16] For Robert Letham, the contribution of Athanasius to the Trinitarian theology consists not only in championing the

The "amazing history" of the Trinity   71

full divinity of the Son and the Spirit and their mutual co-inherence, but also in formulating his doctrine of the Trinity from the economy of creation and salvation.[17] "Defending the Nicene belief in the *homoousion* of the Son (and Spirit) with the Father, their equal deity," claims Pannenberg, "Athanasius vanquished subordinationism, insisting that we cannot think of the Father as Father without the Son and Spirit."[18]

But in spite of these credible achievements, Athanasius' thought about the inner life of the Trinity leaves us with much to desire. He hesitated to probe into the inner life of the Godhead, supposing it to be a mystery to be adored rather than inquired.[19] This explains why he does not venture to discuss the eternal distinctions among the persons of the Godhead. There also is no clear-cut distinction between *ousia* and *hypostasis* in Athanasius' Trinitarian framework. He used the two words interchangeably. This is informed partly by his inability to find a suitable word for "person," as even *prosopon* and *hypostasis* seemed inadequate for him. Fortman rightly argued that Athanasius "was not a speculative systematic theologian, and he lacked a well-constructed vocabulary" with which to fully express his doctrine of the Trinity.[20] But as the forerunner of Eastern Trinitarian thought, these are critical issues which Athanasius left unresolved, but which were addressed by later Eastern theologians, especially the Cappadocian Fathers, to whom we now turn.

The Cappadocian Triad: communion of God

The Cappadocian Triad (Basil the Great, Gregory of Nyssa, and Gregory of Nazianzus) consolidated the legacy bequeathed by Athanasius. As pillars of Greek Trinitarian theology, the Cappadocian Triad articulated with biblical and philosophical creativity a communal vision of God, which laid the foundation on which Orthodox Trinitarian reflection is based.

The Trinitarian reflections of the Cappadocian Triad were largely triggered, on the one hand, by the false teachings of Eunomius and, on the other hand, by the false teaching of the *pneumatomachii*. The former not only claimed to have the rational capacity to utterly comprehend the divine essence, but also believed that God the Father's divine nature, which is absolutely un-relational, cannot communicate such essence by begetting a son. Should God beget a Son, it would mean either that God was not ingenerate prior to begetting the Son or that the Son is absolutely unlike the Father in substance. In other words, God becomes a Father only when he begets the Son. Like Arius, Eunomius claimed there was a time when the Son did not exist and thus the Son, who is begotten in time from God's will, is subordinate to the Father, who alone is truly God. As for the latter – *pneumatomachii* – the Son is divine, but the Spirit is an inferior divine member of the Godhead and does not deserve to be worshipped along with other hypostases of the Trinity.[21]

Reacting to these false teachings, the Cappadocian Fathers propounded the co-divinity and co-equality of the Son with the Father and the divinity of the Spirit as a co-equal member of the Triune God. These Trinitarian responses of

72 The "amazing history" of the Trinity

the Cappadocian Fathers, which are rooted in scripture and philosophy, will be discussed here as well as their specific individual contributions to the emergence and the development of the Trinity.

Basil the Great

Responding to Eunomius, Basil the Great insisted on the consubstantiality of the Son with the Father. Suggesting that the Father and the Son share one deity, Basil argued that the Son is "eternally begotten" by the Father without dividing their indivisible substance. As one who owes his "origin and cause" to the Father, the Son is second from the Father in order and dignity, albeit not second in nature to him.[22] The Son is thus not radically different from the "Unbegotten" Father, as claimed by Eunomius, meaning the Son is not a creature made from nothing in time, but rather, the Son is of one and the same substance *(homoousion)* with the Father and thus eternally and equally divine. Basil adopted the term *homoousion* to remove such impiety because the union between the Son and the Father is without time and interval. Basil succinctly wrote,

> For after saying that the Son was light of light, and begotten of the substance of the Father, but was not made, they went on to add the *homoousion*, thereby showing that whatever proportion of light any one would attribute in the case of the Father will obtain also in that of the Son. For very light in relation to very light, according to the actual sense of light, will have no variation. Since then the Father is light without beginning, and the Son begotten light, but each of Them light and light; they rightly said "of one substance," in order to set forth the equal dignity of the nature.[23]

Basil argued that the Father and Son are not *homoousios* to each other as "brothers," but rather, "when both the cause and that which derives its natural existence from the cause are of the same nature, then they are called 'one substance.'"[24] Appealing to the scripture, Basil argued that the Son is not only the wisdom, power, and justice of God, but also the living and active hypostasis who wholly reveals the Father. "The Son is in the Father and the Father in the Son," Basil argued, "so that according to the distinction of persons, both are one and one, and according to the community of Nature, one."[25] All the divine attributes that are exemplified by the Father could also be assigned to the Son. If, for instance, the Father is referred to as light, then the Son must be spoken of as "light from light."

As for the Spirit, Basil endorsed the co-divinity of the Holy Spirit with the Father and the Son without categorically calling the Spirit "God." According to him, the Spirit is divine in that "in all things the Holy Spirit is inseparable and wholly incapable of being parted from the Father and the Son."[26] Hence, the Holy Spirit must be adored with the Father and the Son in worship, not less than them, or else our worship is in vain. This is because even in worship the Spirit is inexorably linked to the Father and the Son. As one "proceeding out of God" from the Father in eternity, not by generation like the Son, but as "Breath of His mouth" and in the economy of salvation, saving, liberating, sanctifying, and illuminating the world, the Spirit is co-divine with the Father and the Son, Basil claimed. For this reason, Basil maintained that the Spirit existed, pre-existed and co-existed with the Father and the Son, an idea which demonstrates that the divine persons are co-equal.[27] If so, the Spirit should be numbered with the Father and the Son and not subordinated to them. As a full divine person of the Godhead, Basil claimed that the Spirit is of a supreme nature and intelligent essence, unlimited and omnipresent, divine attributes ascribed only to God.

Possessing divine titles such as "holy" and "good," which are attributed to the Father and the Son, the Spirit also is divine, Basil further buttressed his argument. The Spirit, Basil wrote,

> is called holy, as the Father is holy, and the Son is holy, for to the creature holiness was brought in from without, but to the Spirit holiness is fulfillment of nature, and it is for this reason that He is described not as being sanctified, but as sanctifying. He is called good, as the Father is good, and He who was begotten of the Good is good.[28]

Undoubtedly, Basil saw the Spirit not just as the place for those who are being sanctified, but also the peculiar and special place of true worship, hence making the Spirit the true place of the saints and vice versa. Basil also maintained that the Spirit's "natural communion" with the Father and the Son, which is proof of his co-divinity, is expressed in the work of creation. This is evident in the way the Father is the "original cause" of creation, the Son is the "creative cause," and the Holy Spirit is the "perfecting cause." The Spirit is, therefore, "conjoined as He is to the one Father through the one Son, and through Himself completing the adorable and blessed Trinity."[29]

Having established the co-divinity of the Father, Son, and Spirit, the obvious pertinent question for Basil is how to describe that which distinguishes the three from each other and, at the same time, binds them together. He observed that employing the appropriate terms to express accurately the distinction of each divine person and their indissoluble unity is necessary for articulating an authentic Christian doctrine of the Triune God, thus overcoming, he thought, the dangers of polytheism and the abstract monotheism of Judaism. Basil wrote,

> For it is indispensable to have [a] clear understanding that, as he who fails to confess the community of the essence or substance falls into polytheism, as he who refuses to grant the distinction of the hypostases is carried away into Judaism.[30]

Basil claimed that it is not enough to enumerate the distinctions of the divine persons; we must affirm that each divine person has an innate existence in real hypostases! Therefore, critically appropriating the Greek philosophy of taxonomy in service to Christian theology, Basil draws a clear distinction between *ousia* and *hypostasis*, which at the time (as noted on p. 92) remained virtually

74 *The "amazing history" of the Trinity*

indistinguishable, and hence were used interchangeably. As Philip Kariatlis explains,

> in appropriating Greek culture and learning, St. Basil refined all those Greek technical terms that were thought to be good, true and useful to theology in such a way that served the scriptural truth of God. In this way, he was able to formulate successfully a theological vision of the Trinitarian God as revealed in its action for the world's salvation.[31]

Drawing a definite distinction between *hypostasis* and *ousia* to describe the concrete peculiarity of each divine person and what is common to them within the Godhead, Basil likened the distinction between *ousia* and *hypostasis* to the distinction between the general and particular. In the words of Basil,

> The distinction between *[ousia]* and *[hypostasis]* is the same as that between the general and particular; as, for instance, between the animal and the particular man. Wherefore, in the case of the Godhead, we confess one essence or substance so as not to give a variant definition of existence, but we confess a particular hypostasis, in order that our conception of Father, Son and Holy Spirit may be without confusion and clear.[32]

Each of the three hypostases, which are absolutely non-interchangeable distinct modes of being united in one common *ousia*, the Godhead, yet can be distinguished from each other because of particular personal properties. According to Basil, these particular properties are paternity, sonship, and sanctification. The paternity of the Father, as a unique metaphysical reality, lies in the fact that the Father is the "origin and cause" of the Godhead. As the only one whose hypostasis is un-derived from any cause, Basil maintained that the Father begets the Son and breathes the Spirit from His mouth. In other words, the Father, who is the primordial cause of the generation of the Son and the procession of the Spirit, is the ground of personal distinctions and unity in the ontological Trinity. To be the Father is to be related to the Son and the Spirit; without them the Father cannot be Father. For Basil, as Guillermo Hansen posits, "being follows relationship, not the other way around."[33] The ontology of hypostasis (person) and not substance is the foundation upon which the mutual *ousia* of the hypostases rests. The communion of the Trinity is one God not because of the unity of substance, but because the person of the Father, who is the source of the Godhead, is one. "For St Basil," Kariatlis accurately argued, "the Holy Trinity is a unity, not only because there is a unity of substance, but because of the monarchia of the Father, who is himself one of the Trinity and source of the Trinity."[34]

Basil thus rejected any suggestion of understanding the unity of the Trinity in mathematical terms, an idea which is susceptible to tritheism. He contended that in giving the church the baptismal formula of the Father, the Son, and the Spirit, Jesus by no means makes arithmetic an integral part of this gift. "We proclaim

The *"amazing history" of the Trinity* 75

each of the hypostases singly;" Basil said, but "when count we must, we do not let an ignorant arithmetic carry us away to the idea of plurality of Gods."[35] The *ousia* of the divine persons, according to which their inner-Trinitarian life is rooted in the ontological productivity and relatedness of the Father to the Son and the Spirit, is perceived in their common operation in the economy of salvation. As we perceive the operation of the Trinitarian persons in the world without division to be one and the same, said Basil, we necessarily infer from this identity of operation the unity of the *ousia*. Basil wrote "we derive no clear proof of variation in nature, because . . . identity of operations indicates community of nature."[36] In other words, the immanent unity of the divine persons resonates with the outward unity of their action. Such correspondent divine unity is non-negotiable! We come back to this subject of the relation between of divine unity *ad intra* and *ad extra* in Chapter 4.

Gregory of Nyssa

Often called the "most intelligent systematic thinker" of the Cappadocian Triad, Gregory of Nyssa, like Basil, continued to reject the false teaching of Eunomius and championed the oneness of the Son and the Spirit with the Father. Unlike Eunomius, who placed the Son in opposition to the Father as generate to ingenerate, Gregory of Nyssa insisted on the designations "Son" and "Father" to express not just their identity of nature, but their "relational personhood," – an interesting point which I will come to in the next chapter. Claiming that the Father is always a Father essentially in relation to the Son, Gregory of Nyssa argued that the titles "Father" and "Son" repudiate any connotation of generate-ingenerate opposition in the Triune God. What the appellations entail, he claimed, is the intimate relationship that exists between the Father and the Son from all eternity. Gregory of Nyssa wrote,

> When we hear the title "Father" we apprehend the meaning to be this, that the name is not to be understood with reference to itself alone, but also by its special signification indicates the relation to the Son. For the term "Father" would have no meaning apart by itself, if "Son" were not connoted by the utterance of the word "Father."[37]

What this means is that the Father and the Son always mutually indwell each other, such that the Son is in essence what the Father is from eternity. As the Son is eternally generated by the Father without severing the divine nature, Gregory of Nyssa claimed that the Son is not a creature, but co-divine with the Father, sharing everything, including the divine essence in common with the Father except *being* the Father. That is to say, the titles "Father" and "Son" are used to demonstrate that the two are distinct but inseparable hypostases, for there has never been a time when there was the Father without the Son and vice versa. As reciprocal persons permeating each other from eternity, neither the Father nor the Son has

76 *The "amazing history" of the Trinity*

existed apart from the other; they must always be contemplated and known in one another! This is perichoresis – mutual indwelling of the persons of the Trinity. As Gregory of Nyssa expressed it,

> For all the attributes of the Father are beheld in the Son, and the attributes of the Son belong to the Father, in so much as the Son abides wholly in the Father and in turn has the Father wholly in Himself. Thus the person or "hypostasis" of the Son becomes as it were the form and countenance by which the Father is made known, and the person or "hypostasis" of the Father is made known in the form of the Son.[38]

Though I will explore this idea of perichoresis in detail later in the next chapter, it is very important to note that the mutual permeation of the Father and the Son is incomplete without the Spirit. This is because the Spirit is intrinsically related to both the Father and the Son. As the third distinct hypostasis in order *(taxis)* of the Godhead, Gregory argued that the Spirit is always together with the Father and the Son from eternity. Assigning the Spirit third in sequence from the Father and the Son, Gregory of Nyssa is willing to grant that the Spirit possesses an identical nature with them, meaning the Spirit (like the Father and the Son) is divine and not a creature. The worship accorded the Father and the Son should equally be given to the Spirit. He also claimed that the Spirit proceeds from the Father and receives from the Son, even though the nature of such procession remains unfathomable! The Spirit is of God and of Christ and cannot be separated from the Word.[39] The three distinct hypostases are inseparable, divided without separation, and united without confusion. Gregory of Nyssa wrote,

> Thus we perceive no gap between the anointed Christ and His anointing . . . but as there is contemplated from all eternity in the Father the Son . . . so there is also contemplated in Him the Spirit. . . . For which reason we say that to the holy disciples the mystery of godliness was committed in a form expressing at once union and distinction.[40]

According to him, these appellations – Father, Son, and Spirit – are not used to refer to a difference of nature *(ousia)* in the Triune God, but rather, to designate concrete subsistences in the Godhead so that we can recognize each divine person without confusion by their distinctive mark of subsistence and yet without being separated from that by which each is connected. There is definite order in God without discord. To be God is to be related by not just begetting a Son and breathing a Spirit, but to be united inherently to them without dissonance. As mutually dependent persons, every divine work of the one God in the economy of creation and redemption always involved the three divine persons. I will come back to this idea of mutual dependence in Chapter 4. As Gregory of Nyssa saw it, "We do not similarly learn that the Father does anything by Himself in which the Son does not work conjointly, or again that the Son has any special operation apart the Holy Spirit."[41]

The *"amazing history" of the Trinity* 77

Such joint work of creation that begins with the Father through the Son is completed in the Spirit. Even grace flows uninterruptedly from the Father through the Son and the Spirit to those who deserve it. In all this collective action, Gregory claimed that the Father is the fountain of power, the Son is the power of the Father, and the Spirit is the spirit of that power.[42]

As a result of the emphasis that Gregory of Nyssa laid on the three hypostases, he was charged with tritheism. Responding to this accusation in his treatise, "On 'Not Three Gods' to Ablabius," Gregory of Nyssa stressed the unity of the Father, the Son, and the Spirit, likening it to particular individual human persons such as Pasy, Tunary, and Titveren sharing common *(ousia)* humanity. However, he argued that God's nature cannot be named and thus is "ineffable," "incomprehensible," and "infinite." As infinite, he suggested that God's essence "is not limited in one respect while it is left unlimited in another, but infinity is free from limitation altogether. That therefore which is without limit is surely not limited even by name."[43] Such incomprehensibility of the divine essence will further be explored in the next chapter. Gregory of Nyssa warned that what we know of God's *ousia* cannot entirely be derived from human nature that, though it possesses one nature like God, is spoken of as plural.

What we perceive of the *ousia* of the Triune God, according to him, comes from the unity of the divine operation made known to us in the economy of salvation. But recognizing God's unity of action does not entail knowing God's nature in itself, which remains ineffable, but it does entail perceiving communal energies of the hypostases as shown in revelation. Though our appellations of the Triune God come from the perception of the several divine operations *ad extra*, such multiple operations should not be misconstrued as the separate operations of separate Gods. If this were the case, it would be tritheism, not a Trinity. What we perceive from the economy is the indivisible operations of one God operating collectively under the rubric of three real inseparable hypostases. As Gregory wrote,

> The name derived from the operation is not divided with regard to the number of those who fulfill it, because the action of each concerning anything is not separate and peculiar, but whatever comes to pass, in reference either to the acts of His providence for us or to the government and constitution of the universe, comes to pass by the action of the Three [hypostases].[44]

The divine action is a single motion and disposition of good will, which is communicated from the Father through the Son to the Spirit. Unlike human beings, who must be perceived as many because they act separately from each other, the Trinitarian divine persons, in virtue of sharing identical *ousia* and acting in communion with each other, must be perceived as one God. Though the Father is the cause, being the cause does not express the divine essence, but a distinct "manner of existence." Such an idea of a cause is intended to demonstrate that the Son owes his existence from generation, while the Father exists without generation. As Gregory wrote, while "the idea of cause differentiates the persons of the Trinity," the idea of unchangeable and undivided divine nature shows that God's *ousia* is one and is thus to be spoken of in the singular.[45]

78 The "amazing history" of the Trinity

Gregory of Nazianzus

As *the Theologian* of the Eastern Church, Gregory of Nazianzus rooted his Trinitarian reflection in biblical witness to the Triune God. He argued that the scriptures progressively unfold witness to the Triune God, starting initially with the explicit proclamation of the Father and culminating in the full manifestations of the Son and the Spirit. As the Nazianzian expressed it,

> The Old Testament proclaimed the Father openly, and the Son more obscurely. The New Testament manifested the Son, and suggested the Deity of the Spirit. Now the Spirit Himself dwells among us, and supplies us with a clearer demonstration of Himself."[46]

Such gradual unveiling of the Triune God, Gregory of Nazianzus claimed, is necessary because "it was not safe, when the Godhead of the Father was not yet acknowledged, plainly to proclaim the Son; nor when that of Son was not yet received to burden us further . . . with the Holy Spirit."[47] The Nazianzian, therefore, minced no words in asserting the deity of the Son and the Spirit in the monarchy of the Father over against his adversaries who denied their deity. On account of deriving their being from the Father's *ousia* from eternity without severing the indissoluble Godhead, the Son and the Spirit are fully divine persons of the Godhead, Gregory of Nazianzus asserted. Therefore, the Nazianzian claimed that the Son is "the Maker of Time, and is not subject to Time,"[48] and the Holy Spirit is unambiguously God: "is the Spirit God? Most certainly. Well then, is He consubstantial? Yes, if He is God."[49]

Insisting that the Son and the Spirit are divine, Gregory of Nazianzus debunked the view of Eunomius, which regarded the Son and the Spirit either as twin brothers or the Spirit as the grandson of the Father. The Nazianzian claimed that the Spirit differs from the Son as a "difference of manifestation" or "mutual relations one to another" which causes a difference in their respective names.[50] The fact that they derive their being from the Father does not mean they are inferior. In the next chapter, we will critically assess whether such an idea of derivation in the Godhead entails hierarchy.

On the grounds of being the starting point of the biblical witness to the Triune God, Gregory of Nazianzus insisted that the Father is also the origin and cause of the Trinity. What this idea of the monarchy of the Father means first and foremost is that the Father is the source and cause of personal diversity in the Triune God. For the Nazianzian, the personal existence of the Son and the Spirit does not just occur, it stems from the personal productivity and relationality of the Father. As source and origin of the monarchy, the Father is the begetter of the Son and the emitter of the Spirit. The Son and the Spirit are both from the Father, but not after the Father, for to be begotten and to proceed from the Father belongs to the very *ousia* of the Triune God. Answering the question of "when did these come into being?," the Nazianzian claimed that "they are all above 'When'" that is, beyond time and human comprehension.[51] The Father is the Father in the absolute sense of the word; He has always been the Father in that there was never a time when he was not the Father of the monarchy. Such an absolute un-originate Father bestows on the Son and the Spirit personal properties of *begotteness* and *procession* which distinguish them from the Father and yet bind together in the Godhead. As Gregory of Nazianzus claimed,

> The Father is Father, and is Unoriginate, for He is of no one; the Son is the Son, and is not unoriginate, for He is of the Father. . . . The Holy Ghost is truly Spirit, coming from forth from the Father indeed, but not after the manner of the Son, for it is not by Generation but by Procession.[52]

On the account that the Father is the cause and source of the unsubstitutable personal properties of the Son and the Spirit, the Nazianzian did not hesitate to characterize the Father as greater in the monarchy, albeit not greater in being.[53] As distinct persons, the Father, Son, and Spirit are constituted by the way they are intimately related to one another in virtue of their communal source of the divine production, which is the Father. Gregory argued that real distinctions between the three hypostases can be maintained only when we refrain from all attempts at conceiving them, even with the best intention to honor the divine unity, as dissolving into one another; otherwise, the personal distinctions would be undermined and eventually the entire Trinity would be destroyed.[54]

For Gregory of Nazianzus, the Father is not just the origin and cause of personal distinctions in the monarchy; He is also the source and cause of *ousia* in the Triune God.[55] According to him, the "monarchy is not limited to one Person" of the Father alone.[56] In other words, the Father's *ousia* is not an exclusive character of the Father, as Eunomius claimed; it is communal *ousia* that the Father shares in common with the Son and the Spirit. But how does the Father share his *ousia*? Through producing the Son and the Spirit from himself, the Father communicates his entire *ousia* to them, causing them to have an identical nature, which makes them not three, but one God. According to C. A. Beeley,

> Gregory frequently stipulates that there is one God because the Son and the Spirit "refer back" to the Father as a single cause . . . and the origin of everything that they are and do. So when the Scripture speaks of the Son and the Spirit as possessing divine qualities or being generated or being sent by the Father, they are referring ultimately to the Son's and the Spirit's eternal source in the Father.[57]

The consubstantiality of the Son and the Spirit with the Father does not mean for the Nazianzian that the divine persons possess identical nature without a cause, so to speak. Rather, they are consubstantial by virtue of obtaining their divinity from the Father. According to him, the one Godhead is "undivided in separate Persons" who owe their source of being from the Father.[58] In other words, the Son and the Spirit are co-divine persons with the Father in as much as it is the Father who furnishes with them such divinity. The unity of the Triune God, therefore,

80 *The "amazing history" of the Trinity*

does not simply lie in the commonality of essence, but unity in monarchy of the Father, according to which his *ousia* is communicated to the Son and the Spirit. As the Nazianzian accurately explained it,

> The unity of God would be preserved [if] Son and Spirit would be referred back to one original cause, but not compounded or blended with each other; their unity would be based on the single, self-identical movement and will of the divine being – the Father.[59]

This raises the question whether such primacy of the Father, which provides the ontological basis of the unity of the Triune God, does not subordinate the Son and the Spirit to the Father. Beeley vehemently denied such implications. Beeley thinks that

> for Gregory, there is no unity and equality in the Trinity – indeed there is no Trinity – if the Father does not convey his Divinity to the Son and the Spirit by generating them. . . . The monarchy of the Father within the Trinity is thus the sort of causality that produces equality and shared being, rather than inequality.[60]

In the Nazianzian's monarchical framework, Beeley claimed that the equality of the Trinitarian persons is not an equality of substance that exists apart from a first principle cause, but a kind of equality derived from and which involved an origin and first principle!

For Gregory of Nazianzus, the monarchy of the Father does not threaten, but affirms, the unity of the Trinity and the equality of the distinct Persons therein. "For the Godhead is one in three, and the three in one,"[61] the Nazianzian wrote, "each of these Persons possesses Unity, not less with that which is United to it than with itself, by reason of the identity of Essence and Power."[62] The three are one with respect to *ousia* and the One is three with regards to properties. Such an idea of "One" is not that of Sabellius, which obliterates real distinctions in God, nor is the "Three" that of Eunomius, which creates subordination in God. In essence, the monarchy is the Trinity and vice versa. The Trinity is the monarchy even though the latter always takes precedence over the former. We cannot undermine one without harming the other. Therefore, the Father's monarchy, which unfolds itself into a Triad, is virtually the starting of the Trinitarian reflection for the Nazianzian and not the Trinity of the hypostases, as it has traditionally been assumed! I will come back to this hermeneutics of the monarchy of God more critically in the next chapter.

Mainline Western Trinitarian thinkers

In the previous section, I have analyzed the Eastern Trinitarian thinking, in which the monarchy of the Father is the starting of their Trinitarian hermeneutics and the ontology of divine personhood taking precedence over substance. In this section,

The "amazing history" of the Trinity   81

I will investigate the mainline Western Trinitarian thinkers: Irenaeus, Tertullian, Augustine, and Thomas Aquinas, who in many ways made divine substance the center and starting point of their Trinitarian hermeneutics of God rather than ontology of person. Such an approach, which cut the doctrine off from the economic salvation, accounted for the triumph of the immanent Trinity. Therefore, I will specifically demonstrate how such a hermeneutical approach implicitly or explicitly contributed to the demise of the doctrine of the Trinity in the modern period.

Irenaeus: God with "two hands"[63]

Though inquiring into the Trinitarian thinking of Irenaeus takes us back to the second century, we are undertaking the inquiry for important reasons. Apart from being the dominant Trinitarian thinker before Origen, J.N.D. Kelly claimed that Irenaeus articulated a vision of the Godhead that is the most complete and explicitly Trinitarian prior to Tertullian.[64] Though, like the Apologists, he affirmed the Trinitarian *regula fidei* (rule of faith) of the Church, Irenaeus never endorsed it without charting a new path of Trinitarian thought.

Irenaeus' Trinitarian thinking was provoked by the prevailing heresy of Gnosticism. Apart from laying false claim to true knowledge of salvation, Gnosticism also believed that the spirit is essentially good, while the material world is intrinsically evil. As an absolutely remote Spirit, God has nothing to do with this material world, Gnostics claimed. Therefore, they believed that there is a clear-cut distinction between this one transcendent "God" and the inferior "Demiurge" who created the world.[65] Believing in the dualism of good and evil, Gnostics such as Marcion even claimed that the God of the Old Testament is the God of vengeance while the God of the New Testament is the God of love.

Refuting the Gnostic heresy of one abstract supreme God entirely detached from the world, Irenaeus put forward the idea of a loving eternal Triune God intimately and actively involved in the world through God's "two hands" as revealed in the economy of creation and redemption. He suggested that the Triune God who has existed with his two hands from all eternity is the Creator of the human and material worlds. As the absolute Creator, creating everything from nothing and not from any pre-existent stuff, Irenaeus claims the Triune God freely made all things through God's creative "hands," the Son and the Spirit, as God pleased, devoid of any necessity or assistance from any beings from outside.[66] Referring unambiguously to the Son and the Spirit as "the Two Hands of God" in the work of creating the world, without the help of any intermediary Demiurge or angelic beings, Irenaeus wrote,

> It was not angels, therefore, who made us, nor who formed us, neither had angels power to make an image of God, nor any one else, except the Word of the Lord, nor any Power remotely distant from the Father of all things. For God did not stand in need of these [beings], in order to the accomplishing of what He had Himself determined with Himself beforehand should be done, as if He did not possess His own hands. For with Him were always present the

82   *The "amazing history" of the Trinity*

Word and Wisdom, the Son and the Spirit, by whom and in whom, freely and spontaneously, He made all things.[67]

Affirming the Trinitarian doctrine of the Two Hands of God, Irenaeus is willing to say that the Triune God is not remotely, but immanently and immediately, active in creation. There is no way the Triune God could be a living God apart from God's direct involvement in the world through creation and redemption. Convinced that "The Two Hands of God" is an expression of the immediacy of creation, not of its mediacy, John Lawson argues that "it justifies the claim that S. Irenaeus taught the doctrine of creation 'by the whole Trinity.'"[68] As a Trinitarian joint work, Irenaeus insisted that the work of creation, which has as its origin the Father, is accomplished through His Wisdom and the Sophia, who are the vehicles of God's creative work.[69] He spoke of "the Father planning everything well and giving His commands, the Son carrying these into execution and performing the work of creating, and the Spirit nourishing and increasing."[70] Such distinct creative works of the Triune God (according to which the Father forms the creation, nourishes it through His Son, and binds it together by His Wisdom), do not suggest that they are works of three separate gods, but rather, the work of the one and only true God. But does the idea of being agents of the Triune God's work of creation imply the functional subordination of the Son and the Spirit in the Godhead? By no means. Lawson said that Irenaeus' "doctrine of '*The Two Hands of God*' represents immediate action by whole Godhead, and consequently equality between the Son and the Spirit."[71]:

> There is, in fact, no emanationism in the doctrine of "*The Two Hands of God*" nor is there any subordinationism. The *Hands* indeed serve God, but they are not thereby subordinate, for this service is God's own activity in the world. So also the Spirit may be described as a gift, but this does not place the Gift below the Giver, for that which God gives is Himself.[72]

The cooperative work of the Triune God, which begins at creation, continues throughout the economy of redemption. Apart from speaking the of the triadic anointing of Jesus Christ (whom Irenaeus identified with the Logos of God), according to which he claims the Father anoints, the Son is anointed, and the Spirit is the anointing agent,[73] Irenaeus argued that the Triune God cooperatively accomplishes human redemption through the working of the Spirit, the ministering of the Son, and the approval of the Father.[74] The outcome of this joint Trinitarian redemptive work that brings humanity into communion of the Triune God also reflects the cooperative relation of the Triune God. As Irenaeus argued,

> The Lord thus has redeemed us through His own blood, giving His soul for our souls, and His flesh for our flesh, and has also poured out the Spirit of the Father for the union and communion of God and man, imparting indeed God to men by means of the Spirit, and, on the other hand, attaching man to God

The "amazing history" of the Trinity 83

by His own incarnation, and bestowing upon us at His coming immortality durably and truly, by means of communion with God.[75]

For Irenaeus, these distinct operations of the persons of the Godhead as revealed in the economy of creation and redemption are neither mere modes of manifestations nor intermediaries of one and the same personal God. Rather, the three are co-equal divine personal realities in themselves prior to the foundation of the world. As Irenaeus wrote, "I have also largely demonstrated, that the Word, namely the Son, was always with the Father; and that Wisdom also, which is the Spirit, was present with Him, anterior to all creation."[76] Affirming the co-eternal co-existence of the Son and the Spirit with the Father permits Irenaeus to argue that the Word and the Wisdom are not lesser beings, emanating from the Triune God, but rather, these Two Hands are as truly divine as the Father. Though the three are distinct divine realities, they are one identical God. Irenaeus, as Fortman wrote,

> does not regard the Son and the Spirit as creatures but as eternal and divine as the Father, for they are the very Word of God and Wisdom of God who belong to the very life of God and possess the divine, creative, revelative and inspirative power of God.[77]

The Son, who is eternally begotten of the Father, and the Spirit, who is eternally breathed of the Father, exist in mutual relationship with one another.

On account of eternal co-existence, the Son and the Spirit share in the divinity of the Father. Sharing the Godhead with the Father entails that the Word and the Wisdom, who have always been with the Father from all eternity, have never been separated from each other either by time or space. In that case, the Son and the Spirit are exactly what the Father is in a way that makes them one God. J.J. Lashier wrote that

> in Irenaeus' formula, the Logos/Son and Sophia/Spirit exist in a reciprocally immanent relationship with the Father and with one another, such that the same divine nature encompasses all three entities. The one divinity, or the one spiritual nature that comprises all three entities, makes Father, Son, and Spirit one.[78]

Even though Irenaeus did not contribute special concepts to the Trinitarian conversation, his affirmation that the immanent Triune God as revealed in the economy is inexorably involved in the material world with His Two Hands – the Word and Wisdom – paves the way for subsequent Western Trinitarian reflections.

Tertullian: monarchical Trinity

Tertullian was a Western African theologian and lawyer who first invented a normative way of speaking about the triune being of God in Latin theology. As an

84   *The "amazing history" of the Trinity*

apologist defending the triadic being of God, Tertullian sought to debunk the claim of Praxean that there is no compatibility between the unity of God and his triune being as revealed in the economy – the dispensation of the personal relations of the Godhead.[79] The Praxeans, who believed in the abstract unity of God, insisted that expressing faith in the triune being of God would obliterate the unity of the monarchy. For Praxeas, there is no ontological distinction between the Father and the Son, and hence the Father Himself was born, suffered, and proclaimed by the church as Jesus Christ! As a concerned apologist, Tertullian intended to defend the idea that the personal distinctions in God are real and, consequently, compatible with Christian monotheism.

Affirming the *regula*, which constitutes the basis for defending the three-ness and the oneness of God, Tertullian said,

> We . . . believe that there is one only God, but under the following dispensation, or oikonomia [economy], as it is called, that this one only God has also a Son, His Word . . . [and] the Holy Spirit, the Paraclete."[80]

This *regula*, according to him, suggested there is no way Christians can believe that God is one without admitting that this one God revealed in the economy of salvation is a Triune God. This Triune God, who is perceived in three degrees, forms and aspects, must be recognized under the rubric of Father, Son, and the Holy Ghost. The Father proceeds from no one. Though the Son, through whom all things were made, proceeds from the Father (as we will see later), he was non-eternally generated.[81] As for the Spirit, Tertullian suggested that the Spirit proceeds from the Father through the Son. While the Son is second in the Godhead, Tertullian suggested that the Holy Spirit is the "Third Name in the Godhead," the "Third Degree of the Divine Majesty," the "Declarer of the One *Monarchy* of God," "the Leader into all truth," and the "Interpreter of the *Economy*."[82] As the first and the only pre-Athanasian theologian to uphold unambiguously the deity of the Holy Spirit, Tertullian argued that the Spirit is inseparably joined with the Father and the Son in terms of substance, and is thus God.[83]

After analyzing several scriptural passages (Is. 42:1; 43:1; 45:1; 49:6; 61:1; Ps. 2:7, 3:1; 71:18, 110:1; 45:1, Pr. 8:22, Joh. 12:38, and Rom. 10:6), Tertullian concluded that the three distinct divine persons are revealed in the economy. He writes, "in these few quotations the distinction of the *persons in* the Trinity is clearly set forth. There is the Spirit Himself who speaks, and the Father to whom He speaks, and the Son of whom He speaks."[84] Debunking the Praxean interpretation of Jesus' claim that "I and my Father are one" (Joh. 10:30), meaning the Father and the Son are identical persons, Tertullian argued that the declaration means the Father and the Son are not only two distinct persons, but also one "thing" – meaning unity of essence as opposed to numerical unity.[85] As such, Tertullian thought it is erroneous, therefore, to believe that God the Father was the same person who was born, suffered, and proclaimed as Jesus.

Having shown that there are three distinct persons in the Godhead according to the economy, Tertullian invented the word *Trinity* (trinitas), the numeral

The "amazing history" of the Trinity 85

implication of which he knew would offend his opponents, to characterize his understanding of the Triune God. He challenged them to explain how God, who is merely and absolutely One and Singular, could speak in the plural in scripture, saying, "Let us make man in our own image, and after our own likeness." There is no way an absolute one God could have spoken in the plural unless such a God is Trinity! God deliberately uses the plural phrase because God is triune. He wrote,

> It was because He had already His Son close at His side, as a second Person, His own Word, and a third Person also, the Spirit in the Word, that He purposely adopted the plural phrase. . . . For with whom did He make man? And to whom did He make him like? (The answer must be), the Son on the one hand, who was one day to put on human nature; and the Spirit on the other, who was to sanctify man. With these did He then speak, in the unity of the Trinity.[86]

Rejecting the modalistic understanding of the Christian God by Praxeas, Tertullian claimed that the three who are distinct are numerically countable. As he argued it, "for we . . . declare that *Two* Beings are God, the Father and the Son, and, with addition of the Holy Spirit, even *Three*, according to the principle of the *divine* economy, which introduces *number*."[87] This implies that the Father is the "first," the Son is the "second," and the Spirit is the "third." Tertullian continued: "Thus the connection of the Father in the Son, and of the Son in Paraclete, produces three coherent Persons, *who are yet distinct* One from Another. The three are one *essence*, not one *Person*."[88] Tertullian is the first Latin African theologian to characterize the "Three" divine realities as "persons" *(personae)* in the history of the Western Christian theology. Fortman argued that "person" in Tertullian's theological framework means more than just the legal sense of a title bearer, with certain legal rights and privileges. The word means "concrete individual."[89] For Tertullian, the fact that the divine persons are distinct does not mean that they are separate, and hence divided. Rather, the three persons are inseparable from each other just as the root-tree-fruit, the sun-ray-apex, and the fountain-river-stream are inseparable from each other. He argued that God sent forth the Word, which the Holy Spirit proclaims as a root puts forth the tree, the fountain produces the river, and the sun radiates the ray. Describing them as *emanations* of the substances from which they proceed without severing their sources, he suggested each of these original sources is a parent and the emanations are their offspring. As such, none of the emanations are foreign to their source, for each obtains its properties from the source.[90]

Therefore, he maintained that "the Trinity, flowing down from the Father through intertwined and connected steps, does not at all disturb the *Monarchy*, whilst it at the same time guards the state of the *economy*."[91] Tertullian claimed that there is no such thing as absolute human monarchy, which precludes a monarch from either sharing his rule with his son or ruling through agents. The fact that a monarch co-shares his monarchy with his son does not entail that the monarchy is divided. Tertullian wondered why the divine monarchy would suffer

86 The "amazing history" of the Trinity

division and severance by virtue of simply assigning second and third places to the Son and the Spirit in the monarchy. Tertullian insisted that the only thing that would overthrow the divine monarchy is when other gods are introduced in opposition to the Triune Creator![92]

What then did Tertullian mean when he claimed there is only one God, even when there are distinct personae in the Godhead? Tertullian meant that the Father is God, the Son is God, and the Spirit is God, and yet they are not three gods, but one.[93] The three are one God by the virtue of sharing one common indivisible substance. As he saw it, the "three coherent persons . . . are one *essence* . . . in respect of unity of substance."[94] By substance, Tertullian probably meant "body or corporeity," for he suggests that God is a "body" even though God is a "spirit."[95] In other words, substance is thus divine material that constitutes the unity of the members of the Godhead.[96] As the divine persons are one in aspect, condition, substance, and power,[97] Tertullian argued that the unity that flows from the Trinity does not destroy, but affirms it.

Tertullian's contributions to the emergence of the doctrine of the Trinity cannot be overemphasized. Tertullian's creativity and originality, with which he initially uses the words "Trinity" and "personae" to speak of the Triune God, had a profound influence on Western theology and, by extension, the entire history of Christian theology. However, Tertullian's use of the word "persona" should not be misconstrued as the modern understanding of person, an autonomous self-conscious individual. In Tertullian's Trinitarian framework, the personal distinctions in the Trinity do not mean independent existence, but relatedness of the persons to each other in their common Godhead. This lends credence to his use of the formula "the three in One."

Tertullian also radicalized the interpretation of the word "divine monarchy," which had been traditionally misunderstood as the absolute rule by a solitary God, the Father, to the exclusion of the Son and the Holy Spirit. Appealing to the economy of salvation, he argued that God is not a solitary Monarch. The Triune God shares this monarchy with the Son and the Spirit, yet the monarchy is reinforced rather than divided. Tertullian found the basis of this sharing in the kingdom of God, in which the Father delivers up his kingdom to the Son and vice versa, even as the Spirit proclaims the monarchy to the world until "God may be all in all."[98] This interpretation is one of the lasting contributions of Tertullian to the doctrine of the Trinity that is rarely noted, but which most likely impacted Moltmann's and Pannenberg's interpretations of reciprocal relations of the persons of the Trinity within the context of the kingdom of God in the economy of salvation.

Therefore, I do not think that George Leonard Prestige is accurate in claiming that Tertullian's understanding of the "economy" has nothing do with either the economy of redemption or revelation. Rather, it is essentially the "economy of divine being," in which the Father is the sole source of the Godhead.[99] Though we cannot deny that Tertullian may have used the word "economy" to mean the Father as the only fount of deity, it is dubious to suppose that the divine economy is not the economy of salvation or revelation. This begs an epistemological question: how did Tertullian know about the Father as the sole source of the Godhead if the economy is not the economy of salvation? Put differently, how would

The "amazing history" of the Trinity 87

Tertullian have known about the Father as the sole source of the Godhead apart from the economy of salvation? This is not possible, or else he wouldn't have claimed that the coming of Christ into the world reveals the plurality of persons in God.[100] Tertullian even made it clear that the economy (mutual relations in the Godhead) are set forth in the scripture under the name of the Word of God.[101] As the only One who knows the Father, it is the Son who reveals the Father in the Spirit.[102] Thus, we can argue that Tertullian's doctrine of the Trinity is more or less practical rather than theoretical in that it is deeply rooted in the economy of salvation. As H. F. Carl accurately wrote,

> Tertullian's doctrine of the trinity is an "economic Trinity" in that almost every formulation is made in the context of the work of God in creation and redemption. Tertullian is almost always thinking practically and functionally, in terms of role and action, and rarely abstractly.[103]

This does not mean that Tertullian did not pay attention to the immanent Trinity. He affirmed that the distinct persons of the Godhead are eternally co-substantial and co-powerful in a way that does not undermine the monarchy of the Father.[104] However, Tertullian's perception of the inner life of the Trinity is contradictory. He suggested that before all things were created, God had been eternally solitary, though he had in Himself a Reason which the Greeks call the *Logos*, but which the church calls *the Word*. The Word, which was always within God, became a full person at creation. As he put it,

> Then, therefore, does the Word also Himself assume His *own* form and glorious garb, His *own* sound and vocal utterance, when God says, 'Let there be light.' This is the perfect nativity of the Word, when He proceeds forth from God . . . He became His first-begotten Son . . . before all things."[105]

This raises the question of whether the Son was a fully distinct co-eternal, co-equal, and co-substantial person with the Father. Fortman suggested that

> if what is not eternal is not divine in the strict sense, then the Son is not divine. But if the possession of "divine substance" is a norm of divinity, then perhaps the Son will still be divine in Tertullian's theology.[106]

Whichever suggestion we endorse, the truth is that Tertullian's thought about the personality and deity of the Son is not only inconsistent, but also susceptible to subordinationism. This subordinationism is obvious when Tertullian claimed, "for the Father is the entire substance, but the Son is a derivation and portion of the whole."[107]

Augustine: mono-Trinitarian God

St Augustine of Hippo is the most influential Western and African theologian, who in many ways can best be characterized as the pillar of Catholic theology.

88 The "amazing history" of the Trinity

Augustine articulated a doctrine of the Trinity which gave the Western Trinitarian heritage its full-blown and final form in his most celebrated book, *On the Trinity*, which took him more than fifteen years to write. Augustine employs a rather different approach from the Cappadocians in formulating his doctrine of the Trinity. Cappadocians started interpretation of the Trinity with the monarchy before they affirmed the unity of the three hypostases in one and the same person of the Father. On the contrary, St Augustine began where the Cappadocians ended and ended where they started. That is to say, St Augustine started off by establishing the divine unity before reflecting on the problem of the three-ness. We will come to this question of the starting point of the hermeneutics of the doctrine of the Trinity in the next chapter.

Making the one simple divine nature (which is the Trinity itself) the starting point of his Trinitarian hermeneutics, Augustine wrote, "the Trinity is the one and only . . . true God . . . the Father, and the Son, and the Holy Spirit intimate a divine unity of one and the same substance in an indivisible equality; and therefore that they are not three Gods, but one God."[108] Augustine set the unity of the consubstantial Trinity in the forefront to establish the co-equality of the Trinity, which eliminates all forms of subordinationism in the Triune God. He reasoned that whatever is said of the Triune God in the singular, not in the plural, with respect to substance, is said of each of the three persons.[109] Each person is thus identical with the divine substance and the Trinity itself. On the account that each person is constituted by identical substance, Augustine claimed there is "so great an equality in that Trinity, that not only the Father is not greater than the Son, as regards divinity, but neither are the Father and the Son together greater than the Holy Spirit; nor is each several person, whichever it be of the three, less than the Trinity itself."[110] Since each divine person is as great as the entire three persons together, he argues that the Triune God cannot be construed as "three-fold," but as a Trinity.

Like the Cappadocians, Augustine endorsed the idea of mutual inexistence of the divine persons. Suggesting that the divine persons are unlimited in themselves, he argued that they mutually indwell each other so intimately that "both each are in each, and all in each, and each in all, and all in all, and all are one."[111] Therefore, Augustine did not believe that the three persons perform separate functions in the economy of salvation because such a conception tends to undermine the simplicity of God. Like the Cappadocians, he affirmed the indivisibility of the work of the Trinity.[112] As the divine persons share one identical essence, Augustine insisted that they have one will and perform one operation![113] With respect to the creation, Augustine argued the divine persons act as "one Principle" and thus, "as they are indivisible, so work indivisibly."[114] The divine persons work so inseparably with one another such that any distinction of work *ad extra* among them can only be made by appropriation. Nonetheless, Augustine claimed the fact that the divine persons work indivisibly in the economy does not mean that he obliterates the distinctions between the Trinitarian persons. Though the whole Trinity works inseparably, he argued that it was not

> this Trinity [that] was born of Virgin Mary . . . but only the Son . . . nor this trinity [that] descended in the form of a dove upon Jesus . . . but only the

The "amazing history" of the Trinity 89

Spirit . . . nor yet that this Trinity [that] said from heaven, "Thou art my Son . . ." but it was a word of the Father only.[115]

Yet Augustine insisted that they are not separate persons doing separate work without the mutual participation of the other; rather, they all cooperate with each other in doing the work. For example, speaking of the voice of the Father at the Baptism of the Son, Augustine claimed,

> Not that the voice could be wrought without the work of the Son and the Holy Spirit (since the Trinity works indivisibly), but that such a voice was wrought as to manifest the person of the Father only; just as the Trinity wrought that human form from Virgin Mary, yet it is the person of the Son alone; for the invisible Trinity wrought the visible person of the Son alone."[116]

Augustine, therefore, rejected the idea of regarding the theophanies of the Old Testament exclusively as the appearances of the Son. He claimed that the whole Trinity was present in these appearances.

As for the distinction of the divine persons, Augustine argued that the divine persons are distinguished from each other in virtue of their relations of origin in the Godhead. Each person holds a distinct personal and eternal property in relation to the other: the Father in relation to the Son is unbegotten; the Son in relation to Father is begotten; while the Spirit is the common gift of the Father and the Son.[117] Augustine dismissed the cunning proposal of the Arians that these divine distinctions in the Triune God must be seen in terms of substance or accidents. He argued that such divine distinctions are not made in the Triune God in terms of accidents or substance because there are no such things as accidents or separate substances in God. Rather, the distinctions are made in terms of their immutable relations of origin of begetter, begotten, and proceeding.[118] As Augustine saw it, Pannenberg suggested,

> The thesis that there are relations in the divine substance does not contradict the exclusion of accidents, for relations in God are not an expression of mutability but obtain eternally, where accidents are mutable. Hence relations in the divine substance are not accidents.[119]

What are these three relations? Augustine hesitantly referred to them as three *persons* in one substance because the word *personae*, for him, seems to suggest independent individuals. As he writes, "The answer, however, is given, three persons, not that it might be spoken, but that it might not be left unspoken."[120] Like Athanasius, Augustine rejected Eunomius' idea that the Son issues not from the substance, but the will of the Father. He claimed that the Son, who comes forth from the Father's substance, is a Son by nature and not will.

As for the Holy Spirit, unlike the Cappadocians, who claimed the Holy Spirit proceeds from the Father alone, Augustine insisted without reservation on the *filioque*, which means the Holy Spirit proceeds from both the Father and the Son but "principally" from the Father.[121] Augustine claimed that "as the Father has in

90   The "amazing history" of the Trinity

Himself that the Holy Spirit should proceed from Him, so has He given to the Son that the same Holy Spirit should proceed from Him, and be both apart from time."[122]

The procession of the Holy Spirit from both the Father and the Son, Augustine contended, does not entail the Father and the Son are two separate, but one Principle of the Holy Spirit. Rather, as the Father and the Son are one Lord and one Creator in relation to the creature, Augustine suggested that so they are one Principle in relation to the Holy Spirit. Therefore, the Holy Spirit cannot be construed as a Son in virtue of proceeding from the Father, "for the Spirit came forth, not as born, but as given."[123] The Holy Spirit was an eternal gift before He was given to us in time as a gift of God Himself. The Spirit is an unalterable communion that binds the Father and Son in the Godhead. The Spirit who is poured out in our hearts not only communicates to us the love of the Triune God, but also the entire Trinity indwells us.[124]

What has been said to be Augustine's most creative contribution to the doctrine of the Trinity is the finding of vestiges of the Trinity in creation.[125] Augustine's traces of the Trinity, which merely have an illustrative character, have become one of the most distinguishing marks of his Trinity. Augustine did not intend by these analogies to prove from creation that God is Trinity, but to boost our understanding of the oneness and three-ness of God. As Kelly wrote,

> Strictly speaking, according to Augustine, there are "vestiges" of the Trinity everywhere, for in so far as creatures exist at all they exist by participating in the ideas of God; hence, everything must reflect, however faintly, the Trinity Which created it.[126]

Augustine claimed that the immediate creature in which we can find the image of the Trinity is humanity. As humanity is made in the image and likeness of the Triune God, so humanity is a bearer of the image of the Trinity. According to Augustine, the image of the Trinity is specifically located in the human mind, which has been given the capacity to grasp supersensible things.[127] Prominent among the analogies which Augustine discovered are the lover, the beloved, and the love that unites them;[128] the mind knowing and loving itself;[129] memory, understanding and will;[130] and the mind remembering, understanding, and loving God.[131] These three elements within the analogy, which are equal, coordinate with one another in a way that illuminates the mutual relations of the Trinitarian persons. However, finding them wanting, Augustine has no pretension about their inadequacies, remoteness, and imperfection.[132]

Assessing the Augustinian doctrine of the Trinity, Fortman has this say:

> There can be no doubt that Augustine produced a more comprehensive and stimulating synthesis of Trinitarian doctrine than anyone else had before him in the West or East. It summed up the work of his predecessors and laid the foundations for most all subsequent Trinitarian theology in the West.[133]

The "amazing history" of the Trinity 91

One such incredible foundation Augustine established is making the one simple divine substance rather than the Trinity of the personae the starting point of the Trinitarian reflection. This approach has become the normative way to start off almost every West Trinitarian conversation. "With this approach," Fortman wrote, "there is no question of the equality of the three for they have identically the same essence and will and operation."[134]

Another Trinitarian contribution of Augustine is the affirmation of the indivisibility of the works of the divine persons, which permits distinctions of works *ad extra* in the Trinity only by appropriation. Letham argued, "Augustine's first main achievement was to stress that the activity of the Trinitarian persons, flowing from their unity, was inseparable."[135] Such a doctrine of inseparability of the work of the Trinity and appropriation are influential theological motifs that impacted the successive West Trinitarian reflections over an extended period of time. Augustine also broke new ground when he developed a Trinitarian pneumatology according to which the Holy Spirit not only proceeds from both the Father and the Son, but is also an unalterable communion that binds and distinguishes the Father from the Son. The Spirit is a Gift, Love, and Sanctifying Indweller of the saint. Fortman suggested that in many ways Augustine surpassed the Cappadocians in the explication of the Trinitarian indwelling, which has radical ontological consequences for baptismal transformation and perfection of the saints.[136]

Augustine's obsession with the oneness of the divine substance and inseparability of the divine persons no doubt obviates the danger of subordinationism in the Trinity, but makes him either guilty of or open to the charge of modalism. This accounts for why the divine unity is not so much a problem for him as the divine three-ness, which as a matter of necessity he reluctantly called "persons." In Augustine's Trinitarian framework, the divine unity tends to logically and even ontologically precede the divine Trinity such that even when he affirmed the divine Trinity, the divine unity still takes precedence over the Trinity. As Pannenberg wrote, "Augustine so strongly emphasized the unity of God that strictly no space was left for the trinity of persons."[137] Augustine, for instance, is willing to believe that the divine persons are eternally distinct from each other in virtue of personal properties, but is unwilling to assign distinct ontological functions to them in the economy, simply to maintain the abstract unity of God.

This begs the question of whether Augustine is faithful to the Trinitarian theologies of St John and St Paul, who identify the Father, Son, and Holy Spirit as real persons who not only hold distinct personal properties from one another, but also function in quite distinct ways from one another. The distinct functions that divine persons perform in the economy are true replications of the mutual working of their eternal distinct interpersonal relationships. Therefore, affirming that the works of the Trinity *ad extra* are one, that is, there is one relation of the Trinity to creation, Augustine abrogated the diversity of the persons in the economy and in the inner life of the Triune God. Such abrogation leaves Augustine with a mono-Trinitarian God in whom Father, Son, and Spirit are mere abstract realities!

92   *The "amazing history" of the Trinity*

Therefore, for Augustine the divine persons are not ontologically related to each other in that they are mere individuals apart from their real communal relation to each other, an idea in Augustine, which, according to LaCugna, "flows from the ontology that begins from substance rather than person."[138] Such obsession with the simple divine substance tends to make the Triune God an impersonal Being, a Triune God who does not have real relation to the world. As Augustine's essence is impersonal, his Trinity is based on Neo-Platonic philosophy rather the economy of salvation. As such, one wonders whether Augustine bequeathed the Trinitarian legacy largely informed by abstract speculation rather than the economy of salvation in the West. As LaCugna saw it, "Even if Augustine himself intended nothing of the sort, his legacy to Western theology was an approach to the Trinity largely cut off from the economy of salvation."[139] Though Augustine's idea of the *filioque* is creative and fascinating, it de-personalizes the Spirit, obscures the perichoresis of the divine persons, and causes the theological quagmire between the West and the East. As Veli-Matti Kärkkäinen argued, "Augustine's idea of the shared love between Father and Son is problematic ecumenically and biblically. In the Bible, God is love rather than Spirit."[140] I will come back to this idea in Chapter 4.

Thomas Aquinas: triumph of immanent Trinity

Aquinas split his reflection on the Triune God into *De Deo Uno* and *De Deo Trino*. Splitting the two and even starting his hermeneutics of the doctrine of the Triune God with the former, Aquinas perfected the hermeneutical approach to the Trinity that Augustine first initiated in the Western Trinitarian Tradition. Though the separation is reminiscent of Peter Lombard' *Sentences*, LaCugna argued that the entire *Summa* is restructured according to the *exitus-reditus* or the Dionysian circle of emanation and return of everything from and to God.[141] As a Christian philosopher who employs natural reason to explicate the tenets of the Christian faith, Aquinas presumed that the subject matter of Christian dogmatics is first and foremost "God in Himself." Aquinas wrote,

> Because the chief aim of sacred doctrine is to teach the knowledge of God, not only as He is in Himself, but also as He is the beginning of things and their last end . . . in our endeavor to expound this science, we shall treat: (1) Of God: (2) Of the rational creature's advance towards God: (3) Of Christ, Who as man, is our way to God.[142]

Reflecting the circle of emanation and return, undoubtedly Aquinas' theological work moves from God in Himself to the immanent procession of the Trinitarian persons; to their mission in the world; to the work of creation and back to the unity of God in Christ. Though LaCugna argued that Aquinas' division between *De Deo Uno* and *De Deo Trino* does not reflect the distinction between reason and faith,[143] I think that by putting the *former* ahead of the *latter* in his *Summa*, Aquinas believed natural reason can adequately demonstrate the existence and nature of the one God on the basis of God's *effects* in creation without reference to

The *"amazing history" of the Trinity* 93

God's revelation in Christ. This hermeneutical approach stands in sharp contrast to that of the Greek Fathers, whose starting point is the monarchy of the Father (as revealed in Christ), the origin and end of everything in God and in the world. As Karl Rahner argued,

> St. Thomas does not begin with God the Father as the un-engendered origin in the Godhead, the origin of all reality in the world, but with the nature common to all three persons. And the procedure became well-nigh universal. Thus the treatise on the Trinity comes to stand still more in a splendid isolation, which brings it into a still greater danger than that of being found without interest for religious existence: it looks as though everything about God which touches ourselves has already been said in the treatise *De Deo Uno*.[144]

Insisting not just on God as the only object of theological science, but also on God's knowability on account of God's effects in nature, Aquinas is also departing from both Aristotelian thinking, which considers God to be one among many objects of theological inquiry, and the Neo-Platonic premise which posits that God is altogether unknowable except through intermediaries.[145] Therefore, Aquinas advanced cosmological arguments for God's existence to substantiate the claim that God is knowable and even provable, though not from our direct, but indirect, perception of the worldly creatures that are God's effects.[146] As for God's substance, Aquinas claimed that the only way we can obtain knowledge of God's substance is not through positive perception of God's nature in the world, but rather, by a via *negativa*. Aquinas wrote, "Because we cannot know what God is, but rather what He is not, we have no means for considering how God is, but rather how He is not."[147]

Consequently, Aquinas argued that God is not a body, nor is God composed of form and matter, genus and difference, subject and accidents. In God, essence is not one thing and existence another thing, nor are there potentialities in God! Drawing on the ideas of a perfect being in Neo-Platonism and *esse commune*, "common being," in Aristotle, Aquinas argued that God does not have being, nor does God depend on *esse commune* as other things for existence. Rather, God is being itself because in God *esse* (being) and the act of being are one and the same.[148] Characterizing God also as *actus purus*, a pure act without any potentiality, Aquinas maintained that God depends on Godself for existence, as opposed to every other thing that exists by participating in God's act of being, hence the one God is self-sufficient and immutable. On the basis of the preceding arguments, Aquinas submitted that God's nature is absolutely simple. As an absolutely simple being, God is always so identical with his own nature that whatever God is, God is it essentially, and thus "God cannot be part of a compound."[149] Affirming divine simplicity is very decisive because it determines not just Aquinas' treatment of divine attributes, but also the Trinity. Following the explication of God's nature, Aquinas said, "Having considered what belongs to the unity of the divine essence, it remains to treat of what belongs to the Trinity of the persons in God."[150] But this raises the questions of whether or not the Triune God can be known by natural reason, from the

94   *The "amazing history" of the Trinity*

perception of God's effects in nature, and whether or not the doctrine of absolute simplicity of God's nature is compatible with the doctrine of the Triune God.

As for the first question, Aquinas categorically gave a negative reply. He argues that natural reason alone can't furnish us with knowledge of the Triune God. Though natural reason can establish on the basis of God's effects in the created world that God is one,[151] it cannot demonstrate on the same account that God is a Trinity of persons. As the creative power of God is exercised in common by the persons of the Trinity, Aquinas claimed that there is no rational justification for making personal distinctions in God. Therefore, Aquinas wrote,

> It is impossible to attain to the knowledge of the Trinity by natural reason. . . . [Humans] cannot obtain the knowledge of God by natural reason except from creatures. Now creatures lead us to the knowledge of God, as effects do to their cause. . . . Therefore, by natural reason we can know what belongs to the unity of the essence, but not what belongs to the distinction of the persons.[152]

Aquinas argued that though philosophers knew the essential attributes ascribed to the persons of the Godhead, they have failed to recognize them by their proper personal attributes of relations of origin. This task, according to Aquinas, belongs to the realm of faith, which alone on the basis of biblical witness to revelation can perceive the distinct persons in God. As Hansen accurately sees it, "The threefold pattern revealed in Scriptures, and the noetic premises of faith, therefore, disclose for Thomas the truth of God's eternal three-foldness which supersedes philosophical accounts of Supreme Being and its contingent relation with the creatural."[153] Aquinas claimed that securing the knowledge of the divine persons of the Trinity is essential not only for establishing "the right idea of the creation," but also, most importantly, for thinking "rightly concerning the salvation" brought about by the incarnation of the Son and gift of the Spirit![154]

As for the second question, Aquinas did not think that divine simplicity and personal distinction in God are mutually opposed to each other. The latter does not negate, but affirms the former. Aquinas thought that there are only two eternal processions in this absolutely simple God (Q. 27), four real relations (Q. 28), three persons (Q. 29–30), and visible and invisible missions of the Son and the Holy Spirit (Q. 43). Explicating the two divine processions in the Triune God in terms of intellectual nature, Aquinas claimed,

> The divine processions can be derived only from the actions which remain within the agent. In a nature which is intellectual, and in the divine nature these actions are two, the acts of intelligence and of will. . . . It follows that no other procession is possible in God but the procession of the Word, and of Love."[155]

Aquinas claimed that the nature of these intellectual processions, that is, the generation of the Word and procession of the Spirit, should not be construed as multiple immanent acts of God; rather, it is the single act of the simple God by which God understands and wills everything. Positing infinite procession in God

The "amazing history" of the Trinity 95

is unnecessary in that the intellectual nature of such procession accomplished within the agent comes to end with the procession of the will. "Hence," Aquinas wrote, "there cannot exist in Him a procession of Word from Word, nor of Love from Love: for there is in Him only one perfect Word, and one perfect Love; thereby being manifested His perfect fecundity."[156]

Perceiving the divine processions as the basis of relations of origin in God, Aquinas thus affirmed real intrinsic divine relations in God, namely, fatherhood, sonship, and procession. Since God is pure substance, Aquinas argued that these relations should not be mistaken for accidents. These divine relations, though identical with God's nature itself, are distinguished from one another in virtue of their real mutual oppositions in God. As Aquinas argued,

> So as in God there is a real relation . . . there must also be a real opposition. The very nature of relative opposition includes distinction. Hence, there must be real distinction in God, not, indeed, according to that which is absolute – namely, essence, wherein there is supreme unity and simplicity – but according to that which is relative.[157]

How are these distinctions in God described? Aquinas described them as three persons in God. But they are not persons merely in Boethius' sense of "the individual substance of the rational nature," nor in Richard St Victor's sense of "the incommunicable existence of the divine nature." Rather, they are persons in the sense of concrete subsistent relations in God, for "person," according to Aquinas, "signifies in God a relation as subsisting in the divine nature."[158] In other words, the Trinitarian "persons" are relations that subsist really in God because each person is identical with the divine substance.

Rounding off the treatment of *De Deo Trino* with the mission of the divine persons, Aquinas claimed that the mission of the persons of the Trinity is not only grounded in the procession of origin from the sender, but also involves a new way of existing somewhere. Aquinas argued that though it is inappropriate for the Father, who is not from anyone, to be sent, it is appropriate for the Son and the Holy Spirit, who owe their origin from the Father to be sent by the Father on a mission to the world.[159] But neither is the Father, who sends, greater than those He sent (the Son and the Holy Spirit), nor are those sent lesser beings than the Sender. The sending of the Son and the Spirit by the Father does not stem from the hierarchy of command, but rather, it is grounded in the equality of their being. As the Son and the Spirit "proceed" and "go forth" from the being of the Father both in time and eternity, there is no such thing as hierarchy or separation among the divine persons even in their mission *ad extra*. Even though the Father is not sent into the world, Aquinas suggested that the Father graciously gives Himself to be enjoyed by the creature through the mission of the Son and the Spirit in the world.[160] Therefore, the entire mission of the Triune God is nothing but grace, which is the indwelling of the creature. As Aquinas wrote,

> Since the rational creature by its operation of knowledge and love attains to God Himself, according to this special mode God is said not only to exist

96 *The "amazing history" of the Trinity*

in the rational creature, but also to dwell therein as in His own temple. So no other effect can be put down as the reason why the divine person is in the rational creature in a new mode, except sanctifying grace. Hence, the divine person is sent, and proceeds temporally only according to sanctifying grace.[161]

Aquinas claimed that the two-fold nature of the mission of the Triune God does not stem from the two-foldness of the events of the economy of salvation, but from the two processions within the divine persons of the Godhead itself. Thus, the operation of the divine persons in the economy of the mission does not impact the intra-divine life of the Trinity.

There is no doubt that Aquinas has "produced the most perfect metaphysical synthesis of trinitarian doctrine,"[162] but the issues raised by such a metaphysical doctrine of the Trinity must not be ignored. Demonstrating first and foremost the unity of the one God on the basis of creaturely existence followed by an unwarranted focus on the immanent life of the Triune God, Aquinas produced a metaphysical Trinitarian theology that is virtually cut off from the operation of God revealed in Christ through the Spirit in the economy of redemption. The consequence of Aquinas' approach, according to Karl Rahner, is that Aquinas'

treatise of the Trinity locks itself in even more splendid isolation, with the ensuing danger that the religious mind finds it devoid of interest. As a result, the treatise becomes quite philosophical and abstract and refers hardly at all to salvation history.[163]

Though Aquinas undertook this approach to protect divine *aseity* or freedom, it definitely ends up being a mere fanciful speculation about the Triune God. What we thus find in Aquinas is the triumph of the immanent Trinity over against the economic Trinity, a triumph that marks the genesis of the eventual eclipse and diminished significance of the doctrine of Trinity for Christian faith and life, especially in the modern period. S.J. Grenz rightly claimed that "regardless of the extent to which we might want to laud Aquinas's greatness as a theological mind, his proposal not only stood at the apex of medieval trinitarian theology, but it also became the precursor of its demise."[164]

What further betrays Aquinas' Trinitarian theology is the doctrine of the absolute divine simplicity bequeathed to the Western Trinitarian tradition by Augustine. The doctrine of absolute simplicity of God, which Aquinas unquestionably embraces and fully develops, is incompatible with the Trinity. As Tersur Aben rightly saw it, "[Absolute] simplicity is not a faith-determined doctrine, and it needlessly inhibits us from affirming the biblical teaching that Father, Son and Holy Spirit are three distinct persons."[165] Though divine simplicity *per se* does not contradict the Trinity, absolute divine simplicity, which negates all forms of composition in God, does, for where there are personal distinctions in the Triune God, there cannot be absolute divine simplicity. Otherwise, the absolute unity of God that Aquinas jealously safeguarded would be dissolved. Similarly, characterizing

The "amazing history" of the Trinity   97

the persons as subsistent relations fails to square up with the understanding of divine persons as a metaphysical being who possesses knowledge and love. Thus, Aquinas' subsistent relations do not possess such knowledge and love, nor can they generate or proceed from God. According to Aben, "These are quite personal acts that cannot be performed by relations. And these are some of the acts that orthodox Christians assign to divine persons but which may not be assigned to relations."[166] One wonders how Aquinas' absolutely simple God could understand and will all things if that God were not a real person endowed with knowledge and will, but a mere relation. Like Augustine, not only is Aquinas' idea of person vulnerable to modalism, but also his idea of dual procession of the Spirit is capable of blurring the distinct personality and role of the Spirit in the Trinity.[167]

Eclipse and renaissance of Trinitarian theology in the early modern period

The early modern period is one of the most crucial eras in the history of the doctrine of the Trinity. It was during this time that the Trinitarian theology suffered neglect as well as experienced revival. The marginalization of the doctrine of the Trinity, which in many ways began with Aquinas' abstract Trinitarian theology in the Middle Ages, reached its zenith in modern Western theology.[168] The neglect of the Trinitarian theology in the period under investigation is partly due to the emergence of biblical criticism, which challenges the authoritative biblical basis of the doctrine of the Trinity and is partly due to the nonchalant attitude of Friedrich Schleiermacher toward the Trinity. As for the revival, the creative recasting of the doctrine of the Trinity by Karl Barth and Karl Rahner opened new fertile grounds for fruitful theological engagement of the Trinity in contemporary theology, and hence ignited a light of renaissance of the doctrine in the twentieth century. Taking an analytical rather than synthetic hermeneutical approach to the doctrine of the Trinity as God's self-revelation in Christ and the Spirit, they provided the solid basis for the emergence of the New Trinitarian theology. According to Kärkkäinen, "The two Karls, Barth and Rahner, are hailed as the originators of the contemporary worldwide Trinitarian renaissance. They have also shaped much of the agenda of the contemporary discussion."[169] In this section, I will discuss Schleiermacher as the main representative figure responsible for marginalization of the Trinity in the early modern period, and Barth and Rahner as the two representative theologians responsible for its renaissance.

Friedrich Schleiermacher: the Trinity, an unnecessary doctrine

Often acclaimed as "the father of modern theology," Schleiermacher's approach to the doctrine of the Trinity is inexorably shaped by the influence of Immanuel Kant within the context of the nineteenth century. In his famous work *Critique of Pure Reason*, Kant claimed that cognition is made up of two essential elements: the content of knowledge and the forms of understanding, which the human senses give us. Suggesting that the two components are inseparable, he

98   The "amazing history" of the Trinity

argued that "thoughts without content are empty, intuitions without concepts are blind."[170] Kant contended that theoretical knowledge of supersensible objects is inaccessible, hence God is a *noumenon* (as opposed to a *phenomenon*, which is knowable). As a noumenon, God cannot be conceived of, meaning a God who is beyond human conception and is not subject to human categories of experience. Since God is not an object of theoretical knowledge, Kant suggested that the doctrine of the Trinity is beyond human comprehension, hence practically useless! Kant wrote, "The doctrine of the Trinity, taken literally, *has no practical relevance at all*, even if we think we understand it; and it is even clearly irrelevant if we realize that it transcends all our concepts."[171] Continuing, Kant contended that "whether we are to worship three or ten persons in divinity makes no difference . . . because this distinction can make no difference in [our] conduct."[172] Schleiermacher formulated his theology under the influence of this Kantian thinking from human experience. Because he concurred with Kant that religion can't be based on theoretical reason, Schleiermacher insisted that the essence of religion consists in the human feeling of absolute dependence.

What is thus striking about Schleiermacher's approach to the doctrine of the Trinity is not only the place he accorded it in his theological work, but also, most importantly, his interpretation of the doctrine itself. Schleiermacher relegated the doctrine of the Trinity to the appendix of his *Christian Faith*, alleging that the doctrine of the Trinity is an unnecessary addition to the Christian faith.[173] Because Schleiermacher thought that the doctrine of the Trinity was a mere concoction of the early church, he did not think that the doctrine of the Trinity is "an immediate utterance concerning the Christian self-consciousness, but only a combination of several such utterances."[174] Schleiermacher claimed that the doctrine of the Trinity is neither an object of human feeling nor consciousness, but rather, an inference made from a combination of feelings. The doctrine, which is in effect valueless, was framed simply to defend the "the union of the Divine Essence with human nature, both in the personality of Christ and in the common spirit of the church," a union which is needed by the redemption in Christ and the church as its bearer.[175]

Schleiermacher contended that the doctrine of the Trinity does not even emerge from the teachings of the New Testament, but from the combination of testimonies regarding a "supersensible fact," which has nothing to do with human experience. Even if the doctrine stems from the proclamations of Christ and the apostolic teachings about Jesus Christ, our faith and communion with Jesus Christ would ordinarily remain the same without the knowledge of the Trinity. Moreover, the fundamental tenets of the Christian faith, such as the being of God in Christ and in the Church, are virtually independent of the doctrine of the Trinity.[176] Schleiermacher also claimed that eternal distinction in God is not derived from the contents of Christian self-consciousness, but from the absolute feeling of dependence in which we perceive of God as the ultimate object on which we utterly depend. Thus, he argued that "all attributes which we ascribe to God are to be taken as denoting not something special in God, but only something special in the manner in which the feeling of absolute dependence is to be related to Him."[177] For him,

The "amazing history" of the Trinity 99

the being of God *ad intra* and the being of God *ad extra* is a philosophical rather than theological distinction. Schleiermacher wrote,

> We have only to do with the God-consciousness given in our self-consciousness along with our consciousness of the world; hence we have no formula for the being of God in Himself as distinct from the being of God in the world, and should have to borrow any such formula from speculation, and so prove ourselves disloyal to the character of the discipline at which we are working.[178]

Therefore, Schleiermacher contended that there is no real distinction between God's presence in Christ and God's presence in the Church. The two are identical and are thus an integral part of God's universal omnipresence in the world. Persuaded then that the doctrine of the Trinity is worthless for "Christian self-consciousness," Schleiermacher sacrificed the doctrine of the Triune God in favor of an unconditioned and absolutely simple God.[179] In such a God, there are no distinctions and God's attributes merely speak the knowledge of the divine nature. As Schleiermacher saw it,

> For if such [attributes] present a knowledge of the Divine Being, each one of them must express something in God not expressed by others; and if the knowledge is appropriate to the object, then, as the knowledge is composite, the object must be composite. Indeed, even if these attributes only asserted relations of the Divine to the world, God Himself, like the finite life, could only be understood in a multiplicity of functions; and as these are distinct one from another, and relatively opposed to one another, and at least partly exclusive of one another, God likewise would be placed in the sphere of contradiction.[180]

Schleiermacher argued that even if we must accept the doctrine of the Trinity on the account of metaphysical proposition, we must interpret it in the Sabellian sense. That is to say, the Trinity is three successive manifestations of one and the same God in the history of salvation. Put differently, the Trinity of the divine persons exists only in the sphere of divine operation and not in the divine life. God the Father is the divine reality of this operation, while the Son and the Spirit are merely God the Father's means of outward operation.[181] Apparently, in Schleiermacher's schema the doctrine of the Trinity has lost its orthodox scriptural basis and has become more or less a matter of feeling rather than biblical witness to the Triune God's revelation. Schleiermacher has not only discarded the traditional method of developing the Trinity from reason and scriptural data, but also sought to construct it from human experience. Consequently, Schleiermacher reduced the Trinity to what Claude Welch describes as a "second rank" doctrine of the Christian faith.[182]

The impact that Schleiermacher's approach had in the nineteenth century is not hard to perceive. First, as his approach was to establish the nature and parameters of general religious experience and then use that framework to screen in

100   *The "amazing history" of the Trinity*

and out fundamental Christian doctrines, any doctrine that does not fit into that framework was discarded. The doctrine of the Trinity certainly does not fit that general system of absolute dependence, hence Schleiermacher screened out the Trinity as an unnecessary doctrine. Second, Schleiermacher's brief treatment of the Trinity and his overt approval of the Sabellian heresy have contributed in many ways to the neglect of the Trinity in modern Christian theology. In making human feeling the starting point of Christian theology, Schleiermacher made subsequent theological reflections on the doctrine of the Trinity from biblical witness to revelation difficult. It is, therefore, not astounding that later theologians who accepted Schleiermacher's rejection of the orthodox idea of revelation and his starting point of Christian theology found it unfeasible to promote the Trinity on the basis of revelation.[183] Like Schleiermacher, those theologians in the nineteenth century continued not only to neglect the doctrine of the Trinity, but also to develop it on grounds other than salvation history. Hegel, for example, constructed his doctrine of the Trinity from a philosophical standpoint rather than from the economy of salvation. According to Welch, for Hegel, the doctrine of the Trinity is wholly a philosophical discipline. There are no two ways about it. As Welch argued,

> Hegel's doctrine of the Trinity is a philosophical truth, resting entirely on general philosophical premises. The truth of that doctrine can be established and elaborated in complete independence of religion. Indeed, it can be understood and *known* to be true *only* by the speculative reason through the analysis of the nature of logic and concrete actuality. "God" means Absolute Spirit, which posits itself in three forms, according to Hegel.[184]

The contention of Welch about Schleiermacher's philosophical Trinitarian theology is an overstatement because Schleiermacher undertook what could be termed a philosophical interpretation of the economic Trinity.

Likewise, convinced that religious knowledge is determined solely by "value-judgments," like Schleiermacher, Albrecht Ritschl also dismissed the doctrine of the Trinity as useless speculation. Nowhere does the doctrine of the Trinity receive special attention in his theological system.[185] Welch wrote,

> After the manner of Schleiermacher and Ritschl there are those theologians generally . . . who continue to deny that the doctrine of the Trinity is essential to the expression of the Christian faith. . . . They therefore reject the concept or relegate it to a definitely subordinate role in the theological schema.[186]

Though Schleiermacher contributed to the neglect of the Trinity in Western modern theology by instilling a nonchalant attitude toward the doctrine of the Trinity in many theologians (who either neglected or reduced the Trinity to a position of nonentity in their theological works in the nineteenth century), he undoubtedly laid the egg for the renaissance of the Trinity,[187] which Karl Barth hatched in the twentieth century by articulating a provocative reconstruction of the Trinity.

The "amazing history" of the Trinity 101

Karl Barth: revelatory Trinity

What Schleiermacher was to the nineteenth century, Karl Barth was to the twentieth century. If Schleiermacher is the greatest liberal theological thinker of the nineteenth century, Barth is the greatest influential "neo-orthodox" theological thinker of the twentieth century. Barth overturned Schleiermacher's approach to the doctrine of the Trinity. It is safe to claim that the whole work of Barth's *Church Dogmatics*, especially the doctrine of the Trinity, which its editors describe as "the greatest treatise of the kind since *De Trinitate* of St Augustine," is a response to Schleiermacher's theology.[188] Unlike Schleiermacher, who thought the Trinity is an appendix of Christian theology, Barth not only elevated the doctrine of the Trinity to the center of his theological system, but also made it the common thread which holds together all the various parts of his theology. As the center of Christian theology, Barth maintained that the content of the doctrine of the Trinity is "decisive and controlling for the whole of dogmatics."[189] Thus, Barth argued that there is no way the doctrine of the Trinity, which distinguishes the Christian doctrines of God and of revelation, should be regarded as an unwarranted addition to the Christian faith. Though Barth's formulation of the doctrine of the Trinity is rooted in Jesus Christ, it is the replacement of the Hegelian idea of an absolute subject, whose self-reflection coincides with the existence of the world. As Robert Jenson suggests, "Only put Jesus in place of Hegel's 'world,' and you have the doctrine of Barth's Church Dogmatics."[190]

Unlike Schleiermacher, Barth gave exceptional attention and place of pride to the doctrine of the Trinity in his theology by putting it in the prolegomena of his *Church Dogmatics*. In order to justify placing the doctrine of the Trinity in the prolegomena before any other doctrines, Barth argued that the significance of scripture, which is usually examined first and foremost in Christian theology, cannot be justified unless the God whose revelation makes the Scripture Holy is made clear beforehand. As we inquire into the revelation to which the scripture bears witness, Barth argued that we are inescapably led to a three-fold question: who is the self-revealing God according to biblical witness? What does God do? What does God effect in humanity? In answering these questions, we are ineluctably led to the doctrine of the Trinity. According to Barth, the identical answer to all these three questions is: "*God* reveals Himself [as Lord]. He reveals himself *through Himself*. He reveals *Himself*."[191] That is to say, the self-revealing God is identical with the act and effect of God's revelation. God actually reveals what God is in Godself. Insisting that God's Word is identical with God in God's revelation, Barth argued that the God who reveals himself as the Lord is the God with unimpaired unity and difference as Revealer, Revelation, and Revealedness. Grounding the doctrine of the Trinity in revelation, "Barth set in motion a revelation-oriented approach to the doctrine of the Trinity that came to characterize much subsequent trinitarian thinking."[192] In the next chapter, we will further explore analytically such a revelation-oriented approach to the doctrine of the Trinity as expressed in subsequent Trinitarian thinkers.

Barth believed that the doctrine of the Trinity is neither explicitly found in the scripture nor a mere synthesis of essential elements of Christian revelation.

102 *The "amazing history" of the Trinity*

Rather, the necessary investigation into the revelatory event of God in Christ, which is a Trinitarian revelation, constitutes the basis of the doctrine of the Trinity. Barth wrote,

> The statement or statements about God's Trinity cannot claim to be directly identical with statement about revelation or with revelation itself. The doctrine of the Trinity is an analysis of this statement, [that God reveals Himself as Lord]. The doctrine of the Trinity is a work of the Church, a record of its understanding of the statement.[193]

As "a necessary and relevant analysis of revelation" that "translates and exegetes" the text of the biblical witness to that revelation, the statement "God reveals Himself as the Lord," according to Barth, is the "root of the doctrine of the Trinity."[194] Barth argued that the conclusion drawn from the analysis of this statement (which is *unveiling*, *veiling*, and *impartation*) corresponds to the distinctions among the Son, Father, and Holy Spirit. In other words, these three elements of revelation, which are interdependent and inseparable, correspond to the Trinitarian life *ad intra*, and thus, constitute the ground-plan of the doctrine of the Trinity. Therefore, Barth claimed that there is close correspondence (not identity) between the economic Trinity and the immanent Trinity. The economic Trinity describes the Triune God as revealed to us in the economy of creation and redemption, while the immanent Trinity refers to the Triune God in Godself from eternity. However, insisting that the Triune God is recognized nowhere else other than in God's self-revelation in Christ, Barth suggested that there is no other God behind the God revealed in Christ. God revealed to humanity in Christ is the God in himself from all eternity. As Barth sees it,

> The reality of God in his revelation cannot be bracketed by an "only," as though somewhere behind His revelation there stood another reality of God: the reality of God which encounters us in His revelation is His reality in all the depths of eternity. This is why we have to take it so seriously precisely in His revelation.[195]

Barth asked whether the biblical witness to revelation, according to which God reveals Himself in Jesus Christ as the Lord, is the exclusive root of the Trinity. Barth answered in the affirmative. He argued that we couldn't seek to use the world to interpret the Trinity; rather, we should use the Trinity to interpret the world. There is no way from the world to God except from God to creation. Therefore, Barth rejected all searches for *vestiges* of the Trinity in creation, for he suspects they would constitute a second basis of the dogma of the Trinity. He suggested that we should rely exclusively on vestige of the doctrine "which God Himself in His revelation has assumed in our language, world, and humanity . . . [and] is the triply one voice of the Father, the Son and the Spirit."[196]

Explicating the unity of God, Barth asserted that the doctrine of the Trinity is not a denial, but a decisive affirmation of the fact that God is One. The Trinity is

The "amazing history" of the Trinity   103

one God in three-fold repetition and only in this repetition is God One without alteration. Divine unity is not a collective unity of three distinct persons, but a unity in which we have one divine "I" thrice.[197] Thus, the divine Trinity is not in conflict with monotheism because "only the substantial equality of Christ and the Spirit with the Father is compatible with monotheism."[198] Though God's *ousia* is his absolute personality,[199] Barth argued that the unity of God is neither singularity nor isolation, but unity which affirms the distinctions in God. Does this mean personal distinctions? Barth answered in the negative. Since the word "person" means an autonomous self in the modern sense, Barth claimed that speaking of three independent personalities in God would be the worst expression of tritheism.[200] To guard against this heresy, Barth suggested that we should describe the Trinity as one absolute personal God who subsists in three essential *modes of being.*[201]

How then did Barth provoke renewed interest in the doctrine of the Trinity? In developing his doctrine of the Trinity neither from human experience nor from the synthesis of the sporadic New Testament testimonies regarding the divinity of Jesus and the Spirit and their unity with the Father, but from the necessary interpretation of the entire biblical witness to revelation, Barth established a methodological principle for the contemporary revival of Trinitarian theology. Grenz argued that

> In the story of trinitarian theology, Barth must be afforded the place at the head of the train of those responsible for the twentieth-century renaissance because he, more than any of his contemporaries, offered a thoroughgoing trinitarian perspective on the method and content of theology.[202]

Barth's constructive proposals for recasting the doctrine in light of God's self-revelation in Jesus Christ have provoked critical and productive responses from theologians such as Jürgen Moltmann, who made the most influential contribution to hermeneutics of the Trinity in the twentieth century from the standpoint of the cross. Though Moltmann in many ways is critical of Barth, Grenz is correct to suggest "Moltmann's trinitarian theology as a kind of historicizing of Barth's contention that the Christ-event is constitutive for the divine life in all eternity."[203] It is, therefore, not an exaggeration to say that the contemporary business of the entire field of Christian theology owes its inspiration to Barth's creative construction of the doctrine of the Trinity. As Jenson accurately suggested, "It can fairly be said that the chief ecumenical enterprise of the current theology is rediscovery and development of the doctrine of the Trinity. It can also fairly be said that Barth initiated the enterprise."[204]

This does not, however, imply that Barth articulated a perfect doctrine of the Trinity; rather, it is its inadequacies that provoked charting of new lines of Trinitarian thinking by subsequent Trinitarian theologians. These inadequacies are not hard to pinpoint. First, Barth did not end up constructing his doctrine of the Trinity from biblical witness to God's self-revelation in Christ, as he explicitly claimed. Instead, Barth developed his doctrine from the logic of German idealism,

104   *The "amazing history" of the Trinity*

according to which God reveals himself as absolute subject through self-distinction and self-recollection. Moltmann argued that "a reflection of subjectivity like this has not necessarily anything whatsoever to do with the biblical witness to the history of God. The notion of God's reflexively differentiated subjectivity and self-revelation can be conceived even without any biblical reference at all."[205] Therefore, Pannenberg is right to argue that Barth "does not develop the doctrine of trinitarian God from the data of the historical revelation of God as Father, Son, and Spirit, but from the formal concept of revelation."[206]

Second, what we find in Barth's so-called "revelatory Trinitarian theology" is the abstract unity of God, which has virtually no room for plurality of persons in God. This is evident in Barth's starting point of the Trinitarian hermeneutics, according to which the unity of God not only precedes, but also subsumes, the treatment of the Trinity of the Persons. As Barth subjected the doctrine of the Trinity to a predetermined non-scriptural concept of divine unity, Moltmann charged that Barth gave ontological priority to divine unity, regarding the Trinity as something secondary that is to be established and reconciled with the divine unity. He claimed that "According to Barth, the Lordship of God precedes the Trinity, logically speaking" and "that is why Barth presents the 'the doctrine of the Trinity' as Christian monotheism and argues polemically against a 'tritheism' which has never existed."[207] It is this perception of the doctrine of the Trinity as a strict unity of God that compels Barth to speak of the Trinity as one God in three-fold repetition and that only in this repetition is God one without alteration. According to Moltmann, the doctrine of the Trinity is more than just establishing the same thing thrice, for "to view the persons merely as a triple repetition, one and the same God would be somewhat empty and futile."[208] Even Barth's rejection of the classical notion of the person with a view to overcoming the challenge of modern philosophy in favor of a single absolute God subsisting in three modes of being has fallen short of producing a lucid understanding of the Trinity. As a matter of fact, his constructive suggestion made the doctrine of the Trinity more obscure than the classical doctrine of God as three hypostases! As J.J. O'Donnell wrote,

> The trinitarian faith of the church is notoriously difficult for believers to grasp. If there are difficulties in the language of the three persons, it seems probable that there are more difficulties in the language of three modes of being.[209]

Third, Barth's concept of modes of being is not good enough, as it constrains us from perceiving God as a community of three real, loving persons. It allows us only to speak of one God as person who subsists in three modes of being, but if God is not the community of three loving actual persons, then we are stripped of the biblical and ontological basis of God forming personal relationships with humanity. The legitimate question is how modes of being can form a personal relationship with humanity and the whole of the world. Contending that Barth's claim poses for us "kerygmatic and pastoral problems," O'Donnell is right to observe, "One can hardly imagine someone praying to a mode of being."[210] The scripture commands us to pray to the Father through the Son in the Spirit, who are actual persons in relationship, but never to modes of being.[211] As Barth affirmed that God is not only an absolute spirit, but also a single person, an "I" existing in and for itself,[212] it is apparent that the Barthian Trinitarian God is certainly a modern individualistic person who does not care about creating personal relationship with anyone except with itself.[213] Thus, O'Donnell's contention that Barth is not modalist in the classical sense of Sabellius may partly be granted. Barth eschewed assigning personhood to God in the classical sense of the word, thinking that doing so is tantamount to modalism. Barth put it rhetorically: "[B]ut did not *persona, prosopon*, also mean 'mask'? Might not the term give new support to the Sabellian idea of three mere manifestations behind which stood a fourth?"[214] Therefore, Barth thought that Sabellianism could be avoided only if he speaks of one personal God subsisting in and for itself in three modes of being.[215] But is this not a repeat of the Sabellian heresy? Does it not follow that Father, Son, and Spirit are mere masks for this single personal God?[216]

Fourth, without denying the truth that the biblical witness to God's revelation in Christ is the basic ground on which the doctrine of the Trinity rests, Barth's rejection of vestiges of the Trinity raises the question of whether he took God's revelation in humanity and nature seriously. If Christ himself employed vestiges in nature and culture to reveal his identity and mission (for example), and if the communion of the Triune God has a cosmic dimension, there is no basis for detaching the doctrine of the Trinity entirely from vestiges found in nature, history, culture, and human society. Even though the trouble for Barth is not ontological, but epistemological, the triadic divine expressions/traces in nature and communal relations, however dim they are, should not be dismissed as mere camouflage of the Triune character of God. In many ways, they reflect the true character of the Triune God. There is no theological justification whatever for us to just undermine the significance of the confession of the Psalmist that "the heavens declare the glory of God; the skies proclaim the work of his hands" (19:1). Such natural witness to God should equally be viewed as the pre-Christian basis of the doctrine of the Triune God. Thus, biblical witness to the Triune God doesn't quash, but affirms and perfects, nature's witness to God, both of which should be recognized as bases for analyzing the doctrine of the Trinity.

Finally, Barth's sharp emphasis on God's self-revelation as Lord, according to Scriptural testimony, seems to obliterate God's revelation of Godself in Christ through the Spirit as a free servant. In Christ through the Spirit, God deliberately emptied Godself in the world, and in particular, in us through bread and wine as free Servant. The Triune God did not reveal Godself in Christ as Lord who came to be lord over humanity and the world, but rather, to serve and lay down his life in the Spirit for the salvation of humanity and the world. Thus, the Trinitarian God who Barth claimed unveils Godself in Christ through the Spirit in the economy is more of a servant than lord, more immanent than transcendent, and nearer than far from humanity and the world.

106 *The "amazing history" of the Trinity*

Karl Rahner: principle of real identity

Just as Barth was the modern father of the Protestant theology of the twentieth century, so was Rahner the modern father of the Catholic theology of the twentieth century. Like Barth, Rahner's contributions to the renewal of the doctrine of the Trinity are phenomenal and thus, will remain indelible in the history of Trinitarian theology. LaCugna argued that "in contemporary Catholic theology no one has done more than Karl Rahner to reawaken interest in trinitarian theology."[217] Rahner's hermeneutical approach to the doctrine of the Trinity is that of critique as well as reconstruction. Critiquing classical theology for excluding the Trinity from Christian piety, Rahner lamented that such isolation has resulted in Christians being "almost just 'monotheists' in their actual religious experience" despite "their orthodox profession in the Trinity."[218] Continuing, Rahner contended that "if the doctrine of the Trinity were to be erased as false, most religious literature could be preserved almost unchanged throughout the process!"[219] Rahner also charged that Augustine's classical doctrine of the indivisibility of the work of the Triune God in the economy has undermined the non-interchangeable character of each person of the Trinity. Accordingly, ever since Augustine, it was believed that any person of the Trinity could have become human.[220] God became human, without admitting specifically that it was the Logos, the second person of the Trinity, who actually became human, as if his incarnation "in particular throws no light on [his] special character [as a unique] person within the divine nature."[221] An explicit consequence of this assumption is that it not only makes the incarnation an external event to God's inner life, but throws the whole theology into confusion.

Rahner argued that in the treatises of classical theology a strict distinction is not only drawn between *De Deo Uno* and *De Deo Trino*, but to make matters worse, the latter is treated without reference at all to the entire salvation history. Though such division did not begin with Aquinas so to speak, it eventually became a normative hermeneutical approach to the doctrine of God in Christian theology. The explicit effect of this division, according to Rahner, is not hard to perceive. Rahner wrote,

> The treatise on the Trinity comes to stand still more in a splendid isolation, which brings it into a still greater danger than that of being found without interest for religious existence: it looks as though everything about God which touches ourselves has already been said in the treatise *De Deo Uno*.[222]

Rahner contended that such a treatment isolates the doctrine of the Trinity not just from the entirety of dogmatic theology, but more crucially, from salvation history, hence rendering the doctrine of the Trinity quite philosophical and abstract.

As a reconstruction, Rahner suggested that the treatise on the Trinity cannot and must not be separated from soteriology, "for the Trinity is a mystery of *salvation*. Otherwise it would never have been revealed!"[223] In other words, the economy of salvation reveals the mystery of the Triune God. The doctrine of the Trinity and

The "amazing history" of the Trinity   107

the economy of salvation are indistinguishable;[224] God with us in Christ through the Spirit is identical with God in Godself from all eternity. Uniting together what classical theists put asunder, Rahner submitted that "the Trinity of economy of salvation is the immanent Trinity and vice versa."[225] This "principle of real identity" does not mean that the doctrine of the Trinity first and foremost finds expression in the revelation of God in Jesus before finding its way back into the eternal essence of the Triune God, but rather, the eternal Triune essence of God must constantly be linked to his historical revelation. Otherwise, the revelation of the triune nature of God in the economy is unconnected to the inner life of the Triune God![226] For Rahner, the principle of real identity means that Jesus is exclusively the Logos (not the entire Godhead), who actually became human, a reality which is proper to him and is neither merely appropriated to him nor a collective act of the divine persons. As Rahner convincingly wrote,

> For Jesus is not simply God in general, but the Son; the second divine Person, the Logos of God is man, and he alone. So there is at least one "sending", one presence in the world, one reality in the economy of salvation which is not merely appropriated to certain divine person, but is proper to him. . . . Here something takes place in the world itself, outside the immanent life, which is not simply the result of efficient causality of the triune of God working as one nature in the world. It is an event proper to the Logos alone, the history of one divine person in contrast to the others.[227]

Rahner argued that the human nature, which Jesus assumed, is not an outward mask concealing the Logos in the world, but rather, the symbol of the Logos itself on account of its origin. Therefore, he contended,

> What Jesus is and does as man, is the self-revealing existence of the Logos as our salvation among us. Here the Logos with God and the Logos with us, the Logos of the immanent Trinity and the Logos of the economy of salvation, is strictly one and the same.[228]

Appealing to the doctrine of grace, Rahner claimed that "each of the three divine persons communicates himself as such to man, each in his own special and different way of personal being, in the free gift of grace."[229] "These three self-communications," Rahner claims, "are the self communication of the one God in the threefold relative way in which God subsists."[230] Thus, Rahner contended that God's relationship to humanity is three-fold, as opposed to classical theism, which posits only one relation of the Triune God to the world. Rahner argued the three-fold communication of the one God is not an analogy, but the immanent Trinity itself, which is exactly replicated in the economy of salvation, hence inner communications and temporal missions are identical events!

The immanent Trinity, which is enacted through eternal mutual relation of the Word and the Spirit with the Father, is mediated to humanity in the economy of salvation. Nonetheless, the Trinity, Rahner argued, "is not merely a reality

108   *The "amazing history" of the Trinity*

to be expressed in purely doctrinal terms: it takes place in us, and does not first come to reach us in the form of statements communicated by revelation."[231] As such, the Trinity is not an abstract, but a practical doctrine. The starting point of any Trinitarian hermeneutics must be the economy of salvation. But how are the three self-communications of the one God revealed to us in the economy described? Rahner replied that the church has classically described these three self-communications as "persons." Since the danger of conflating the immanent and economic Trinity is massive (tritheism rather than modalism), Rahner argued that the use of the term "person," which means "individual" in the modern sense of the word, could be misunderstood as meaning there are three independent centers of consciousness and action in God. This is tritheistic and, therefore, inaccurate. Should the word "person" then be replaced? Unlike Barth, Rahner answered in the negative. He reasoned that the notion has been in use for more than 15 centuries, and it is hard to find a better word that would today be less controversial. However, should the church seek for a better replacement of the concept to obviate the said danger, Rahner suggested the phrase "distinct manner of subsisting." He argued that we can overcome the dilemma when we affirm that in God "there are not three consciousnesses; rather, the one consciousness subsists in a threefold way. There is only one real consciousness in God, which is shared by the Father, Son and Spirit, by each in his own proper way."[232]

This raises the question of whether Rahner's proposal has produced an intelligible understanding of the Trinity. It is hard to judge, but I don't think so. Rahner has undoubtedly accelerated the renewed interest in the Trinitarian theology initiated by Barth with his "principle of real identity," which, according to Ted Peters, "marks a decisive watershed in twentieth-century trinitarian thinking."[233] Consequently, Rahner has restored the Trinity to its rightful place in Christian faith and life. Rahner nonetheless spoiled his brilliant recasting of the Trinity when he suggested the concept of person should be replaced by "distinct manner of subsisting." This is because, as I argued earlier, we cannot afford to discard the concept completely in developing the doctrine of the Trinity without paying for its disastrous kerygmatic and pastoral consequences. Preaching the Father, the Son, and the Spirit who are mutual persons of the Triune God as mere distinct manners of subsisting contradicts the biblical witness to God and is, therefore, meaningless. The valid question is how a distinct manner of subsisting, for example, as Rahner told us, can assume human nature and save humanity. Put differently, how can distinct manners of subsisting know and love each other? This is a personal function which the scripture ascribes to real divine *personae*, but which the scripture does not assign to distinct manners of subsistence. Rahner alone did this, but what is his biblical basis for doing so?

While it is true that the concept of "person" may be misunderstood to mean an autonomous individual, suggesting a distinct manner of subsisting as a suitable alternative to "person" complicates the problem, and is, therefore, misleading. According to Moltmann, Rahner's understanding of "person" is not vibrant, but a

The *"amazing history" of the Trinity*   109

polished form of the extreme individualism on which modern bourgeois society is established. As he wrote,

> What Rahner calls "our secular use of the word person" has nothing in common with modern thinking about the concept of person. What he describes is actually extreme individualism: everyone is a self-possessing, self-disposing centre of action which sets itself apart from other persons.[234]

If the Triune God is not three actual reciprocal persons, but one center of consciousness operating in three distinct manners of subsistence, what we are left with in Rahner is not massive danger of tritheism, as he feared, but massive danger of modalism.

As Moltmann accurately saw, what we find in Rahner's doctrine of the Trinity is nothing but the enthronement of German idealism, which replaces the orthodox understanding of the Triune God with the Hegelian idea of absolute subjectivity. Moltmann contended,

> Rahner's reinterpretation of the doctrine of the Trinity ends in the mystic solitariness of God. It obscures the history of the Father, the Son and the Spirit to which the Bible testifies, by making this the external illustration of that inner experience.[235]

Contemporary African hermeneutics of the Trinity

The doctrine of the Trinity that has hitherto been formulated with Western and Eastern philosophical and academic tools by Latin and Greek theologians for their own audiences, appears irrelevant to the African context. Confronting the task of contextualizing the doctrine relevant for African peoples, a good number of contemporary African theologians have employed African metaphysical and intellectual resources to recast the doctrine of the Trinity for the African audience. Here three of these African theologians, A. Okechukwu. Ogbonnaya, James Henry Owino Kombo, and Agbonkhianmeghe E. Orobator, will be examined.

A. Okechukwu Ogbonnaya: communitarian divinity

A. O. Ogbonnaya is a Nigerian theologian and a pastor in the United Methodist Church in the United States. Ogbonnaya, who received his Ph.D. from the School of Theology at Claremont, also serves as adjunct professor at the University of La Verne Extension Program. The fundamental concern which spurs Ogbonnaya to undertake the task of reinterpreting the doctrine of the Trinity from an African perspective is the massive failure of African theologians who, according to him, are merely good at criticizing the concept of the Divine which the West imposed on them, often without proffering a truly liberating alternative proposal. Ogbonnaya

110 *The "amazing history" of the Trinity*

contends that such a failure has led these African theologians to continue to speak of the Divine in the same way as Western theologians. To shatter this "cycle of hermeneutical bondage" which "stifles the imagination" and "robs Africans of their authentic contribution to theological discourse," Ogbonnaya suggests that "Africans must begin using their own experience and traditional philosophical 'categories'" to recast the dominant Western doctrine of the Triune God.[236]

Therefore, in his *On Communitarian Divinity*, Ogbonnaya attempts to reinterpret the doctrine of the Trinity from an African worldview of community, drawing inspiration from Tertullian's Trinitarian theology. According to him, the African traditional understanding of community is a comprehensive network of communal relationships, involving not only human beings, but also ancestors and spirits across distant spans of time-space. The physical and spiritual web of relationships among the members of the community is permanent and inescapable. Ogbonnaya claims that the African concept of community characterized by "communality, and fundamental interconnection underlie the African mode of seeing and being in the world."[237] Thus, the doctrine of God in the African context must be viewed from the concept of community. As Ogbonnaya argues it, the "idea of personal interconnection within the community is foundational to a theological understanding of God."[238]

Ogbonnaya maintains that there are two prevailing conceptions of the Divine in African theology. One holds that Africans believe in one singular and personal God, which is monotheism. The other argues that polytheism, which sees the Divine as separate and unrelated gods, is that which describes the African concept of the Divine. However, Ogbonnaya contends that the two conceptions are inaccurate because both fail to take into consideration the African understanding of the oneness and manyness of the Divine. Ogbonnaya suggests that a third category, which describes accurately the African view of the Divine and provides a solid basis for understanding the Trinity, is *communotheism*, a community of gods.[239] Though Africans believe that there is one great God among many gods, Ogbonnaya contends that to construe such a God as the one and only true God in African thought is not only foreign to Africa, but is erroneous. As "one god is inextricable related to other gods by virtue of the Divine nature," Ogbonnaya argues that in African traditional religion, a god is god regardless of whether the god in question is great or small![240] Therefore, he contends that Africans believe in many gods but never see them as separate and unrelated; rather, they believe that these gods are connected by a single divine nature as members of the same family, thereby forming an inseparable community. As Ogbonnaya states, "The Divine is a community of gods who are fundamentally related to one another and ontologically equal while at the same time distinct from one another by their personhood and functions."[241]

Ogbonnaya acknowledges that functional subordination, which exists in the African concept of the Divine, does not entail hierarchy of divinity; rather, it shows a mere distribution of responsibility among members of the Divine community. Ogbonnaya contends each god, by virtue of possessing an inherent Divine force, has the capacity to reproduce other gods of their own substance without diminishing either their divinity or personhood. In ancient Egypt, such "belief

The "amazing history" of the Trinity   111

in the substantial active force and its differentiation into a multiplicity of gods is the basis . . . of the notion of the unity and diversity of the Divine."[242] Therefore, Ogbonnaya argues that it is this African idea of human communality and the community of gods which shapes Tertullian's formulation of the Trinity.

Drawing on biblical revelation, Ogbonnaya contends that Tertullian nuanced his African traditional religious idea of the oneness and manyness of the Divine into the doctrine of the Trinity. Tertullian began to speak of the Trinity in terms of the community of equal divine persons within the one God, even though his "emphasis on Divine communality was eclipsed, however, by the debates that ensued after his death, which fostered concepts of ontological hierarchy instead of equality."[243] Ogbonnaya asserts that, for Tertullian, the notion of the Trinity is bound up with the economy of salvation. Describing Tertullian's doctrine of the Trinity as the Divine community, in which there are three fully distinct divine realities, according to the biblical witness to God, Ogbonnaya claims that Tertullian uses social metaphors of *Monarchia, Dispositio,* and *Oikonomia* to illustrate the unity, diversity, and function in the Divine community. Ogbonnaya argues that Tertullian's divine monarchy is not a kingdom ruled by one single individual, but by a community of inseparable persons, and thus "the monarchy belongs equally to all the members of the family, including children . . . forever."[244] Thus, he suggests that in Tertullian's Trinity, there is one community with one power that all the inseparable divine members mutually exercise in virtue of sharing a common divine nature. The power of the divine community, which is evenly shared among them, is not concentrated in the hands of an individual member of the Divine community.

In accordance with Tertullian's Trinitarian thinking, Ogbonnaya insists that the members of the Divine community also share a common Spirit as substance (vital force), which not only binds them together, but also distinguishes them from each other. Hence, all the divine members are equal. Ogbonnaya claims that, "equality in [the Divine] community is tied to substance, nature, and power. . . . All the members of the Divine community, by virtue of their inner connection . . . are naturally equal."[245] Though there is functional subordination of the Son and Spirit to the Father in the economy of salvation, Ogbonnaya contends such subordination is historical and temporal and not substantial. The fact that they are of the same substance and power disallows ontological subordinationism in the Divine life. Ogbonnaya writes, "Communality of the Divine is a community of equality. This equality is based on the fact that all share in one nature. . . . This concept of shared nature and power disallows ontological subordination."[246]

Undoubtedly, Ogbonnaya's reinterpretation of the dominant Western doctrine of the Trinity through the African framework of community is creative. This creativity is evident from the way Ogbonnaya makes the African rather than European concepts of community and God a sufficient starting point for the construction of African Trinitarian theology. As we have seen in Chapter 1, such communitarian reinterpretation of Trinitarian theology shows there is a correlation between the African communality and the relationality in the Triune God. However, there are challenges that Ogbonnaya's African understanding of the Trinity invites. He makes claims that seem to be misleading. Ogbonnaya uses words like "Gods,"

112   *The "amazing history" of the Trinity*

"gods," and "persons" interchangeably to refer to both the African concept of the Divine and the Tertullianic understanding of the Christian God without distinguishing between them. For example, he says that for Tertullian, "Gods or persons emerge . . . for the purpose of specific functions. The gods are no longer alone as community in time and space."[247] This begs the question whether Tertullian employs these words interchangeably to speak of the divine persons of the Trinity.

If, as Ogbonnaya claims, African religious thought has no distinction between God and god because every god is divine by virtue of sharing the same divine nature, one wonders whether it is appropriate to ascribe these words arbitrarily to divine persons of the Godhead. Do they convey the same idea when they are used of the Trinity? I do not think so. Using these words, especially "gods," even deliberately (as he suggests) to speak of the Trinity, not only distorts the significance of the Trinity, but also is awkward. As a matter of fact, if Ogbonnaya's proposal were accepted, what we would have in the end is not even tritheism, but multi-theism. Therefore, Kärkkäinen is right to suggest that "it would be more helpful [for Ogbonnaya] to talk about the 'communitarian divinity' (singular) rather than 'community of gods' (plural) when speaking of the Christian God."[248] I concur with Kärkkäinen that the Christian tradition and the biblical witness permit us to speak of the Triune God as the community of three divine persons, but do not allow us to describe them as a community of gods.

Similarly, Ogbonnaya claims that in Tertullian Trinitarian theology, the three divine persons are equal in virtue of sharing the same divine nature and subordination of the second and the third persons of the Trinity are functional rather than ontological. But such an argument does not seem to hold water because (as demonstrated earlier), Tertullian's Trinitarian theology exemplifies not just temporal, but ontological subordinationism in view of the undue priority which Tertullian gave to the Father over the Son and Spirit.[249]

Finally, Ogbonnaya applies the African view of community and community of gods to the doctrine of the Trinity without stating points of convergence and divergence between them. For example, one would ordinarily desire to know whether or not Ogbonnaya's community of gods is identical with the Trinitarian communion of God. If yes, what are the scriptural bases and the limits for such claim? How are the two compatible or incompatible? Indeed, Ogbonnaya is right to argue that the African concept of communality is essential for rethinking of the doctrine of Trinity, but fails to tell us how the Trinitarian theology is also crucial for recasting the African concept of community. What we need is a dynamic reciprocal hermeneutical approach to the doctrine of the Triune God according to which the African concept of community impacts and is impacted by the doctrine of the Trinity. The question of how the doctrine of the Trinity could impact the African concept of community will be addressed in Chapter 5.

James Henry Owino Kombo: the Triune God as Great Muntu

J.H.O. Kombo is a Kenyan Anglican priest and professor of systematic theology at Daystar University, Kenya. Kombo obtained his D.Th. in systematic theology

The "amazing history" of the Trinity   113

from Stellenbosch University in South Africa. In his book *The Doctrine of God in African Christian Thought: The Holy Trinity, Theological Hermeneutics and the African Intellectual Culture*, Kombo addresses the question of translating the doctrine of the Trinity to the roots of the African cultural context through African tools or symbols. Kombo argues that Christian theologies, as handed down through the ages, view God within the perplexity of unity and plurality. The Christian faith presents the Father as God, the Son as God, and the Holy Spirit as God, and yet the three are not understood as three gods, but one God. Kombo maintains that the fundamental task of the African Christian theology is to articulate ways by which this cardinal "truth" of the Christian faith can be translated into African thought-forms using African conceptual frameworks rather than the Western ontology of Neo-Platonism and Hegelianism.[250] Thus, undertaking the task of translating the doctrine is necessary in Africa. As the doctrine of the Triune God has practical value, Kombo argues that entrenching the doctrine of the Trinity in the African culture would be of great benefit to the wider Christian audience in Africa. Kombo contends that the trouble of understanding the doctrine of the Trinity lies squarely with the wrong hermeneutical starting point. Rather than starting off the interpretation of the doctrine with "the fact that God has revealed himself as one, and yet we in the Christian faith have experienced him as the Father, the Son and the Holy Spirit," Kombo contends most hermeneutics of the Trinity begin with the formula "One God, three Persons."[251]

Kombo alleges that such a Western starting point of interpreting the doctrine of the Triune God often characterized by Neo-Platonism and German idealism makes the Trinity too complicated for non-Western people to comprehend. Therefore, as the early church fathers employed philosophical concepts of Greek metaphysics to interpret their faith in the Triune God, African Christian theologians should draw on African metaphysics to interpret their Christian faith in the Triune God in a way that is not just intelligible to Africans, but is in harmony with the Catholicity of the church.[252] Thus, Kombo believes that the Christianization of the African concept of God is of fundamental importance in this project of reinterpreting the doctrine of the Triune God in Africa. Convinced that the African peoples were deeply religious even before the advent of Christianity, as evident in the names which each ethnic nationality gives to God, such as *Modimo*, *Nyame*, and *Mulungu*, Kombo notes that these names have already been used by African Christians to speak of the Christian God. Though this is a welcome step toward Christianization of the African concept of God, Kombo contends that how these names (for instance, *Modimo* (God)) have come to be revealed in the Son and the Spirit have not been adequately explained in inculturated African theology. Moreover, there is no clear explanation in African theology about the distinction between the African concepts of God and the Christian view of God. This, according to Kombo, is problematic because African Christians continue to comprehend the Christian God in the African traditional religious sense, while what they need is not the African concepts of God, but a clear picture of the Christian view of God.[253] To present such a crystal clear Christian view of God, Kombo argues that the Christian idea of God should be translated into the

114 *The "amazing history" of the Trinity*

conceptual framework of African culture in such a way that people can comprehend. Kombo writes,

> A fully Christianized concept of *Mulungu*, for example, should indicate how *Mulungu* (God) has made himself known in the Son and the Spirit. And, moreover, such a view of *Mulungu* should be articulated within the infrastructure of metaphysics that the Nyanga as a people can decipher.[254]

Kombo claims that African metaphysics is quite different from Western metaphysics. Unlike Europeans, Africans do not perceive reality from the perspective of either Neo-Platonism or philosophical idealism. The studies done by Tempels, Kagame, and Mbiti reveal that Africans have quite a unique way of interpreting reality, which is not learned from anywhere else around the world. The existence of such African metaphysics debunks the myth by the European missionaries regarding the African mind as "tabula rasa."[255] Kombo argues that the Africans' thought pattern is thus complex and well-developed enough to deal with matters requiring logic, creativity, and reflective thinking. Kombo contends that in spite of the multiplicity of African languages and cultures, Africa has a common well-formed "conceptual framework" with which it makes sense of the world and God. Kombo claims that embracing Christianity does not mean that this rich African traditional legacy of intellectual framework is destroyed; rather, it is not only transformed and redirected to Christ, but it must also be used to better explicate the Christian faith.[256] This African conceptual framework is often characterized as "Ntu-metaphysics," an ethno-philosophy found among the Bantu people of Africa which perceives the universe as a hierarchy of "forces" arranged according to their power.

Kombo argues that the highest force in the ladder of the forces is God, who is the ultimate explanation of the origin and sustenance of humanity and all things. God is followed in the hierarchy by spirits of superhuman beings and the living dead. Under them are human beings, followed by animals and plants, and then the lowest in the hierarchy is phenomena and inanimate objects. Kombo argues that all things in the hierarchy are forces, a concept which replaces the idea of "being" in the Western philosophy. Though human beings belong to the category of "muntu," plants, animals, and inanimate things to "kintu," and phenomena to "kuntu," Kombo argues that they are collectively categorized as "Ntu" in virtue of their relationship to each other.[257] Above all these forces is God as the greatest force, the first cause and sustainer of everything, and hence the starting point of the African intellectual framework. Kombo claims that this accounts for why the existence of Africans is inexorably bound up with God, for they "believe that if God does not exist, then the reality outside of him also does not exist."[258] Such a God is spoken of not merely as a concept, but the "Great Muntu" (Person), the ultimate source and explanation of humanity and other created things. The African conceptions of this God have been studied in African inculturation theology to include "diffused monotheism, *preparatio evangelica, mysterium tremendum et fascinans* ('awesome mystery and fascination')."[259] Kombo claims that these concepts of God demonstrate that African people had acquired knowledge of God from the natural order (even if such knowledge is distorted and non-salvific) prior to Christian faith.

In effect, Kombo argues that African inculturation theologians have done extremely well in articulating the African concepts of God, but have failed in articulating a clear understanding of the God we encounter in Christ. This is because these theologians have not only relied extensively on comparative interpretation of the scripture, which merely highlights the similarities between the African concepts of God and the Christian view of God, but also have emphasized how African people understand God rather than how that God is revealed in Christ, making no attempts at utilizing the indigenous African philosophical symbols as a medium for translating the Christian message. The explicit consequence is that it has constrained African Christian theologians from raising and discussing the Trinity as a distinctly Christian way of perceiving God. In the words of Kombo, "The issue of cultural identity and focus on the African concepts of God place the African inculturation theology within a paradigm that makes it structurally difficult to raise and address the idea of the Trinity with passion."[260] Kombo concurs with African theologians who insist the God that Africans worshipped is identical with the Christian God. However, Kombo argues that how this God has made himself known to the whole of the world in the incarnation of the Son and the outpouring of the Holy Spirit has not been clearly articulated. African inculturation theology needs to explain to its African audience what it means to say, for example, *Modimo* – God – reveals himself in the Son and the Holy Spirit.

Therefore, to accomplish such a project, Kombo suggests "moving beyond the African notion of God" and the African doctrine of God based on comparative interpretation and the cultural identity paradigm to the formulation of an African Christian doctrine of the Trinity which Christianizes "the African concepts of God" and utilizes "African metaphysics."[261] As Christianity borrowed the names of God from among other cultures in history and filled them with new content, Kombo argues that Christianization of the African concepts of God means filling the African ideas of the divine with Christian content. The explicit implication of such Christianization, said Kombo, is that the God African peoples have perceived in creation, such as *Nyasaye*, *Modimo*, or *Mulungu*, would no longer refer to their respective native referents, but to the Triune God of the Bible who revealed Godself in Christ through the Spirit.[262] But he warns that the Christianization of the African concepts of God without regard for native metaphysics would lead to African Christians not knowing what to make of the Christian content. Thus, this calls for expressing the Trinity in "ntu" metaphysics and speaking of the Triune God as the "Great Muntu." This translation, however, cannot be understood by African Christians unless the name "Great Muntu" is "Yahwehized" and expressed in Trinitarian terms! Therefore, the Christianization of the African concepts of God demands that "Christianized Nyasaye" (God), is expressed "Nyasaye Wuro" (God the Father), "Nasaye Wuowi" (God the Son) and "Nyasaye Roho Maler" (God the Holy Spirit).[263] As a self-existent God, Nyasaye Wuro is the *principium* of the "Nyasaye Wuowi" and the "Nyasaye Roho Maler." They

116   The "amazing history" of the Trinity

are not three Nyiseche (gods), but one Nyasaye (God) in virtue of sharing the common *ntu* (nature) of the Great *Muntu*. Thus, each is a perfect reflection of the Great *Muntu*. Thus, the Great *Muntu* is not a monad, but a "community in unity." As Kombo suggests, "Persons cannot exist in isolation. These ultimate persons have always and will always exist in community."[264]

What an amazing African reinterpretation of the doctrine of the Triune God! Kombo has to be given credit for creatively drawing on African metaphysical and intellectual frameworks to recast the doctrine of the Trinity for an African audience. Kombo's originality is evident. Unlike Ogbonnaya, who found African concepts of community and God a sufficient starting point for the construction of an African doctrine of the Triune God, Kombo finds the starting point inadequate and suggests moving beyond the predominant "African notion of God" to Christianization of the pre-Christian African understanding of God, utilizing *Ntu*-metaphysics. Unlike Ogbonnaya, Kombo has succeeded to a large extent in Christianizing the African concepts of God without losing sight of its continuity and discontinuity.

However, there appears to be no significant difference between Kombo's proposed African doctrine of the Trinity and the Western one, except for the African categories he uses in his proposal. Thus, Kombo's proposed doctrine of the Triune God may be viewed as the African "dynamic equivalent" (of the Western doctrine of the Trinity), which simply replaces the Western Trinitarian categories with the African categories. A. M. Mbuvi charges accurately that Kombo approaches "the table with little *resistance* to the Christian doctrine as received from the West. As a result, he perhaps too quickly jettisons the [three-tiered] categories of African cosmology (God, Spirits/Divinities, and Humans) as insufficient for articulating meaningfully the Trinitarian doctrine."[265] Undoubtedly, like many of the Western patriarchal Trinitarian theologies, Kombo's doctrine of the Triune God is more or less the African corresponding patriarchal Trinity rooted in the monarchy of the Father as the source of the divine community and is thus susceptible to subordinationism.

Agbonkhianmeghe E. Orobator: African symbol for the Triune God

A. E. Orobator is a Jesuit priest who hails from Nigeria. Orobator received his licentiate from the Jesuit School of Theology at Berkeley, California, and Ph.D. in Theology and Religious Studies from the University of Leeds in England. Currently, Orobator works as the Rector and professor of Theology and Religious Studies at the Hekima College of Jesuit School of Theology and Institute of Peace Studies in Nairobi, Kenya. In his tome *Theology Brewed in an African Pot*, Orobator attempts to explicate cardinal doctrines of the Christian faith from an African perspective for lay African Christian women and men engaged in reflecting on the contents of their Christian faith and its implications for everyday Christian living. Orobator attempts to present his African reinterpretation of the doctrine of the Trinity in Chapter 3, entitled "The Mad Preacher and the Three Persons in One God."[266]

The "amazing history" of the Trinity   117

There is every reason to believe that Orobator's style of writing is influenced by Chinua Achebe's best-selling classic *Things Fall Apart*, which contains the vivid account of the encounter between European culture and religion and African culture. The influence is evident from what Orobator claims to be the central theme in exploring the doctrine of the Trinity. Borrowing the central theme from the novel in presenting the Trinity, Orobator writes of "the encounter between the African way of life, in its native beauty and earthly innocence, and missionary Christianity, with its disruptive intrusion and baggage of bewildering concepts and doctrines of religion."[267]

Orobator retells a scene from Achebe's novel where a European missionary struggles in vain to explain to his African audience what appears to be an absurd notion of three persons in one God. Realizing that the explanation of the Trinity by the missionary and his interpreter made no sense at all, the main representative character of the audience in the person of Okonkwo went away disappointed, thinking that the missionary was mad. This is because the argument of the missionary that God has a Son without a wife sounds ridiculous to him.

Therefore, Orobator admits from the onset of his presentation of the Trinity that this is very difficult to explain, especially to African Christians, in that the Trinity is not only a unique Christian doctrine, but also a Christian notion of God, which is different from the African conception of God. As a new Catholic convert, Orobator says he experienced the same frustration with his catechist, who struggles during catechetical instruction to explain the doctrine of the Trinity as a mathematical formula. Like Okonkwo, the doctrine of the Trinity left him baffled and thus he decided to accept the doctrine as a mystery for the sake of being a faithful Catholic, even though he knew that the methodology of the catechist was wrong.[268]

Therefore, Orobator contends that the hermeneutical starting point of the doctrine of the Triune God should not be mathematical (How many persons are there in one God?) Rather, it should be "What does [the Trinity] tell us about God's relationship with us? How do we understand this relationship?"[269] Orobator argues that viewing the Trinity as a mathematical puzzle leads to tritheism, which contradicts the orthodox Christian faith that God is one. He, therefore, suggests perceiving of the Trinity as a symbol which "points the way and allows us the possibility of expanding our horizon of thought; it does not pretend to contain everything that it attempts to represent."[270] Orobator argues that as a symbol the Trinity points to the event and nature of our salvation accomplished by God through Jesus Christ in the power of the Holy Spirit. Viewed from this perspective, Orobator claims that the Trinity is not a mathematical puzzle to be solved in God, but rather, it is about the living and salvific relationship which the Triune God has established with Christians – their own special way of speaking of that salvific relationship which God has accomplished and continues to accomplish in their lives. Convinced that the doctrine of the Triune God is inseparable from the church's teaching of salvation, Orobator accepts without question the doctrine of the Trinity as taught by the church, and thus makes no original attempts at reconstructing the Trinity.

118 *The "amazing history" of the Trinity*

Speaking of the biblical basis of the Trinity, Orobator warns against appealing to biblical quotations such as Gen. 1:26 and Is. 6 as proof texts for the doctrine of the Triune God. He argues that biblical texts may enlighten our Trinitarian faith, but they do not contain the doctrine of the Trinity. Though there are quite a few unambiguous New Testament texts bearing Trinitarian formulas, which refer to plurality in God, Orobator contends that they are by no means to be confused with the developed form of the doctrine of the Trinity, as we know it today. He claims that the binitarian and Trinitarian formulas found in several references of the New Testament, which the early church used to summarize the key elements of their faith, developed out of their liturgical life.[271] Though the developed form of the doctrine is not found in the scripture, the doctrine of the Trinity is scriptural. Orobator notes that the developed form of the doctrine of the Trinity (with all its theological jargon) emerged as the orthodox teaching of the church at the time of the great Trinitarian heresies, largely during the fourth century. Orobator observes that the Trinitarian language drew so heavily on the dominant forms of the Greek abstract and speculative philosophy of Neo-Platonism that our present-day manner of speaking of the Triune God sadly bears the unavoidable mark of this Greek philosophy. As a result, Orobator notes that the Trinity has not only become very technical and complicated, but also, most importantly, barely adaptable to the contemporary context and circumstances of Christians, especially for African Christians whose metaphysics is quite different from the context where the doctrine was developed.[272]

The question then for Orobator is, "As an African[,] how do I understand the idea of the Triune God? Is there anything in my African background that gives me a unique insight into the meaning of three persons in one God?"[273] He answers emphatically in the affirmative. Then what is it? Orobator claims it is the imagery of the African mother as a metaphor or symbol of a Triune God. Orobator uses the symbol of "Obirin Meta, a Many-sided Character." As "Obirin" means "woman" and "meta" means "three," Orobator argues that the two words symbolize "a woman who combines the strength, character, personality, and beauty of three women."[274] He uses various known scenarios in Africa to describe the multi-sided character of "Obirin Meta." First, Orobator speaks of an African woman carrying a basket of produce on her head with a baby strapped on her back rushing to prepare dinner for her family. Second, he refers to a *painting* of an African woman returning from the fields with bundles of produce and firewood piled up on her head and a baby strapped on her back. Orobator contends that "Obirin Meta" does not describe outward physical attributes, but the essence of a woman exemplified by combined inner qualities of largeness of heart, strength of character, and wisdom.[275]

Orobator argues that the symbol "Obirin Meta" is way of naming and understanding God that will draw Africans to the Triune God rather than alienating them as does the missionary interpretation of the Trinity. This alienated Okonkwo, forcing him to prefer the pleasure of drinking afternoon palm-wine over listening to the European explaining the madness of the Trinity. The imagery of "Obirin Meta" symbolizes the abundant and radical open-endedness of God in Godself

The *"amazing history" of the Trinity*   119

and his encounter with humanity. As Obirin Meta, the Triune God exemplifies the many-sided character in his open-ended radical relation with us. Orobator writes,

> Like *Obirin meta*, God is *unbreakable stone*, when we need God to be strong for us; the *eye that sees the four corners of the world*, when we are overwhelmed by the complexities of our existence; the *river that never ceases to flow*, when we need God to shower us with blessings; the *slender arm pregnant with kindness*, when we need God to be generous; the *deep pot*, when we need God's unfathomable wisdom to unravel the mysteries of life; the *great nursing mother*, when we need God's love like we have known that of a nursing mother.[276]

Orobator claims the significance of naming the Triune God in this way is that it demystifies whatever mystery beclouds our imagination from understanding the Trinity and brings the Triune God closer to us in the reality of our everyday living. As a result, what we find in the doctrine of the Trinity is no longer a mystery, but a radically open-ended Triune God, who is everything to us both *intra* and *ad extra*. Orobator concludes that explicating the doctrine of the Trinity in a practical sense such as this would not have alienated Okonkwo, but rather, drawn him closer to the Triune God.

The strength of Orobator's African understanding of the doctrine of the Trinity is two-fold. First, the use of a maternal symbol to speak of the Triune God is rarely used in predominantly masculine Western and African Christian theologies. Such Trinitarian hermeneutics is gender sensitive and thus reverses the patriarchal understanding of God, which dominant male theologies seem to propagate in the church and society. Second, it is the use of not just African maternal imagery to talk about the Triune God, but also speaking of how pragmatically God is involved in the daily existential needs of the people. Speaking of the Triune God in such a pragmatic way undoubtedly illuminates the doctrine of the Trinity better than the Western notion of the Trinity, imbued with sophisticated and abstract Greek philosophy.

While we commend Orobator's African reinterpretation of the Trinity, we should not lose sight of the weakness of that reinterpretation. Though Orobator is right to contend that the starting point of any Trinitarian hermeneutics should not be a mathematical question about how many persons there are in God, but rather, what the Trinity tells about God's relationship to us, he fails to raise and address the question of what the Trinity also tells about our relationship with others in the African community and all of God's cosmic community. Second, Orobator claims that the doctrine of the Trinity is a symbol. But instead of Orobator unpacking the symbol in reinterpreting the Trinity, he simply uses another symbol to explain the symbol, making the Trinity even more conceptually complicated to understand. For instance, using the symbol "Obirin Meta," Orobator says that "Obirin" means "woman" and "meta" means "three," which when put together ordinarily means three women, but in his explanation, he claims this means "a many-sided character." One wonders what exactly "Obirin Meta" theoretically means? Does "Obirin

120   *The "amazing history" of the Trinity*

Meta" mean three women with a many-sided character or one woman with many attributes or one woman with the many-sided attribute of three women? Whichever one endorses, the indisputable fact is that Orobator's African maternal symbol for the Triune God, rather than illuminating the notion of the Trinity, makes it more conceptually ambiguous and baffling to grasp than is the Western notion of the doctrine of the Trinity he criticizes as too abstract and philosophical. Though "Obirin Meta" as an African symbol for the Triune God has a practical implication for Christian daily living, one finds it conceptually wanting.

Summary and conclusion

The Bible does not contain the doctrine of the Trinity, but bears faithful witness to the Triune God, who is revealed in Christ through the Spirit. The classical doctrine emerged from the synthetic and speculative reflection about the sporadic biblical witness to the deity of the Son and the Spirit and their unity with the Father, while the new Trinitarian theology developed from the sustained critical analysis of this entire biblical witness to God's self-revelation. As an authoritative biblical doctrine of the Church, the historical emergence and development of the doctrine of the Trinity are bound up with the history of the early church. The fourth and fifth centuries were indeed the critical formative stages in the history of the doctrine of the Trinity. It was during these centuries that the Trinity was finally "baptized" and even flourished as an orthodox doctrine of the Christian faith. In the Eastern Church, Athanasius and the Cappadocian Fathers were very instrumental in making this a reality. As the stalwart defender of Nicene faith, Athanasius championed the divinity of the Son and the Holy Spirit, which eventually culminated in establishing the consubstantiality and co-equality the persons of the Trinity. In stating without ambiguity that the indivisible Godhead exists simultaneously in a consubstantial and co-equal Triad, Father, Son, and Spirit, he not only produced a well-formed doctrine of the Trinity, but also laid the foundation for reciprocal understanding of the Godhead.

Following Athanasius, the Cappadocians affirmed the divinity of the Spirit and established the common substance of the Father, the Son, and the Spirit, which put an end to the Trinitarian controversy started by Arius. They made a clearcut distinction between *ousia* and *hypostasis*. The Cappadocians also stressed the monarchy of the Father, which expresses itself in three hypostases, and made it the starting point of their Trinitarian hermeneutics. For them, the monarchy is the Trinity and vice versa; the Trinity is the monarchy in as much as the latter is always the source and origin of the former. As a result, any Trinity without monarchy is not a Trinity at all. I will return to this question of monarchy in the next chapter. They also investigated the distinctions between the hypostases ontologically in terms of "cause," "relation," and "mode of being," which became the basis for later Trinitarian reflections. As originators of perichoretic theology, the Cappadocians invented the doctrine of mutual inexistence, perichoresis, περιχωρεσισ, which still plays a huge role in the new Trinitarian theology, as we will see in the next chapter. In Eastern Trinitarian thinking, to be a Triune God is

The *"amazing history" of the Trinity* 121

to be a community of divine hypostases in mutual communion. However, their massive emphasis on the Trinity of the hypostases leaves them open to the charge of tritheism. Again, though the Eastern Trinitarian hermeneutics was based the economy of salvation, LaCugna is right to argue that "Greek [Fathers] . . . exaggerated agnosticism that relegated the trinitarian persons to a region far beyond our capacity to experience or understand. Hence, the defeat of the doctrine of the Trinity."[277]

In the Western Church, the doctrine of the Triune God is perceived more from the perspective of substance than hypostasis. Unlike in the East, to be a God in Trinitarian terms in the West is to be a community of three *personae* sharing one and the same substance. Irenaeus, who spoke of the Trinity as the Triune God with "Two Hands" within the context of the economy of creation and salvation, is the forerunner of the Western orthodox doctrine of the Trinity. Unlike the God of the Gnostics, who is alienated from the material world, Irenaeus articulated the doctrine of the eternal loving Triune God who is proactively involved in the world with his "Two Hands," the Son and the Spirit. As the first Latin African theologian to reflect analytically about the Triune God in the Western theology, Tertullian affirmed that there are three real, distinct, but related divine personae in the Godhead according to God's revelation in the economy of creation and salvation. He argued that the Triune nature of God does not divide, but rather, strengthens God's monarchy in virtue of the divine personae, not only sharing mutually the monarchy, but also having a common undivided substance. Tertullian's lasting contribution to the doctrine of the Trinity is two-fold. The first is his creative invention of words such as the *Trinity*, *substance*, and *persona* in the interpretation of the triune nature of God. The other is the radical reinterpretation of the divine monarchy not as absolute rule by a single divine monarch, but as reciprocal kingdom of God, collectively ruled by the divine personae of the Trinity. Though Tertullian's thoughts about the inner life of the Trinity are inconsistent and even vulnerable to subordinationism, they have had a profound influence on subsequent Trinitarian theology.

As the pillar of Catholic theology, Augustine contributed a different approach to the Trinity that begins with simple divine substance rather than the Father as the source of the Godhead. In affirming the one and the same divine substance and inseparability of the work of the divine personae *ad extra*, he established the co-equality of the divine persons that repudiates all forms of subordinationism. But Augustine's stress on the unity of God reduced the personae to mere abstract realties in God and produced a mono-Trinitarian theology, which is hardly absolved from modalism. Moreover, Augustine constructed the unbiblical doctrine of *filioque*, which had devastating consequences on the personality of the Spirit, *perichoresis* of the divine persons, and the unity of the Western and the Eastern Church. In the Middle Ages, Thomas Aquinas took Augustine's doctrine of divine simplicity and developed it into a full-blown abstract speculative doctrine of the Triune God. Aquinas drew a strict distinction between "On the One God" and "On the Triune God" in his treatise on God, and treated the latter as if it were the tributary (arm) of the former. The strict distinction not only

122   The "amazing history" of the Trinity

severed the doctrine of the Trinity from the economy of redemption, but also reduced the doctrine simply to a science of the inner life of the Triune God. As LaCugna contends,

> In scholastic theology, the doctrine of the Trinity was identified as the science of God's inner relatedness. The result of this was a one-sided theology of God that had little to do with the economy of Christ and the Spirit, with the themes of incarnation and grace, and therefore, little to do with the Christian life.[278]

There is no wonder that such a one-sided hermeneutics of the doctrine set the stage for the marginalization of the Trinity in the modern period.

Therefore, in the modern age the doctrine of the Trinity was pushed into possible oblivion (if not rejection) in Christian theology. Under the impact of the Kantian distinction between noumenon and phenomenon, according to which the doctrine of the Triune God is dismissed as supersensible and practically useless for Christian conduct, Schleiermacher relegated the doctrine of the Trinity to the appendix of his *Christian Faith*. Because Schleiermacher thought that the doctrine of the Trinity was a mere concoction of the early church, he thought that the doctrine of the Trinity had nothing to do with Christian self-consciousness. Consequently, Schleiermacher discarded the Trinity in favor of a God who is "unconditioned and absolutely simple" and overtly approved the Sabellian heresy as the appropriate interpretation of the Trinity. Though Schleiermacher's approach contributed in effect to the neglect of the Trinity in modern Western theology, it undoubtedly prepared the way for the rediscovery of the Trinity by Barth and Rahner in the twentieth century.

Reacting to Schleiermacher's hermeneutical approach to the doctrine of the Trinity, Barth placed the Trinity at the prolegomenon of his *Church Dogmatics* and grounds it in the Biblical witness to God's self-revelation in Jesus Christ. Barth contended that biblical witness to God's self-revelation in Jesus Christ, rather than human feeling, must be the starting point for any valid Trinitarian hermeneutics of God. Even though Barth contradicted himself by formulating his doctrine of the Trinity from the formal concept of revelation based on the Hegelian logic of reflective structure, thereby making him vulnerable to modalism, Barth's analytical rather than synthetic hermeneutical approach to the Trinity, coupled with a relentless emphasis on God's self-revelation in Christ as the exclusive starting point of the doctrine of the Trinity, rescued the doctrine from its total eclipse and ignited the flames of its revival in the twentieth century. Rahner accelerated this Trinitarian renaissance by identifying the economic Trinity with the immanent Trinity. But Rahner did not develop his Trinitarian theology from the economy of redemption as he claimed. This is evidenced in his rejection of the word "person" in favor of "distinct manner of subsistence," and which makes him guilty of modalism. However, his "principle of real identity" restores the doctrine of the Trinity to the center of the Christian faith and piety, as a practical rather than an abstract doctrine, and provides the normative principle for new Trinitarian reflection. This became the guiding norm for most new Trinitarian hermeneutics of God.

Finding the Western doctrine of the Trinity quite abstract and knotty for a non-Western audience to understand, contemporary African theologians have reinterpreted the Trinity by utilizing an African intellectual legacy and metaphysics. Drawing on the African concept of human and divine community, Ogbonnaya contends that the doctrine of the Trinity should be reinterpreted as a "communotheism," a community of gods. Though the reinterpretation suggests a close correlation between the African notion of community and the doctrine of the Triune God, it is an unbiblical proposal. This is because Ogbonnaya's rethinking of the Triune God contradicts the faithful testimony of the scripture to God which permits us to speak of community of persons *in* God, rather than a community *of* gods. Appealing to what he terms "the African intellectual culture" and "ntu" metaphysics, Kombo also argues for a formulation of the African doctrine of the Trinity, which not only transcends the predominant "African notion of God," but also Christianizes the African concept of God. To Christianize the African concept of God, according to him, is to fill the African idea of the divine with Christian content. That is to say, the African idea of God such as "Nyasaye" would no longer be used to refer to any native African god, but to the God of the Bible who is revealed in the incarnation of Jesus Christ and the outpouring of the Spirit. Kombo contends that expressing the Trinity in "ntu" metaphysics requires speaking of the Triune God as the "Great Muntu" (Person), *Yahwehizing* and naming it in a Trinitarian way. As the Yahwehized "Great Muntu," a "Christianized Nyasaye" (God) should be translated as "Nyasaye Wuro" (God the Father), "Nyasaye Wuowi" (God the Son) and "Nyasaye Roho Maler" (God the Holy Spirit). Though Kombo produces an amazing African reinterpretation of the Western Trinitarian doctrine with African categories, he brings little or no change to the Western traditional notion of the Trinity. Kombo's reinterpretation of the Trinity is simply the African dynamic equivalent of the Western doctrine of the Triune God.

Using the African maternal symbol of "Obirin Meta," Orobator argues that the doctrine of the Triune God is not a mathematical question to be solved in God, but a symbol, which points to God's salvific relationship with us in Christ through the Spirit. As "Obirin Meta" is a symbol of an African woman who exemplifies a "many-sided character" of largeness of heart and wisdom engaged with meeting the daily existential needs of her family, Orobator contends that the doctrine of the Trinity points to the radical open-endedness of a many-sided character of God who is concerned in various ways to responding to the everyday existential needs, concerns and struggles of the African people. Practically speaking, Orobator's maternal metaphor for the Triune God has not only made the doctrine of the Trinity intelligible to African Christians, but also has deconstructed the dominant patriarchal understanding of God which is often promoted by the male-dominant Trinitarian theology. However, Orobator's African maternal metaphor for the Triune God remains quite ambiguous and difficult, just like the Western notion of the Trinity, failing also to address the crucial question of what the doctrine of the

124 *The "amazing history" of the Trinity*

Trinity has to say about our relationship with fellow Africans, the realities confronting them today, and the world God so loves.

What the aforementioned mainline Trinitarian thinkers have not adequately addressed is not only the relation of the Trinity to the cross, time, history, eschatology, and the entire cosmic community. They also have not unpacked the radical implications of the doctrine of the Triune God for the transformation of church and society. These crucial dimensions of the Trinity are addressed by the new Trinitarian theology, analyzed in the next chapter.

Notes

1 Edmund J. Fortman, *The Triune God: A Historical Study of the Doctrine of the Trinity* (Grand Rapids, MI: Baker Book House, 1972), xv.
2 Ibid., 35.
3 Athanasius, "Four Discourses Against the Arians," in *Nicene and Post-Nicene Fathers*, ed. Philip Schaff and Henry Wace, trans. John Henry Newman and Archibald Robertson, vol. 4 (Peabody, MA: Hendrickson Publishers, 1994), Discourse 3, Chapter 25, Paragraph 15.
4 Ibid., 3, 23, 3.
5 Ibid., 2, 21, 59.
6 Guillermo C. Hansen, The Doctrine of the Trinity and Liberation Theology: A Study of the Trinitarian Doctrine and Its Place in Latin American Liberation Theology (Ann Arbor, MI: UMI Dissertation Services, 1995), 109.
7 Athanasius, "Four Discourses Against the Arians," 3, 30, 62.
8 Athanasius, *The Orations of S. Athanasius Against the Arians* (London: Griffith Farran Okeden & Welsh, 1889), 259.
9 Athanasius, "Four Discourses Against the Arians," 3, 30, 66.
10 Ibid.
11 Athanasius, *The Orations of S. Athanasius Against the Arians*, 77.
12 Ibid., 184.
13 John Norman Davidson Kelly, *Early Christian Doctrines* (New York, NY: Harper, 1959), 257.
14 Ibid., 258.
15 Ibid.
16 Fortman, *The Triune God*, 72.
17 Robert Letham, *The Holy Trinity: In Scripture, History, Theology, and Worship* (Phillipsburg, NJ: P & R Pub., 2004), 145.
18 Wolfhart Pannenberg, *Systematic Theology*, trans. Geoffrey W. Bromiley, vol. 1 (Grand Rapids, MI: Eerdmans, 1991), 275. Italics in the original.
19 Athanasius, *The Orations of S. Athanasius Against the Arians*, 124. He even thought that whoever dares inquire into the inner life of the Godhead is insane!
20 Fortman, *The Triune God*, 74.
21 Letham, *The Holy Trinity*, 146–7.
22 Fortman, *The Triune God*, 76.
23 Basil, "Letters," in *Nicene and Post-Nicene Fathers of the Christian Church*, ed. Philip Schaff and Wace Henry, vol. 8 (Peabody, MA: Hendrickson Publishers, 1994), 52, 2. Emphasis added.
24 Ibid.
25 Basil, "On the Spirit," in *Nicene and Post-Nicene Fathers of the Christian Church*, ed. Philip Schaff and Wace Henry, vol. 8 (Grand Rapids, MI: W. B. Eerdmans Publising Company, 1955), 18, 45.
26 Ibid., 16, 37.
27 Ibid., 19, 49.

The *"amazing history" of the Trinity* 125

28 Ibid., 19, 48.
29 Ibid., 18, 45.
30 Basil, "Letters," 210, 5.
31 Philip Kariatlis, "St Basil's Contribution to the Trinitarian Doctrine: A Synthesis of Greek Paideia and the Scriptural Worldview," *Phronema* 24 (2010): 62.
32 Basil, "Letters," 236, 6.
33 Hansen, The Doctrine of the Trinity and Liberation Theology, 121.
34 Kariatlis, "St Basil's Contribution to the Trinitarian Doctrine," 67.
35 Basil, "On the Spirit," 18, 44.
36 Basil, "Letters," 189, 8.
37 Gregory of Nyssa, "Against Eunomius," in *Nicene and Post-Nicene Fathers*, ed. Philip Schaff and Henry Wace, vol. 5 (Grand Rapids, MI: W. B. Eerdmans Publishing Company, 1954), Book 2, Chapter 2.
38 As cited in Catherine Mowry LaCugna, *God for Us: The Trinity and Christian Life* (San Francisco, CA: HarperSanFrancisco, 1991), 73.
39 Fortman, *The Triune God*, 78–9.
40 Gregory of Nyssa, "Against Eunomius," Book 2, Chapter 2.
41 Gregory of Nyssa, "On Not Three Gods," in *Nicene and Post-Nicene Fathers*, ed. Philip Schaff and Henry Wace, vol. 5 (Grand Rapids, MI: W. B. Eerdmans Publishing Company, 1954), 334.
42 Gregory of Nyssa, "On the Holy Spirit," in *Nicene and Post-Nicene Fathers*, ed. Philip Schaff and Henry Wace, vol. 5 (Grand Rapids, MI: W. B. Eerdmans Publishing Company, 1954), 320.
43 Gregory of Nyssa, "On Not Three Gods," 335.
44 Ibid., 334.
45 Ibid., 336.
46 Gregory of Nazianzen, "The Fifth Theological Oration: On the Spirit," in *Nicene and Post-Nicene Fathers*, ed. Philip Schaff and Henry Wace, vol. 7 (Grand Rapids, MI: W. B. Eerdmans Publishing Company, 1955), 5, 26.
47 Ibid.
48 Gregory of Nazianzen, "Oration on the Holy Lights," 39, 12.
49 Gregory of Nazianzen, "The Fifth Theological Oration: On the Spirit," 5, 10.
50 Ibid., 5, 9. The Nazianzian said the fact that the Father is not the Son is not due to any deficiency of substance, but that properties of Unbegotteness or Begotten or Proceeding designate the name "Father" to the first Person, "Son" to the second Person, and "Spirit" to the third Person in a way that maintains their personal distinction in the one *ousia*.
51 Gregory of Nazianzen, "The Third Theological Oration on the Son," in *Nicene and Post-Nicene Fathers*, ed. Philip Schaff and Henry Wace, vol. 7 (Grand Rapids, MI: W. B. Eerdmans Publishing Company, 1955), 29, 3.
52 Gregory of Nazianzen, "Oration on the Holy Lights," 39, 12.
53 Nazianzen, "The Third Theological Oration on the Son," 29, 15.
54 Brian E. Daley, *Gregory of Nazianzus* (New York, NY: Routledge, 2006), 101.
55 Though Gregory of Nazianzus stressed that essence of God is incomprehensible in contradiction to Eunomius' claims that God's essence is utterly knowable, he insisted the Jesus Christ became human that God might be comprehensible. Gregory of Nazianzen, "On the Words of the Gospel," in *Nicene and Post-Nicene Fathers*, ed. Philip Schaff and Henry Wace, vol. 7 (Grand Rapids, MI: W. B. Eerdmans Publishing Company, 1955), 37, 3.
56 Nazianzen, "The Third Theological Oration on the Son," 29, 2. To Nazianzen, the name "Father" does not mean an essence or action. Rather, it is a relational term used to indicate relation of the Father in respect to the Son and the Spirit and vice versa.
57 Christopher A. Beeley, *Gregory of Nazianzus on the Trinity and the Knowledge of God* (New York, NY: Oxford University Press, 2008), 206.
58 Gregory of Nazianzen, "The Fifth Theological Oration: On the Spirit," 5, 14.

126   *The "amazing history" of the Trinity*

59 Daley, *Gregory of Nazianzus*, 101. Emphasis added.
60 Beeley, *Gregory of Nazianzus on the Trinity and the Knowledge of God*, 210.
61 Gregory of Nazianzen, "Oration on the Holy Lights," 39, 11.
62 Gregory of Nazianzen, "The Fifth Theological Oration: On the Spirit," 5, 16.
63 Although Irenaeus wrote his theological treatises in Greek, he is often considered to be a Western Father. Fortman, *The Triune God*, 101.
64 Kelly, *Early Christian Doctrines*, 107.
65 Fortman, *The Triune God*, 101.
66 Irenaeus, "Irenaeus Against Heresies," in *The Ante-Nicene Fathers: Translations of the Writings of the Fathers Down to A.D. 325*, ed. Alexander Roberts, Donaldson James and Coxe A. Cleveland, vol. 1 (New York, NY: Christian Literature Pub. Co., 1885), Book 2, Chapter 30, Paragraph 9; Book 3, Chapter 8, Paragraph 3. It is important to note that Irenaeus not only used the Word and the Son interchangeably, but also always identified the Spirit with Wisdom, as we shall see later.
67 Ibid., 4, 20, 1.
68 John Lawson, *The Biblical Theology of St. Irenaeus* (London: Epworth Press, 1948), 125.
69 Irenaeus, "Irenaeus Against Heresies," 2, 30, 9.
70 Ibid., 4, 38, 3.
71 Lawson, *The Biblical Theology of St. Irenaeus*, 127. Italics in the original.
72 Ibid., 132. Italics in the original.
73 Irenaeus, "Irenaeus Against Heresies," 3, 8, 3; 3, 9, 3.
74 Ibid., 4, 19, 6.
75 Ibid., 5, 1, 1.
76 Ibid., 4, 20, 3.
77 Fortman, *The Triune God*, 106.
78 Jackson Jay Lashier, "The Trinitarian Theology of Irenaeus of Lyons" (Dissertation, Marquette University, 2011), 242.
79 Tertullian, "Against Praxeas," in *Ante-Nicence Fathers: The Writing of the Fathers Down to A.D. 325*, ed. Alexander Roberts and James Donaldson, trans. Peter Holmes, vol. 3 (Peabody, MA: Hendrickson Publishers, 1994), 2, 598.
80 Ibid.
81 Fortman, *The Triune God*, 111.
82 Tertullian, "Against Praxeas," 30, 627. Italics in the original.
83 Fortman, *The Triune God*, 111.
84 Tertullian, "Against Praxeas," 11, 606. Italics in the original.
85 Ibid., 22, 618.
86 Ibid., 12, 606–7.
87 Ibid., 13, 608. Italics in the original.
88 Ibid., 25, 621. Italics in the original.
89 Fortman, *The Triune God*, 113. However, the persona has traditionally been understood to mean a "mask" which was worn by actors in theater.
90 Tertullian, "Against Praxeas," 8, 603.
91 Ibid. Italics in the original.
92 Ibid., 3, 559.
93 Ibid., 13, 608.
94 Ibid., 25, 621.
95 Ibid., 7, 602.
96 Fortman, *The Triune God*, 114.
97 Tertullian, "Against Praxeas," 2, 589.
98 Ibid., 4, 559–600; 30, 627.
99 George Leonard Prestige, *God in Patristic Thought* (London: S.P.C.K., 1956), 105–6.
100 Tertullian, "Against Praxeas," 13, 608.
101 Ibid., 6, 601.
102 Ibid., 8, 603.

The *"amazing history" of the Trinity* 127

103 Harold F. Carl, "Against Praxeas—How Far Did Tertullian Advance the Doctrine of the Trinity?," *Global Journal of Classic Theology* 7, no.1 (2009): 1–18. www. phc.edu/UserFiles/File/_Other%20Projects/Global%20Journal/7-1/HaroldCarl.pdf (accessed May 26, 2014).
104 Fortman, *The Triune God*, 113.
105 Tertullian, "Against Praxeas," 7, 601. Italics in the original.
106 Fortman, *The Triune God*, 111.
107 Tertullian, "Against Praxeas," 9, 603–4.
108 Augustine, "On the Trinity," in *The Works of Aurelius Augustine, a New Translation*, trans. Arthur West Haddan, vol. 7 (Edinburgh: T&T Clark, 1873), Book 1, Chapter 2, Paragraph 4; Chapter 1, Book 4, Paragraph 7.
109 Ibid., Book 5, Chapter 8.
110 Ibid., 8, 1.
111 Ibid., 6, 10, 12.
112 However, unlike Augustine, who claimed that the substantial unity of the Trinity corresponds to undifferentiated divine outward work, for the Cappadocian Triad generally, unity of the work of the Godhead *ad extra* is indivisible in as much as such work flows from the Father through the Son and is eventually completed by the Spirit. See Hansen, *The Doctrine of the Trinity and Liberation Theology*, 132.
113 Augustine, "On the Trinity," 2, 5, 9.
114 Ibid., 1, 4, 7.
115 Ibid.
116 Ibid., 2, 10, 18.
117 Ibid., 5, 6, 7; 5, 12.
118 Ibid., 5–7.
119 Pannenberg, *Systematic Theology*, 284.
120 Augustine, "On the Trinity," 5, 10.
121 Ibid., 15, 17, 29.
122 Ibid., 15, 26, 47.
123 Ibid., 5, 15.
124 Fortman, *The Triune God*, 146.
125 Ibid. Kelly, *Early Christian Doctrines*, 276.
126 Kelly, *Early Christian Doctrines*, 277.
127 Augustine, "On the Trinity," 15, 27, 49.
128 Ibid., 8, 12–19, 2, 15, 5, 10.
129 Ibid., 9, 12, 17–18.
130 Ibid., 13–14.
131 Ibid., 14, 10, 13; 14, 12, 15.
132 Fortman, *The Triune God*, 149.
133 Ibid., 153.
134 Ibid., 152.
135 Letham, *The Holy Trinity*, 199.
136 Fortman, *The Triune God*, 152.
137 Pannenberg, *Systematic Theology*, 287.
138 LaCugna, *God for Us*, 102.
139 Ibid.
140 Veli-Matti Kärkkäinen, *The Trinity: Global Perspectives* (Louisville, KY: Westminster John Knox Press, 2007), 50.
141 LaCugna, *God for Us*, 146–7.
142 Thomas Aquinas, *The "Summa Theologica" of St. Thomas Aquinas*, trans. Fathers of the English Domican Province, 2 ed., vol. 1 (London: Burns Oates & Washbourne, 1920), Question 2, Article 1.
143 LaCugna, *God for Us*, 147.
144 Karl Rahner, *Theological Investigations*, trans. Kevin Smyth, vol. 4 (Baltimore, MD: Helicon Press, 1961).

128 *The "amazing history" of the Trinity*

145 See LaCugna, *God for Us*, 148; Hansen, The Doctrine of the Trinity and Liberation Theology, 174.
146 For the five cosmological arguments which Aquinas employed to prove the existence of God from motion (efficient cause, necessary existence, gradation and governance of the world), see Aquinas, *The "Summa Theologica" of St. Thomas Aquinas*, Part 1, Question 2, Article 3.
147 Ibid., 1, 3, 1.
148 Ibid., 1, 3, 4.
149 Ibid., 1, 3, 8.
150 Ibid., Part 1, Question 27.
151 One in this sense does not mean addition to or division of being, because Aquinas claimed that "one does not add any reality to *being*; but is only a negation of division: for *one* means undivided being." Ibid., 1, 11, 1. Emphasis in the original. He, therefore, thought one is identical with being and thus being is simple and undivided.
152 Ibid., 1, 32, 1.
153 Hansen, The Doctrine of the Trinity and Liberation Theology, 180.
154 Aquinas, *The "Summa Theologica" of St. Thomas Aquinas*, 1, 32, 1.
155 Ibid., 1, 27, 5.
156 Ibid.
157 Ibid., 1, 28, 3.
158 Ibid., 1, 29, 4.
159 Ibid., 1, 43, 4.
160 Ibid.
161 Ibid., 1, 43, 3.
162 Fortman, *The Triune God*, 210.
163 Karl Rahner, *The Trinity* (New York, NY: Herder and Herder, 1970), 16–17.
164 Stanley J. Grenz, *Rediscovering the Triune God: The Trinity in Contemporary Theology* (Minneapolis, MN: Fortress Press, 2004), 13.
165 Tersur Aben, *Is Absolute Simplicity Compatible with the Trinity?* (Bukuru: TCNN Publications, 2002), 21.
166 Ibid., 23.
167 Kärkkäinen, *The Trinity*, 53.
168 Ibid., 55.
169 Ibid., xx.
170 Immanuel Kant, *Immanuel Kant's Critique of Pure Reason*, trans. Norman Kemp Smith (New York, NY: St Martin's Press, 1963), 93.
171 Immanuel Kant, *The Conflict of the Faculties*, trans. Mary J. Gregor (New York, NY: Abaris Books, 1979), 65–7. Emphasis in the original.
172 Ibid., 67.
173 Grenz argued that Schleiermacher's consigning of the Trinity to the appendix of his tome does not mean that the doctrine is unimportant! Rather, it marks the conclusion of Schleiermacher's entire systematic theological treatise. See Grenz, *Rediscovering the Triune God*, 21.
174 Friedrich Schleiermacher, *The Christian Faith*, ed. Hugh Ross Mackintosh and James Stuart Stewart (Berkeley, CA: The Apocryphile Press, 2011), 738.
175 Ibid.
176 Ibid., 740–1.
177 Ibid., 194.
178 Ibid., 748.
179 Ibid., 392.
180 Ibid., 195–6.
181 Robert W. Jenson, *The Triune Identity: God According to the Gospel* (Eugene, OR: Wipf and Stock Publishers, 2002), 134.

The *"amazing history" of the Trinity* 129

182 Claude Welch, *In This Name: The Doctrine of the Trinity in Contemporary Theology* (New York, NY: Charles Scribner's Sons, 1952), 9.
183 Ibid.
184 Ibid., 11. Emphasis in the original.
185 Ibid., 18–19.
186 Ibid., 47.
187 Grenz, *Rediscovering the Triune God*, 23.
188 Karl Barth, "Editors' Preface," in *Church Dogmatics*, ed. Geoffrey William. Bromiley and Thomas F.Torrance, vol. 1 (London: T&T Clark International, 2004), ix.
189 Karl Barth, "The Doctrine of the Word of God," in *Church Dogmatics*, ed. Geoffrey William Bromiley and Thomas F. Torrance, vol. 1 (London: T&T Clark International, 2004), 303.
190 Jenson, *The Triune Identity*, 136.
191 Barth, "The Doctrine of the Word of God," 296. Italics in the original.
192 Grenz, *Rediscovering the Triune God*, 51.
193 Barth, "The Doctrine of the Word of God," 308.
194 Ibid., 307.
195 Ibid., 479.
196 Ibid., 347.
197 Ibid., 351.
198 Ibid., 353.
199 Ibid., 358. To substantiate his claim, Barth cited F. Diekamp that "in God, as there is one nature, so there is one knowledge, one self-consciousness."
200 Historically, Barth claimed that the meaning of "person" was so controversial in the early church that the Eastern and Western churches never agreed on what exactly it means. Each party was content with its definition. He argued that even Augustine declared that he used "person" as a matter of necessity because a suitable word in lieu of "person" does not exist. In the Medieval Ages, Barth claimed that the controversy surrounding the meaning of "person" persisted. While Boethius defined "person" as an "individual substance of the rational nature," Aquinas saw "person" as a subsistent relation in the divine nature. Barth contended the introduction of the modern concept of "personality" as meaning "autonomous self" has complicated the problem. Therefore, ascribing the word "person" to God became difficult to accomplish without risk of tritheism. He argued that Schleiermacher decided to remain silent about God's personality. Ibid., 355–8.
201 Ibid., 359.
202 Grenz, *Rediscovering the Triune God*, 34.
203 Ibid., 75.
204 David Ford, *The Modern Theologians: An Introduction to Christian Theology in the Twentieth Century* (New York, NY: B. Blackwell, 1989), 1, 47.
205 Jürgen Moltmann, *The Trinity and the Kingdom: The Doctrine of God*, 1st ed. (Minneapolis, MN: Fortress Press, 1993), 142.
206 Pannenberg, *Systematic Theology*, 296.
207 Moltmann, *The Trinity and the Kingdom*, 140, 144.
208 Ibid., 141–2.
209 John J. O'Donnell, *The Mystery of the Triune God* (New York, NY: Paulist Press, 1989), 105.
210 Ibid.
211 Ibrahim Bitrus, "The Trinity in Karl Barth" (Master's Thesis, Theological College of Northern Nigeria, Bukuru, 2005), 113.
212 Barth, "The Doctrine of the Word of God," 358.
213 Even when such a God creates fellowship with humanity and the world, such fellowship is strictly monotheistic rather than Trinitarian!

130　*The "amazing history" of the Trinity*

214　Barth, "The Doctrine of the Word of God," 355. Italics in the original.
215　It is important to note that there is a significant difference between the Greek Fathers' and Barth's usage of the term "modes of being." Unlike the Greek Fathers, who maintained that each mode of being subsists in God, Barth spoke of one personal God who subsists in these modes of being.
216　Bitrus, "The Trinity in Karl Barth," 111.
217　LaCugna, *God for Us*, 210.
218　Rahner, *Theological Investigations*, 79.
219　Ibid. Emphasis added.
220　Ibid., 80.
221　Ibid.
222　Ibid., 83–4. Italics in the original.
223　Ibid., 87. Emphasis in the original.
224　Rahner, *The Trinity*, 24.
225　Rahner, *Theological Investigations*, 87.
226　Pannenberg, *Systematic Theology*, 328.
227　Rahner, *Theological Investigations*, 87–8.
228　Ibid., 94.
229　Ibid., 95.
230　Ibid., 96.
231　Ibid., 98.
232　Rahner, *The Trinity*, 107.
233　Ted Peters, *God as Trinity: Relationality and Temporality in Divine Life* (Louisville, KY: Westminster/John Knox Press, 1993), 102.
234　Moltmann, *The Trinity and the Kingdom*, 145.
235　Ibid., 148.
236　A Okechukwu Ogbonnaya, *On Communitarian Divinity: An African Interpretation of the Trinity* (New York, NY: Paragon House, 1994), x.
237　Ibid., 1.
238　Ibid., 10.
239　Ibid., 28.
240　Ibid., 24–5. Ogbonnaya contended there is no strict distinction in African religious view between "God" with an upper case and "god" with a lower case. The two are essentially one and the same.
241　Ibid., 23.
242　Ibid., 41.
243　Ibid., xiii.
244　Ibid., 66.
245　Ibid., 85.
246　Ibid., 89.
247　Ibid., 70.
248　Kärkkäinen, *The Trinity*, 378.
249　Ibid. See the subheading titled "Tertullian: Monarchical Trinity."
250　James Henry Owino Kombo, *The Doctrine of God in African Christian Thought: The Holy Trinity, Theological Hermeneutics and the African Intellectual Culture* (Leiden; Boston, MA: Brill, 2007), 7–8.
251　Ibid., 9.
252　Ibid., xi.
253　Ibid., 11–12.
254　Ibid., 10–11.
255　Ibid., 142.
256　Ibid., 144.
257　Ibid., 145–63.

The *"amazing history" of the Trinity* 131

258 Ibid., 160.
259 Ibid., 169, 173, 186.
260 Ibid., 201.
261 Ibid., 25.
262 Ibid., 233.
263 Ibid., 260.
264 Ibid., 246.
265 Andrew M. Mbuvi, "Review of the Doctrine of God in African Christian Thought: The Holy Trinity, Theological Hermeneutics, and the African Intellectual Culture," *Modern Theology* 25 no. 3 (2009): 512. Emphasis added. However, I prefer the word "change" to "resistance."
266 Agbonkhianmeghe E. Orobator, *Theology Brewed in an African Pot* (Maryknoll, NY: Orbis Books, 2008), 26.
267 Ibid.
268 Ibid., 27.
269 Ibid., 28.
270 Ibid.
271 Ibid., 29.
272 Ibid., 30.
273 Ibid.
274 Ibid., 31.
275 Ibid., 32.
276 Ibid., 33. Italics in the original.
277 LaCugna, *God for Us*, 210.
278 Ibid.

Bibliography

Aben, Tersur. *Is Absolute Simplicity Compatible with the Trinity?* Bukuru: TCNN Publications, 2002.

Aquinas, Thomas. *The "Summa Theologica" of St. Thomas Aquinas.* Translated by Fathers of the English Dominican Province. 2 ed. Vol. 1. London: Burns Oates & Washbourne, 1920.

Athanasius. "Four Discourses against the Arians." Translated by John Henry Newman and Archibald Robertson. In *Nicene and Post-Nicene Fathers*, edited by Philip Schaff and Henry Wace. Vol. 4. Peabody, MA: Hendrickson Publishers, 1994.

———. *The Orations of S. Athanasius Against the Arians.* London: Griffith Farran Okeden & Welsh, 1889.

Augustine. "On the Trinity." Translated by Arthur West Haddan. In *The Works of Aurelius Augustine, a New Translation.* Vol. 7, xiii, 448. Edinburgh: T&T Clark, 1873.

Barth, Karl. "The Doctrine of the Word of God." In *Church Dogmatics*, edited by Geoffrey William Bromiley and Thomas F. Torrance. Vol. 1. London: T&T Clark International, 2004.

———. "Editors' Preface." In *Church Dogmatics*, edited by Geoffrey William Bromiley and Thomas F. Torrance. Vol. 1. London: T&T Clark International, 2004.

Basil. "Letters." In *Nicene and Post-Nicene Fathers of the Christian Church*, edited by Philip Schaff and Wace Henry. Vol. 8. Peabody, MA: Hendrickson Publishers, 1994.

———. "On the Spirit." In *Nicene and Post-Nicene Fathers of the Christian Church*, edited by Philip and Wace Henry Schaff. Vol. 8. Grand Rapids, MI: W. B. Eerdmans Publishing Company, 1955.

132 The "amazing history" of the Trinity

Beeley, Christopher A. *Gregory of Nazianzus on the Trinity and the Knowledge of God.* New York, NY: Oxford University Press, 2008.

Bitrus, Ibrahim. "The Trinity in Karl Barth." Master's Thesis, Theological College of Northern Nigeria, Bukuru, 2005.

Carl, Harold F. "Against Praxeas – How Far Did Tertullian Advance the Doctrine of the Trinity?" *Global Journal of Classic Theology* 7, no. 1 (2009): 1–18, www.phc.edu/UserFiles/File/_Other Projects/Global Journal/7–1/HaroldCarl.pdf (accessed May 26, 2014).

Daley, Brian E. *Gregory of Nazianzus.* New York, NY: Routledge, 2006.

Ford, David. *The Modern Theologians: An Introduction to Christian Theology in the Twentieth Century.* New York, NY: B. Blackwell, 1989.

Fortman, Edmund J. *The Triune God: A Historical Study of the Doctrine of the Trinity.* Grand Rapids, MI: Baker Book House, 1972.

Gregory of Nazianzen. "The Fifth Theological Oration: On the Spirit." In *Nicene and Post-Nicene Fathers*, edited by Philip Schaff and Henry Wace. Vol. 7. Grand Rapids, MI: W. B. Eerdmans Publishing Company, 1955.

———. "Oration on the Holy Lights." In *Nicene and Post-Nicene Fathers*, edited by Philip Schaff and Henry Wace. Vol. 7. Grand Rapids, MI: W. B. Eerdmans Publishing Company, 1955.

Gregory of Nyssa. "Against Eunomius." In *Nicene and Post-Nicene Fathers*, edited by Philip Schaff and Henry Wace. Vol. 5. Grand Rapids, MI: W. B. Eerdmans Publishing Company, 1954.

———. "On the Holy Spirit." In *Nicene and Post-Nicene Fathers*, edited by Philip Schaff and Henry Wace. Vol. 5. Grand Rapids, MI: W. B. Eerdmans Publishing Company, 1954.

———. "On Not Three Gods." In *Nicene and Post-Nicene Fathers*, edited by Philip Schaff and Henry Wace. Vol. 5. Grand Rapids, MI: W. B. Eerdmans Publishing Company, 1954.

Grenz, Stanley J. *Rediscovering the Triune God: The Trinity in Contemporary Theology.* Minneapolis, MN: Fortress Press, 2004.

Hansen, Guillermo C. *The Doctrine of the Trinity and Liberation Theology: A Study of the Trinitarian Doctrine and Its Place in Latin American Liberation Theology.* Ann Arbor, MI: UMI Dissertation Services, 1995.

Irenaeus. "Irenaeus Against Heresies." In *The Ante-Nicene Fathers: Translations of the Writings of the Fathers Down to A.D. 325*, edited by Alexander Roberts, Donaldson James and Coxe A. Cleveland. Vol. 1. New York, NY: Christian Literature Pub. Co., 1885.

Jenson, Robert W. *The Triune Identity: God According to the Gospel.* Eugene, OR: Wipf and Stock Publishers, 2002.

Kant, Immanuel. *The Conflict of the Faculties.* Translated by Mary J. Gregor. New York, NY: Abaris Books, 1979.

———. *Immanuel Kant's Critique of Pure Reason.* Translated by Norman Kemp Smith. New York, NY: St Martin's Press, 1963.

Kariatlis, Philip. "St Basil's Contribution to the Trinitarian Doctrine: A Synthesis of Greek Paideia and the Scriptural Worldview." *Phronema* 24 (2010): 57–83.

Kärkkäinen, Veli-Matti. *The Trinity: Global Perspectives.* Louisville, KY: Westminster John Knox Press, 2007.

Kelly, John Norman Davidson. *Early Christian Doctrines.* New York, NY: Harper, 1959.

Kombo, James Henry Owino. *The Doctrine of God in African Christian Thought: The Holy Trinity, Theological Hermeneutics, and the African Intellectual Culture.* Leiden; Boston, MA: Brill, 2007.

LaCugna, Catherine Mowry. *God for Us: The Trinity and Christian Life*. San Francisco, CA: HarperSanFrancisco, 1991.

Lashier, Jackson Jay. "The Trinitarian Theology of Irenaeus of Lyons." Dissertation, Marquette University, 2011.

Lawson, John. *The Biblical Theology of St. Irenaeus*. London: Epworth Press, 1948.

Letham, Robert. *The Holy Trinity: In Scripture, History, Theology, and Worship*. Phillipsburg, NJ: P & R Pub., 2004.

Mbuvi, Andrew M. Review of the Doctrine of God in African Christian Thought: The Holy Trinity, Theological Hermeneutics, and the African Intellectual Culture. *Modern Theology* 25, no. 3 (2009): 510–12.

Moltmann, Jürgen. *The Trinity and the Kingdom: The Doctrine of God*. 1st ed. Minneapolis, MN: Fortress Press, 1993.

Nazianzen, Gregory of. "On the Words of the Gospel." In *Nicene and Post-Nicene Fathers*, edited by Philip Schaff and Henry Wace. Vol. 7. Grand Rapids, MI: W. B. Eerdmans Publishing Company, 1955.

———. "The Third Theological Oration on the Son." In *Nicene and Post-Nicene Fathers*, edited by Philip Schaff and Henry Wace. Vol. 7. Grand Rapids, MI: W. B. Eerdmans Publishing Company, 1955.

O'Donnell, John J. *The Mystery of the Triune God*. New York, NY: Paulist Press, 1989.

Ogbonnaya, A. Okechukwu. *On Communitarian Divinity: An African Interpretation of the Trinity*. New York, NY: Paragon House, 1994.

Orobator, Agbonkhianmeghe E. *Theology Brewed in an African Pot*. Maryknoll, NY: Orbis Books, 2008.

Pannenberg, Wolfhart. *Systematic Theology*. Translated by Geoffrey W. Bromiley. Vol. 1. Grand Rapids, MI: Eerdmans, 1991.

Peters, Ted. *God as Trinity: Relationality and Temporality in Divine Life*. Louisville, KY: Westminster/John Knox Press, 1993.

Prestige, George Leonard. *God in Patristic Thought*. London: S.P.C.K., 1956.

Rahner, Karl. *Theological Investigations*. Translated by Kevin Smyth. Vol. 4. Baltimore, MD: Helicon Press, 1961.

———. *The Trinity*. New York, NY: Herder and Herder, 1970.

Schleiermacher, Friedrich. *The Christian Faith*. Edited by Hugh Ross Mackintosh and James S. Stewart. Berkeley, CA: The Apocryphile Press, 2011.

Tertullian. "Against Praxeas." Translated by Peter Holmes. In *Ante-Nicene Fathers: The Writing of the Fathers Down to A.D. 325*, edited by Alexander Roberts and James Donaldson. Vol. 3. Peabody, MA: Hendrickson Publishers, 1994.

Welch, Claude. *In This Name: The Doctrine of the Trinity in Contemporary Theology*. New York, NY: Charles Scribner's Sons, 1952.

4 The new hermeneutics of the Trinity

The emergence of the new Trinitarian hermeneutics of God is one of the most promising developments in contemporary theology. The new Trinitarian hermeneutics rescues the doctrine of the Triune God from bondage to speculative Trinitarian theology. This recovery not only stresses the relationality of the Triune God, but also reclaims its radical pragmatic consequences for Christian living in church and society. In this chapter, I will describe analytically and thematize the ideas of the contributors of the new hermeneutics of the Trinity. Pannenberg, Moltmann, Zizioulas, LaCugna, Boff, and many others, influenced by the initiators of new Trinitarian theology, charted new lines of thought quite different from their predecessors. For most of them, it is the economy of salvation rather than abstract metaphysics that is the starting point of an authentic Trinitarian hermeneutics of God. Second, I will explore their understanding of the personal distinctions and relationships of the members of the Trinity while affirming the unity of the Trinitarian communion as perichoresis. Finally, I will demonstrate that their hermeneutics of the perichoresis of the divine persons in the economy of salvation and in God's inner life does not exclude, but includes the whole cosmic community. I will argue that the new Trinitarian hermeneutics of God teaches that this divine communion, which takes place in Christ through the Spirit, is an ongoing and eschatological reality.

Starting point of the new Trinitarian theology

According to the new Trinitarian theologians, the doctrine of the Trinity is bound up with salvation history. God revealed Godself in Jesus Christ through the Spirit as three distinct persons in communion. The economy or history of salvation is the contact point between the Triune God and the whole of creation. It is, therefore, in the economy that humanity in particular recognizes the Trinitarian divine persons for who they are in their inner divine communal life. As Jesus says, "If you knew me, you would know my Father also. . . . Anyone who has seen me has seen the Father. . . . I am in the Father and the Father is in me" (Joh. 8:19, 14:9–11).

As an access point into the intra-Trinitarian life, the economy is the normative platform to begin every Trinitarian hermeneutics of God. The Trinity cannot be divorced from the economy of salvation, which is the road map to the inner divine

The new hermeneutics of the Trinity   135

life. According to Rahner, one of the initiators of contemporary Trinitarian theology, the mystery of human salvation and of God is bound up with the Trinity. The dividing wall between humanity and God has been collapsed through hypostatic union (i.e., the union of both divine and human natures in one person of Christ); hence, their destiny is inseparable: "The Trinity of the economy of salvation is the immanent Trinity and vice versa."[1] This Rahnerian "principle of real identity" is not a pantheistic truism, which claims that the Triune God is identical with the world and vice versa. On the contrary, it is an epistemological maxim according to which the economy of salvation is the access "road" to the inner life of the Triune God. In the words of LaCugna, this principle means that "*theologia* is fully revealed and bestowed in *oikonomia*, and *oikonomia* truly expresses the ineffable mystery of *theologia* [knowledge of God in Godself]."[2]

Pannenberg puts it more emphatically: the doctrine of the Trinity must be grounded in the divine economy and the immanent Trinity must flow from the economic Trinity. He contends that one cannot fathom the inner distinctions and the relations of the divine persons from the different operations of the one God in the World. "One can know the inter-trinitarian distinctions and relations, the inner life of God, only through the revelation of the Son," he asserts.[3] Pannenberg suggests that only when we affirm with Rahner that the immanent Trinity is the economic Trinity can we overcome the temptation of separating God's inner life from God's work and modes of existence in the world. This "from economic to immanent" approach to the Trinity reverses the "top-down" traditional Latin approach to the doctrine of the Trinity, which often begins with the eternal unity of God rather than the Trinity from the economy of salvation.

Pannenberg argues that the "from below-up" approach, according to which the divine unity is derived from the Trinity rather than the reverse, is more justifiable. He writes, "A systematic grounding and development of the doctrine of the Trinity must begin with the revelation of God in Jesus Christ."[4] That is to say, what constitutes the basis of the doctrine of the Trinity is the historical Sonship of Jesus and not the abstract concept of revelation. Thus, Pannenberg contends that the doctrine of the Trinity cannot be treated as a mere addition or appendix to the general doctrine of God. That is, the persons of the Trinity cannot be derived from the idea of one God. He writes, "Any derivation of the plurality of trinitarian persons from the essence of one God, whether it be viewed as spirit or love, leads into the problem of modalism on the one hand or subordinationism on the other."[5] Therefore, Pannenberg argues that the Trinitarian hermeneutics of God must begin with the manner in which the divine persons came to the scene and relate to one another in the event of revelation. Though Pannenberg follows Barth in constructing the Trinity from God's revelation, Pannenberg distances his approach from that of Barth, charging that Barth formulates his doctrine of the Trinity as a "formal concept of revelation."[6]

Bemoaning the marginalization of the doctrine of the Trinity in Christian theology and ethics, Moltmann charges that the undue emphasis on the unity of God has reduced the doctrine of the Trinity to mere abstract monotheism. He also contends that the Christian faith affirms three real persons in one God. Moltmann

136 *The new hermeneutics of the Trinity*

argues that such a Trinitarian concept of God, which is derived not from abstract speculation, but from the history of Jesus, is bound up with history of the Father and the Spirit. Thus, the doctrine of the Trinity is inseparable from Christology and pneumatology and vice versa. As opposed to the tradition that begins the Trinitarian hermeneutics with the oneness of God, Moltmann proposes, "We are beginning with the trinity of the Persons and shall then go on to ask about the unity."[7] The God revealed in Jesus Christ in the economy of salvation is neither a supreme substance nor an absolute subject, but a community of three persons-in-relationship. "It is in his historical and eschatological history that we can perceive the differences, the relationships and the unity of the Father, the Son and the Spirit."[8] Continuing, Moltmann wrote, *"The New Testament talks about God by proclaiming in narrative the relationships of the Father, the Son and the Spirit, which are relationships of fellowship and are open to the world."*[9]

In effect, we do not know if there was divine Trinitarian communion in God prior to this economic perspective. Even if there was, we have come to know of this divine communion as it is given to us in the economy of salvation. That is to say, all we know about the inner divine life is via the economic life, through which God fully communicates this communion with Godself and the cosmic community. We comprehend and interpret the inner life of the communion of the Trinity on the basis of what is revealed about God in the economy of salvation. LaCugna writes, "The doctrine of the Trinity is the attempt to understand the eternal mystery of God on the basis of what is revealed in the economy of redemption."[10] She argues that this economy is the normative basis for making any valid claim about the Triune God. We have no access to divine life whatsoever except through the economy of redemption. Yet what we know of God in the economy is true of God in God's self. What faith perceives of God from outside in the economy is a true reality of who God is from eternity. That is, the revelation of the immanent divine life in the economy attests to God's eternal faithfulness in time. Whatever God has revealed about God's communion rooted in Christ and the Spirit in the economy is the reality of God from eternity. There is no other Triune God than the One revealed in this way. We cannot get behind the economy and find a different God. As LaCugna sees it,

> God's saving activity through Jesus Christ and the Spirit fully expresses what God is already "in Godself." More accurately, God's actions reveal who and what God is. The possibility of a *deus absconditus* (hidden God) who lurks behind *deus revelatus* is banished once and for all. There is no God who might turn to be different from the God of salvation history, even if God's mystery remains absolute.[11]

The economy is not only faint reflection of the intra-divine relations of God, but God's tangible existence in Christ and the Spirit. The Triune God has wholly revealed Godself in the economy; hence, the Triune God is no longer incomprehensible. Even when the Triune God seems to be incomprehensible, it is not because God's revelation through Christ and the Spirit is partial. Rather, it

The new hermeneutics of the Trinity 137

is because the fallen human mind, marred by sin, cannot fully comprehend the revealed God. Humanity did not seem to have such limitations before the fall. Drawing on St Paul's claims, we "know in part" (1 Cor. 13:12), and not in whole. It is the total depravity (corruption) of human nature by sin that has hampered us from fully comprehending God in divine economic activity. Since here God's being as communion is revealed in Christ through the Spirit, then we are obliged to begin articulating the doctrine of the communion of the Trinity with the three-ness of God before God's oneness. As John Zizioulas writes,

> It would be unthinkable to speak of the "one God" before speaking of the God who is "communion," that is to say, of the Holy Trinity. The Holy Trinity is a *primordial* ontological concept and not a notion which is added to the divine substance. . . . The substance of God, "God," has no any ontological content, no true being, apart from communion.[12]

What is this economy and where do we perceive by faith the Triune God as three distinct persons in communion? The economy is the execution of God's entire eternal plan of salvation in time and history through Jesus Christ in the power of the Spirit.[13] The realization of this divine plan, which begins from creation through incarnation, and redemption finds, fulfillment at the eschaton. As LaCugna writes, "*Oikonomia* [economy] is not the Trinity *ad extra* but the comprehensive plan of reaching from creation to consummation, in which God and all creatures are destined to exist together in the mystery of love and communion."[14] Boff also claims that this economy is the incarnation of the Son and the actions of the Spirit in history.[15] Nonetheless, there is more to this than only comprehending divine order/salvation in the world. For Moltmann and Pannenberg, the economy is not merely the *ordo cognoscendi* of the Triune God, that is, the epistemological ground for the explication of the Trinity. What happens in the economy of salvation retroactively impacts the inner life of the Triune God in *ordo essendi*.[16] However, according to new Trinitarian theologians, whatever we comprehend of the Triune God is a result of the economic activity of God because it is there that the Triune God has made Godself known to us.

I will analyze in detail three specific ways in which three of these theologians perceive distinct persons of the Trinity to begin their new Trinitarian hermeneutics:

In Jesus' message of the kingdom

Pannenberg argues that the distinctions between the divine persons are revealed in Jesus' proclamation of the Kingdom. In the revelatory message of the Kingdom, Pannenberg claims, Jesus calls the God of Israel, "Father," which became a proper name for God in the New Testament.[17] As the entire mission of Jesus is to glorify the Father and his lordship, Pannenberg argues that the utterances of Jesus are directly linked to the nearness of the Father's lordship and the summoning of humanity to submit all other concerns to the "dawning future of God."[18] In establishing the Father's lordship, which is the fundamental content and primary

138   *The new hermeneutics of the Trinity*

goal of his mission, Jesus shows himself to be the Son who is obedient to the will of the Father. Pannenberg argues that by proclaiming the Father's lordship and subjecting himself to his will as a creature, Jesus distinguishes himself clearly as the counterpart of the Father. Such self-distinction and subjection, which is constitutive of Jesus' Sonship, creates room for the Father's claim of lordship. In Jesus' self-distinction as a creature, according to which he fulfills the first commandment (unlike the first Adam, who wanted to be like God), Jesus corresponds to the fatherhood of God. Pannenberg writes unambiguously,

> As Jesus glorifies the deity of the Father by sending and in his own relation to the Father, he himself, in corresponding to the claim of the Father, is so at one with the Father that God in eternity is Father only in relation to him. This distinguishes Jesus from all other human beings who follow his call and by his mediation share in his fellowship with the Father. . . . As the one who corresponds to the fatherhood of God, Jesus is the Son, and because the eternal God is revealed herein as Father, and is Father everywhere only as he is so in relation to the Son, the Son shares his deity as the eternal counterpart of the Father.[19]

Jesus' resurrection from death is the divine confirmation of his self-distinction from the Father and his claim to eternal Sonship. As Pannenberg writes, "As the resurrection of Jesus was seen as a divine confirmation of the claim implied in his earthly ministry, Jesus in the light of Easter had to appear as the Son of the Father whom he proclaimed."[20] He claims that it was by the power of the Spirit that Jesus was raised and instituted into divine Sonship.

For Pannenberg, God is not just a Son related to his Father; rather, God is also the Spirit who is the medium of communion of Jesus and the Father, as well as the mediator of our participation in Christ. Suggesting that the Jesus' proclamation of his relationship with God in the message of the kingdom is accomplished through the work and the presence of the Spirit in and with Jesus, Pannenberg maintains that the presence of the Spirit is essential for determining the intimate relation between Jesus and his Father. As the mode of God's presence in Jesus, the Spirit is indeed the indispensable medium of fellowship of Jesus with the Father. Otherwise, the Spirit's deity would merely be an extraneous addition to the church's confession of the relation of the Son to the deity of the Father. Pannenberg argues that "the fellowship of Jesus as Son with God as Father can obviously be stated only if there is reference to a third as well, the Holy Spirit."[21] Stated in brief, the mutual subordination of Jesus to the Father, which forms the Trinitarian self-distinction, involves also the self-distinction of the Spirit from and unity with the Father and the Son. Such self-distinctions of the divine persons and their unity should not simply be based on their different modes of operations, but on the Trinitarian message of Jesus about God's kingdom. As Pannenberg writes, "The differentiation of Father and Son is grounded in one and the same event, in the message of Jesus concerning God and his kingdom. What is said about the Holy Spirit also relates to this event."[22] Though Pannenberg starts his Trinitarian

The new hermeneutics of the Trinity   139

hermeneutics with the Trinity of persons, as proclaimed in the kingdom message, he has never lost sight of the unity of God. Convinced that the Trinity is not a contradiction, but a confirmation of the unity, Pannenberg describes the doctrine of the Trinity as "concrete monotheism," as opposed to abstract unity of God, which has no room for plurality of persons.[23]

In Jesus' cry of dereliction

In distinction from Pannenberg, who locates the distinctions among the divine persons in Jesus' proclamation of the Kingdom, Moltmann locates their personal distinctions in the cross-event. Moltmann maintains that Christian faith perceives the Triune God himself in the passion of Christ and vice versa. He claims, "we are to understand the suffering of Christ as *the suffering of the passionate* God."[24] The cross is the crucial Trinitarian event, which radicalizes our understanding of who God is as a communion of three loving persons. What the cross reveals is the inner life of the Triune God. As Moltmann writes,

> If Christ is weak and humble on earth, then God is weak and humble in heaven. For "the mystery of the cross" is a mystery which lies at the center of God's eternal being. . . . The cross on Golgotha has revealed the eternal heart of the Trinity.[25]

The cross reveals that the Christian God is neither an impassible God nor an unmoved divine monarchial being, unaffected by the suffering of the world. Rather, God is a communion of persons moved and implicated by the world's pain, agony, and suffering.

Thus, the cross not only reveals the communal diversity in unity of the Triune God, but also constitutes the inner life of the Trinitarian persons. In other words, what takes place in the cross not only reveals God's triune being, but also retrospectively impacts the intra-divine life of God. Moltmann writes, "What happens on Golgotha reaches into the innermost depths of the Godhead, putting its impress on the trinitarian life in eternity."[26] Elsewhere, he argues, "The pain of the cross determines the inner life of the triune God from eternity to eternity."[27] Implied by this claim is that the Triune God has always been passible and not an impassible God.

As a communion of distinct "passible divine persons," Moltmann suggests they mutually participate in the suffering of creation and humanity in Christ through the Spirit on the cross. Moltmann roots the Trinitarian mutual suffering of the divine persons in Jesus' cry of dereliction on the cross. In the act of forsaking of the Son to death by the Father, Moltmann argues that not only does the Son lose his sonship, but also the Father loses his fatherhood. Such a mutual loss, he contends, retroactively affects the innermost life of the Triune God, transforming the love that binds them together into a dividing curse and infinite pain. But in this forsakenness, which cracks the relationship between them, the Spirit, who is the link in this separation, becomes the bond uniting the Father and the Son.

140 *The new hermeneutics of the Trinity*

Moltmann writes, "The common sacrifice of the Father and the Son comes about through the Holy Spirit, who joins and unites the Son in his forsakenness with the Father."[28]

Speaking of this agony in which " 'God' is forsaken by 'God,' " Moltmann is willing to describe it as " 'eternal death,' 'the death of God.' "[29] Indeed, the whole community of God is involved in Christ's suffering on the cross, but one wonders whether it is dogmatically appropriate to speak of this communal divine passion as the death of God. To speak of the suffering of the *Father* with the *Son* on the cross as the death of God is (prone to) patri-passianism. Yet affirming the death of the Son is dogmatically fitting, for the Son completely died on the cross, as both as human and as God.[30] As Pannenberg sees it, the cross affects "eternal placidity of the Trinitarian life of God,"[31] but to speak of Christ's passion especially in terms of Hegelian philosophy, as the death of God, suggesting divine death is God's self-realization in the world, is dogmatically erroneous. As such, Pannenberg argues,

> We can say only of the *Son of God* that he was "crucified, dead, and buried". . . . The cross throws doubt not merely on the divine power of Jesus but also on deity of the Father as Jesus proclaimed him. To this extent we may speak of the Father's sharing of the suffering of the Son, his sympathy with passion.[32]

Pannenberg contends that ultimate humiliation and acceptance of death by the Son on the cross is not only the ultimate consequence of his self-distinction from the Father, but also calls into question the deity of the Father. He argues that the cross is not just the manifestation and consequence of the Son's eternal self-distinction from the Father. The cross refers also to the work of the Spirit raising Jesus Christ from the dead. Therefore, the resurrection of Jesus, he insists, is an event in which all three persons of the Trinity are at work.[33] Thus, the cross is where God incorporates the suffering of the world into his own Trinitarian history and the resurrection opens up a new future for the world, while the Spirit moves world history toward attainment of that future.

It is significant to note at this point that the Triune God suffers with and for the suffering cosmic community in the Son through the Spirit on the cross because his abundant triune being is love. As loving persons, the divine persons are not immune from suffering; they confront and overcome suffering through death for all eternity. Thus, their divine freedom does not contradict, but affirms that the Triune God is love. The Triune God, who is love, is always free to love and to be loved and hence is free to respond to the suffering of others. Otherwise, such a community of the Triune God who is love is not truly free; it is, rather, a bound community. Moltmann rightly states,

> God's freedom is his vulnerable love. . . . God demonstrates his eternal freedom through his suffering and his sacrifice, through his self-giving and his

The new hermeneutics of the Trinity 141

patience. Through his freedom he waits for man's love, for his compassion, for his own deliverance to his glory through [humanity].[34]

The freedom of the Triune God is not that which dominates and arrogates every lordship, power, and possession to God's self, but rather, that which creates community, friendship, and fellowship with God's self and the whole world.

In human society

This is a social starting point of the Trinitarian hermeneutics according to which the three distinct divine persons are perceived neither in Jesus' proclamation of the kingdom nor in his cry of forsakenness on the cross, but in the context of human society. The social approach to the Trinity, which Boff draws on superbly, seeks to make the social connections that bind women and men together in human community and society the starting point of Trinitarian reflection. Boff charges that the new approach is informed by the failure of the classical hermeneutical approaches to the Trinity. These not only are founded on the categories of substance and person, but also make metaphysics and personalism the means for recognizing the social dimension of the Trinity.[35] Though this social starting point carries the danger of tritheism, Boff insists on it because of its social benefit. He argues that the social approach views the society as not only the sum total of its individual members, but also the network of relationships among them, the functions and institutions that constitute that social and political community. The social benefit of cooperation and teamwork among the members is that it produces collective good for the entire society. Boff claims that these social qualities of human society, which carry the traces of the Trinity, embody the Trinity interpreted as the divine society. As Boff claims,

> Human society is a pointer on the road to the mystery of the Trinity, while the mystery of the Trinity . . . is a pointer toward social life and its archetype. Human society holds a *vestigium Trinitatis* since the Trinity is "the divine society."[36]

Boff claims that Trinity understood in terms of communion of Persons provides the foundation for a democratic society where dialogue and consensus are the fundamental ingredients for co-existence in the world and the church.

Not only does Boff contend that there is correlation between the divine society and human society, but he also believes the divine community is the "prototype of human community dreamed of by those who wish to improve human society."[37] Thus, the divine society provides inspiration for oppressed people in their struggle for liberation. A corollary of making human society the starting point of Trinitarian reflection is what Boff calls "the trans-sexist theology of the Maternal and the Paternal Mother."[38] Such a trans-gender approach, he contends, is a critique of dominant patriarchal and sexist views of God.

142   *The new hermeneutics of the Trinity*

These three specific economic starting points of the new Trinitarian theology are not mutually opposed to each other. They are no doubt intimately related to each other, as each complements the other. Each brings a unique voice to the Trinitarian conversation, but all insist on starting with the Trinity of the persons as revealed in the economy, whether we encounter them in Jesus' proclamation of the kingdom, his cry of abandonment on the cross, or in the context of human community and society.

Therefore, all are opposed to the Latin hermeneutical method, which usually starts the Trinitarian conversation with the unity of the divine persons, while approving the Greek Trinitarian legacy. In other words, divine personhood takes precedence over essence in the new Trinitarian hermeneutics. To this new Trinitarian hermeneutics as a divine community of mutually related persons we now turn.

Hermeneutics of Trinitarian mutual relations of the Triune God

The new Trinitarian theology rejects the modern characterization of the constituent members of the Trinity, whether as "modes of being" or as "manners of subsistence." This conflicts with the biblical witness to the Triune God and thus is tantamount to modalism. According to them, there is no better alternative to understanding the Triune God as relational persons in communion.[39] LaCugna writes, "God is *immutably personal*. God cannot be anything but personal. God cannot revert to impersonal or pre-personal existence, or act in a way that is contrary to who God is. God is not ultimately a substance but a person."[40] Therefore, the Triune God is perceived as three distinct real persons existing in communion with each other. LaCugna contends that "the 'essence' of God," is relational, meaning "God exists as diverse persons united in a communion of freedom, love and knowledge."[41] As distinct persons, each person is unique in God. No person can be exchanged for another. Particularity is indispensable to divine personhood. Each divine persona is exactly their own being and not another. Yet they are not three independent individuals unrelated to each other. Rather, communal interpersonal relations with each other constitute the persons, that is, the being of each divine person is nothing but a being in communion.

Zizioulas argues that there is no true being without communion; nothing exists as an "individual," conceivable in itself except in communion with others. Thus, he contends that the Triune God is inconceivable apart from communal relationship. Zizioulas writes, "Father, Son and Spirit are all names indicating relationship. No person can be different unless he is related. Communion does not threaten otherness; it generates it."[42]

Drawing on the Hegelian idea of self-distinction according to which a person gains identity through self-surrender and mutual dependence on another, Moltmann and Pannenberg argue that divine persons are essentially constituted by their mutual relationships with each other. Moltmann maintains that the divine persons do not exist in themselves separately prior to entering into communion with one another; this view would be tritheism. Moltmann writes, "The divine Persons exist in their particular . . . relationships to one another, and are determined

The new hermeneutics of the Trinity   143

through these relationships. It is in these relationships that they are persons. Being a person in this respect means existing-in-relationship."[43] For him, relation is constitutive of person; that is a "person" cannot be divorced from "relation." Moltmann contends, "There are no persons without relations; but there are no relations without persons either."[44] Appealing to Richard of St Victor's understanding of a person seen through the perspective of love, Moltmann argues that the divine persons "exist totally in other: the Father exists by virtue of his love, as himself entirely in the Son; the Son, by virtue of his self-surrender, exists as himself totally in the Father; and so on."[45] Thus, Moltmann argues that each Person of the Triune God not only finds his existence and joy in the other, but also receives fullness of life from the other.

Stated more emphatically, Pannenberg argues that it is reciprocity that constitutes the Triune God. He maintains that divine persons are mutually dependent on each other both for their personal identity and divinity, such that each cannot be truly personal and divine without the other. Each person is a catalyst in the Trinitarian co-dependent reciprocal relationships.[46] Peters gets Pannenberg right when he claims that in Pannenberg's theological framework, the "divinity of each of the three persons is *dependent* divinity [because] divinity comes to each as the result of personhood in relationship."[47] Continuing, Peters contends, "Pannenberg stressed that God is not personal except in one or another of the three persons. . . . *God is personal only through one or another of the three hypostases, not as a single ineffable entity.*"[48] Though the divine persons are "living realizations of separate centers of action,"[49] Pannenberg insists that such claims should not be construed as tritheism because the divine persons are constituted by reciprocal relationships, which distinguish them from one another and bring them into communion with one another.

How can we, therefore, account for the origin of these mutual relations of the divine persons in the Triune God? There are two main explanations regarding the relation of origin of the divine persons in God in new Trinitarian theology.

Asymmetrical relations of origin in the Triune God

Standing in the Cappadocian Trinitarian tradition, Zizioulas in many ways can be seen as the most influential contemporary proponent of this theory. Contending that "the being of God could be known only through personal relationships and personal love," Zizioulas claims that "Being means life, and life means *communion.*"[50] Thus, the Triune God exists always in communion of three persons such that outside the Trinity there is no God. Zizioulas insists such communion does not just exist by itself; it is caused, but not by *substance* of God. Rather, the person of the Father who alone is the source of the being and life of the Triune God causes it. The hypostasis of Father causes the existence of the Son and the Spirit out of love, without reference to time and necessity. He writes,

> Father out of love – that is, freely – begets the Son and brings forth the Spirit. If God exists, He exists because the Father exists, that is, He who out of love freely begets the Son and brings forth the Spirit."[51]

144   *The new hermeneutics of the Trinity*

In other words, if the Father does not exist, there cannot be the Triune God, that is, God cannot be a communion of three hypostases without the Father. As such, the Father is the embodiment of the whole Trinitarian communion. "If the Trinity is God," Zizioulas contends, "it is only because the Father makes it Trinity by granting it *hypostases*."[52]

Zizioulas contends that this Trinitarian communion is a product of freedom of the Father. As a person, the Father freely wills the communion, which the divine nature is not ecstatic enough to cause. Convinced that freedom and love are one and the same, Zizioulas claims that the exercise of this freedom finds full expression in the fact that "God is love."[53] Love is, therefore, neither an emanation nor secondary property of God's being, but rather, it is the essential quality that hypostasizes and constitutes God's being. He argues that this love that hypostasizes God is not the divine nature, which all the three divine persons share in common. Rather, Zizioulas argues, when we say, "God is love," we mean *only* the person of the Father – who hypostasizes God and makes God three persons.[54] As the ontological ground of divine being, the Son and the Spirit find their existence only through the Father, without whom they would not exist. As a result, the Father is inconceivable as a relational entity apart from them. That is to say, unlike human fatherhood, divine Fatherhood and its causal relations with the Son and the Spirit coincide. Thus, Zizioulas contends that the freedom of the Father is not a moral freedom of the will, but an ontological freedom to be the *other* who bestows irreplaceable personal identities on the Son and the Spirit without imposing himself on them. Zizioulas writes,

> His freedom in bringing them forth into being does not impose itself upon them, since they are not already there, and their freedom does not require that their consent be asked, since they are not established as entities before their relationship with the Father. This is the difference between moral and ontological freedom: the one presupposes individuality, the other causes individuality, or rather personhood.[55]

On the account that the Father is the only person who freely initiates this Trinitarian existence of the Son and the Spirit, Zizioulas argues that the Father exists in an unconditional freedom. The Father is not constrained by the necessities of substance, not even his own substance. As such, the Father is truly free, that is, his freedom is the freedom of personhood and the freedom from all forms of mutability.

Unlike Western Trinitarian thinking, the *arche* of the Father is not shared in common with other members within the Triune God, but rather, it is given to them by the Father. However, Zizioulas warns that this idea of divine Fatherhood has nothing to do with human fatherhood, which presupposes individuality prior to relationality, nor does it have any connection with paternalistic and sexist philosophy, which justifies domination in the church and human society. In such relational ontology of the Triune God, Zizioulas contends that all of these dangers are allayed. He writes,

> All fears that by maintaining the biblical language of God the Father we encourage sexism in religion and society are dissolved in such a relational

ontology. [This is because] the Fatherhood of God is incompatible with individualism and, therefore, with notions of oppression and so on.[56]

Zizioulas insists, therefore, that the scriptural appellation God the Father must not be jettisoned in theological conversation. Instead, it should be maintained, for it not only demonstrates the way the Triune God calls himself in his revelation, but also is the only way by which we name and experience Jesus Christ, our savoir, and the Holy Spirit, our sanctifier, as God. On the account that the Father is the ontological ground of the existence of the Trinitarian persons, Zizioulas also claims that the Father is always greater than the Son and the Spirit, not with respect to divine nature, but with respect to hypostasization of the divine nature.

As a result, Zizioulas contends that affirming anything else other than the Father, not even the idea of reciprocal causation among the divine persons as the ontological cause of the Triune God, endangers biblical monotheism. What this claim implies is that there is an irreversible hierarchy in the Trinity according to which the Father always comes first, the Son second, and the Spirit third. But such Trinitarian order is not incompatible with equality of the divine persons. As Zizioulas rightly sees it, the Trinitarian causation and *taxis* (order) protect, rather than threaten the equality and full divinity of the divine persons, when a clear-cut distinction is made between the divine nature and the person of the Father and between personal causation and the process of imparting of the divine nature by the Father to the Son and the Spirit.[57] In other words, the Son and the Spirit are co-equal with the Father not because they are mutually dependent on each other for divinity, as Pannenberg sees it, but in as much as they receive their divinity from the Father.

As for Moltmann, who also affirms the asymmetrical origin of the Persons of the Trinity, the Father, who is without origin, is the origin of the Son and the Spirit. He argues that affirming the eternal origin of the Trinity in the Father is the only way to protect the doctrine of the Triune God from degenerating into the Sabellian heresy. The Father is first the source of the Triune God and second the Father who begets the Son and brings forth the Spirit. "The Father is therefore defined through himself and through his relations to the Son and to the Spirit," Moltmann contends, continuing, "The Son and the Spirit, on the other hand, are defined through the Father and through their own relations."[58] However, he argues that what constitutes the Triune God *ad intra* is not the monarchy of God as a universal Father, but rather, the inner-Trinitarian monarchy of the Father as the origin of the Son and the Spirit. "In spite of the 'origin' of the Son and the Spirit in the Father," Moltmann warns, "we have to adhere to the equally primordial character of the Trinitarian Persons . . . because otherwise the Trinity threatens to dissolve in monotheism."[59] Though the Father is the fount of deity, Moltmann believes in the mutual workings of the Father and the Son in transferring of the kingdom of God from one person to another in the economy and changing of its form in that process. "*So God's triunity*," Moltmann argues, "*precedes the divine lordship.*"[60]

Undoubtedly, Zizioulas' theology of the being of the Triune God as divine persons in communion is a crucial aspect of his Trinitarian theology, which is partly significant for our project of recasting African concept of community. Yet his

146 *The new hermeneutics of the Trinity*

insistence on the primacy of the person of the Father over the divine substance as the source of this communion raises the question of whether the Son and the Spirit are co-equal divine persons with the Father. Though Zizioulas has insisted that affirming the Father alone as the cause of the Trinitarian communion safeguards rather than endangers the equality of the divine persons, such asymmetrical communion tends to create hierarchy in the divine communion, which undermines mutual dependence between the divine persons. Thus, Zizioulas' emphasis on the monarchy of the Father has a propensity to render his Trinitarian doctrine as gender exclusive, which often perpetuates gender inequality in the church and human society. Even if the Greek Fathers and their contemporary followers, especially Zizioulas and Moltmann, never intended anything of this sort, their hierarchal ontology of relations of origin in the Triune God has been used to legitimatize unwarranted hierarchy in the church and society.[61]

While the significance of stressing the Father as the cause of Trinitarian communion is that it safeguards biblical monotheism from being destroyed, it at the same time endangers the Christian doctrine of the Triune God, that is, it creates subordination in God. As Pannenberg rightly sees it, the argument that the Father is the fount of deity, without qualifying that the Father is the principle of deity only from the perspective of the Son, endangers the equal deity. "Without the addition of this qualification," Pannenberg contends, "the Son and the Spirit are ontologically inferior to the Father."[62] Even Moltmann's insistence on the primordial character of the divine persons and their reciprocal workings in the process of establishing the kingdom does not surmount this danger in as much as he insists that the Father is the sole cause of the Trinity. It is a contradiction for Moltmann to say that the divine persons, who are unequal in their inner life, are equal in virtue of mutual workings *ad extra* in the establishment of the kingdom. The legitimate question is whether the Triune God revealed in the economy is different from the Triune God in his immanent life. Finding Moltmann's "idea of the Father as 'origin' and 'monarchy' of the Deity" as "theologically misguided," Kärkkäinen wonders whether "this represent[s] subordinationism, an idea Moltmann claims to refute with his idea of perichoresis."[63] In such asymmetrical divine causation, we have no option but to conclude that the Son and the Spirit receive deity and personhood from the Father without the Father getting anything in return from them. What a lopsided Trinitarian causation! Besides, Zizioulas' ontology of the being of the Triune God as communion seems to be based on abstract speculation, lacking expression or basis in the economy of salvation. On this point, against Zizioulas, I side with LaCugna and Pannenberg, who, in order to avert the propensity toward subordination in the Trinity, give a radical interpretation to the divine relations of origin in God from salvation history.

Symmetrical relations of eschatology in the Triune God

Boff, while rejecting the monarchy of the Father on the account that it justifies inequality and oppression, suggests that the only way to deal with such abuse of

The new hermeneutics of the Trinity   147

the monarchy is to argue that "the divine Persons are simultaneous in origin and co-exist eternally in communion and interpenetration."[64] Boff claims that

> Each one of the Persons is "without beginning" and is therefore revealed simultaneously. . . . The three have their origin from all eternity, none being anterior to the others. Their relationship is one of reciprocal participation rather than production and procession.[65]

This proposal is cogent to overcome the dilemma, which the *arche* of the Father poses. Nonetheless, because Boff's idea of the simultaneous origin of the divine persons in God is based on "dynamic and relational substance," LaCugna charges that it "altogether bypasses the *taxis* of the divine persons in the economy."[66] Therefore, LaCugna contends that the authentic understanding of the Trinitarian *arche* of God must be based on what is revealed of God in the economy through Christ and the Spirit, devoid of subordination, unitarianism, and primacy of substance over person. LaCugna contends that the Persons of the Trinity are co-equally God because of what they have accomplished in our salvation. "To think of Jesus Christ as ontologically subordinate to God," LaCugna argues, "vitiates the reality of our salvation through him. Likewise with the Holy Spirit."[67] LaCugna claims that even if the orthodox Trinitarian theology has succeeded in obviating subordinationism "within" the Triune God, it has sadly replicated it *ad extra* in their vision of social and personal relations, a tragedy which makes a mockery of their metaphysical claims. This accounts for why the *arche* of God has been used to perpetuate all sorts of unjust patriarchal, racial, clerical, and political hierarchies in the church and society. "When the Christian doctrine of God is trinitarian, explicitly rooted in the revelation of God in Jesus Christ and the Spirit," LaCugna writes, "God's *arche* is seen as the antithesis of tyrannical, solitary, or patriarchal rule. The *arche* of God is understood to be personal life; person, not substance is the root *(radix)* of reality."[68] To say the Father is "Un-originate Origin," as LaCugna argues, means that God's personhood is the source and norm for any other personhood and love. Thus, the monarchy of the Father is the distributive *arche of* personhood, love, and communion, which the divine persons have in common, as opposed to exclusive property of a single person.

Unlike Zizioulas, who thinks the act of begetting of the Son and breathing of the Spirit takes place in God, LaCugna contends it takes place "outside" God in the economy of salvation.[69] She argues that "the *arche*, the origin and ruling principle of God's life with us[,] is a person who loves another, who suffers with another, a person who unites himself or herself with another in communion of love."[70] The *arche* of God is, therefore, not a metaphysical claim about the communion in the inner life of the Triune God so to speak. Rather, it is the Trinitarian reign of God revealed by Christ and the Spirit that promises the life of communion among all humanity and creatures. As the ground of communion, the *arche* of God is an experiential and eschatological reign of God that incorporates everyone and everything into the communion of the personal life of the Triune God. While the

148 *The new hermeneutics of the Trinity*

divine *arche* is a critique of patriarchal, sexist, and racial structures and ideologies, LaCugna argues that God's *arche*, which excludes all forms of subordination among persons, is a solid foundation for mutuality, equality, and a non-hierarchal social order. LaCugna writes, *"any theological justification for a hierarchy among persons also vitiates the truth of our salvation through Christ."*[71] That approach also perpetuates subordination, domination, and exploitation on the basis of the monarchy of the Father.

Undoubtedly, we concur that the *arche* of the Triune God, which is rooted in the economy, not only affirms the equality and communion of the divine persons, but also critiques and serves as the archetype of restructuring an imbalance in sociopolitical and religious order. However, LaCugna has not properly demonstrated the mutual dependence among the divine persons, as expressed in the economy, which provides the fundamental basis for that claim. Without properly rooting the relationality and mutuality of the Triune God in God's revelation in Christ, LaCugna's hermeneutics of the Trinity can be construed as our mere treasured ideas about human community, which are projected onto God. There is no other theologian who roots the mutual dependence of the divine persons in the economy of salvation like Pannenberg.

According to Pannenberg, the relation of Jesus to his Father through the Spirit in the revelatory event demonstrates reciprocal "self-distinction-in-unity," which constitutes the inner life of the Triune God. Such revelatory relation, says Pannenberg, expresses more accurately the diversity and unity in God than the traditional concepts of *begetting* and *breathing*, which are not only exegetically unsustainable, but also create hierarchy in the Trinity.[72] First, unlike LaCugna, who contends that the eternal begetting of the Son and the breathing of the Spirit take place in God's economy, Pannenberg argues that the scriptures speak of begetting of the Son and breathing of the Spirit without reference to the same eternal acts of begetting and breathing. In other words, Pannenberg is suspicious of affirming the act of begetting of the Son and breathing of the Spirit, which scriptures speak of as taking place in the inner life of the Triune God. Second, Pannenberg charges that the traditional idea according to which the Father alone is the source of deity excludes mutual relations between the divine persons. As Pannenberg succinctly puts it,

> Tradition has it that the Father alone is without origin *(anarchos)* among the three persons of the Trinity, that he is the origin and fount of deity for the Son and Spirit. . . . This view seems to rule out genuine mutuality in the relations of the trinitarian persons, since it has the order of origin running irreversible from Father to Son and Spirit.[73]

While Pannenberg concurs with the Greek Fathers that the Son neither begets nor sends the Father, the order of which is irreversible, he does suggest that the personal relationships in the Trinity, as seen in Jesus' relationship to the Father and the Spirit, are reciprocal. Unlike Moltmann, he claims that perichoresis points to this reality but "had only a limited impact because of the one-sided viewing of the intra-trinitarian relations as relations of origin."[74] Drawing on Athanasius' insight that the Father would not be the Father without the Son, he suggests that the deity of the Father also must be dependent on his relation to the Son, thus providing a basis for "true reciprocity in the trinitarian relations."[75] Pannenberg locates such a basis in the mutual establishment of the Father's lordship, in which the Father gives the kingdom to the Son. The Son reigns until all enemies are put beneath His feet, at which point He returns the kingdom to the Father in consummation (I Cor. 15:24–8). As the Father hands over his lordship to the Son, the Father makes his eternal kingdom contingent on whether or not the Son glorifies him and delivers his lordship in the world.

Pannenberg argues that such mutual relationship of handing the kingdom over and back between the Father and the Son is not seen in begetting: "The self-distinction of the Father from the Son is not just that he begets the Son, but that he hands over all things to him, so that his kingdom and his own deity are now dependent upon the Son."[76] Pannenberg argues that it is unimaginable to think of the rule or kingdom of the Father as an external reality distinct from his deity, as if God can be God without his kingdom.[77] Though the world as the object of God's lordship is not essential to God's deity on the account that it owes its existence from divine freedom, the reality of its existence is not compatible with his deity apart from his lordship over the world.

But Pannenberg contends that the mutual establishment of the monarchy or the kingdom in the world would have been unsuccessful without the third divine person, the Holy Spirit. As the origin of life, the Spirit distinguishes himself as a distinct person not just by raising Jesus from the dead. Pannenberg claims that by glorifying the Father through the Son, the Spirit also distinguishes himself from the Father and the Son and relates to both.[78] The Father does not just breathe the Spirit; the Father makes deity contingent on the Spirit's work of creating communion between the Father and the Son via raising Jesus from the death and ushering humanity into their communion. Therefore, Pannenberg writes,

> Relations among the three persons that are defined as mutual self-distinction cannot be reduced to relations of origin. The Father does not merely beget the Son. He also hands over his kingdom to him and receives it back from him. The Son is not merely begotten of the Father. He is obedient to him and he thereby glorifies him as the one God. The Spirit is not just breathed. He also fills the Son and glorifies him in his obedience to the Father, thereby glorifying the Father himself.[79]

Pannenberg argues that the reciprocal dependency of the divine persons on each other for the establishment of the kingdom does not tear down, but builds up the monarchy of the Father. As the work of the Son establishes the Father's monarchy in creation, so the work of the Spirit consummates his monarchy in creation. Pannenberg contends that "by their work the Son and Spirit serve the monarchy of the Father. Yet the Father does not have his kingdom or monarchy without the Son and Spirit, but only through them."[80] Thus, the monarchy of the

150   *The new hermeneutics of the Trinity*

Father, which is not the presupposition, but the outcome of their joint work, is "the seal of their unity."[81] The symmetrical relationships among the divine persons in establishing the monarchy in the economy is an ongoing reality which finds final consummation at eschaton. Though according to biblical testimony, the Father is the only one *proper* God in this mutual monarchy, Pannenberg asserts that this by no means implies that the Son and the Spirit are ontologically inferior to the Father. Rather, the Father is known as the one God by means of the Son in the Spirit.

Though Pannenberg asserts that perichoresis does not capture the mutual relations of the Trinity, I believe perichoresis is one of the appropriate categories to express the vibrant divine unity of the community of the divine persons as one God. To this we now turn.

Hermeneutics of the unity of the Triune God

The unity of the Triune God is one of the most fascinating themes in the new Trinitarian theology. It is a theme that has witnessed a revolutionary departure from the abstract classical understanding of the unity of the Triune God. Affirming the orthodox Trinitarian hermeneutic of unity of the Triune God, Zizioulas claims that the unity of the Triune God lies in the person rather than the substance of the Father, who is the cause of the Son and the Spirit. The persons of the Trinity are united not in virtue of their identical divine substance, but in virtue of the commonality of their cause, that is, the Father. As Zizioulas writes,

> Among the Greek Fathers the unity of God, the one God, and the ontological "principle" or "cause" of the being and life of God does not consist in the one substance of God but in the *hypostasis*, that is, *the person of the Father*. The one God is not the one substance but the Father, who is the "cause" both of the generation of the Son and of the procession of the Spirit.[82]

Zizioulas claims that what safeguards the unity of the Triune God is not the unity of substance, but rather, the monarchy of the Father, who is one of the integral persons of the Trinity. This unity of the Triune God, which finds complete expression "through the unbreakable *koinonia* that exists between the three persons," says Zizioulas, demonstrates that "otherness is not a threat to unity, but a *sine qua non* condition of it."[83] Implied by this claim is that even when the person of the Father alone is said to constitute the unity of the Trinity, this does not mean that the unity of the Triune God is a unity of independence or isolation. Rather, it is a unity that expresses itself in an indissoluble Trinitarian communion that precludes every kind of individualism and separation in the Triune God. Zizioulas writes,

> The three constitute such an unbreakable unity that individualism is absolutely inconceivable in their case. The three persons of the Trinity are thus one God, because they are so united in an unbreakable communion *(koinonia)* that none of them can be conceived apart from the rest.[84]

The new hermeneutics of the Trinity   151

But the world, which came from the free act of the personal and transcendent God, is precluded from this unbreakable ontological unity of the Triune God. In other words, the unity of the Triune God, which is the unity of the divine persons *in* the person of God the Father, has nothing to do with the world.

Unlike the Eastern Trinitarian hermeneutic of the divine unity, according to the Western Trinitarian teaching, the unity of the Triune God is that which is common to the persons of the Trinity, which is substance. The divine persons who are distinct from each other in virtue of their relations of origin are united in their indivisible one and the same substance. The substance that unites the persons of the Trinity is their uncreated divine nature, for that "which is not divine essence is a creature."[85] Therefore, as a self-sufficient and immutable divine nature, the classical interpretation of the unity of the Triune God in the Western Trinitarian tradition (including the East) is construed strictly as the independence of the Triune God from the world. It is the unity of the Triune God *in itself* – even when such unity finds expression in the common action of the Triune God *ad extra*. That is to say, humanity and the entirety of God's creation are excluded from the divine unity as co-sharers!

Barth is perhaps the most prominent contemporary Western Trinitarian representative of such a classical interpretation of the unity of the Triune God. According to Barth, divine unity is not a collective unity of three distinct persons, but a unity of triple repetition of one personal God existing in three modes of being. Hence, he thinks that the divine Trinity is not in conflict with monotheism because "only substance equality of Christ and the Spirit with the Father is compatible with monotheism."[86] God's unity, for Barth, is nothing but God's self-sufficiency. That is, the Trinitarian God does not "need" the world and humanity in order to be One.[87] As Barth writes,

> God is One, but not in such a way that as such He needs a second and then a Third in order to be One, nor as though He were alone and had to do without a counterpart, and therefore again . . . as though He could not exist without the world and man, as though there were between Him and the world and man a necessary relation of reciprocity.[88]

Such a claim, as plausible as it is, seems to be at odds with the biblical witness to the Triune God's relation to the world and humanity for at least three reasons. First, God characterized the world and humanity, which God created from his abundant loving freedom, as "very good" (Gen. 1:31). Second, when the world and humanity were estranged from God, God continued to love the world and humanity so much that God gave his only Son to die for its salvation (Joh 3:16). Above all, God promised to eschatologically transform the existing creation to a new heaven and a new earth (2 Pet. 3:10; Rev. 21).

Therefore, if God can be God without the world and humanity, one wonders why God has created such a "very good" world and humanity in the beginning and even redeemed them when they were estranged from God? Why didn't God let them perish forever if God does not actually "need" them? Besides, this raises the question of why God promises to eschatologically renew the existing world and humanity if God does not need them. While I concur with Barth that

152   *The new hermeneutics of the Trinity*

the divine Trinity does not contradict, but affirms concrete monotheism, I fail to see why vibrant communal divine unity is closed rather than open, exclusive rather than inclusive. This practical understanding of unity of the Triune God (as we shall explain in this chapter) is what marks the radical departure of the new Trinitarian theology from traditional exclusive construal of the unity of the Triune God.

Eschewing the traditional method of basing the unity of the Triune God either on the unity of "homogeneous substance or identical subject," Moltmann constructs the unity of the Triune God in Trinitarian terms in light of Trinitarian history. Moltmann contends that what emerges from such construction is the "concept of divine unity as the union of the tri-unity."[89] He says that the divine persons are co-active in the Trinitarian history of God; hence, the unity of the Trinity is not "monadic unity." Rather, it is the sort of unity that lies not just in the *union* of the divine persons, but also in their *fellowship*.[90] Drawing on the idea of perichoresis, reciprocal permeation, Moltmann argues that such unity is "the unitedness, the at-oneness of the three Persons with one another, or: the unitedness of the triune God."[91] Perceiving such unity in the perichoresis of the divine persons, he argues that the unity of the Triune God drawn from the divine Trinitarian history must be understood as "open, unifying at-oneness of the divine Persons in their relationships to one another," hence the "transcendent primal ground" which does not lie in the identical divine substance or absolute subject. Rather, it lies in the eternal perichoresis of the divine persons according to which they "form their own unity by themselves in the circulation of the divine life."[92] Perichoresis is the expression of the perfect unity in distinctions among the divine persons in their inner life, for he writes, "in the perichoresis, the very thing that divides them becomes that which binds them together."[93] He claims that the divine persons are so united with and in one another that there is no distinction between their personal and social relationships.

The perichoretic divine persons permeate and co-mingle with one another in their divine perichoretic life without confusion or separation. The Father, Son, and Spirit mutually interpenetrate themselves so deeply that wherever the one is, the other two are found. One does not exist apart from the other two, yet the unsubstitutable personal identity of each is not lost, but maintained. Even as a community of three unique and non-interchangeable persons, Father, Son, and Holy Spirit co-exist in communion. In the words of Boff, "The greatness of trinitarian communion . . . consists precisely in its being a communion of three different beings; in it mutual acceptance of differences is the vehicle for the plural unity of the divine persons."[94] He argues that the communion of the Trinity involves their co-presence with one another, their reciprocity, the intimacy of immediacy, and community life. This trinitarian union means each Person contains the other two; each one penetrates the others and is penetrated by them; one lives in the other and vice versa. The interpenetration also involves self-surrender of each person to others, which forms the Trinitarian union of the persons. Boff argues that the intrinsic characteristic of each person is *for, through, with*, and *in* the others, such that the divine persons do not exist just in themselves for themselves, but also for others. He states,

> Diversity-in-communion is the source-reality in God, whose unity can only be the union of this personal diversity. . . . The unity is the actualization of the process of one Person communing with others, of one Living sharing in the lives of the others.[95]

As LaCugna sees it, perichoresis is an eternal divine movement characterized by the mutual and reciprocal permeation of each person *in, with, through*, and *by* the other divine persons without abrogating their individuality. As a divine dance, LaCugna describes the perichoretic Trinity as "an eternal movement of reciprocal giving and receiving, giving again and receiving again" in which there are no leaders or followers.[96] Everyone is equal. No one is marginalized. Everyone is significant. But perichoresis is not simply a glorious jamboree about the inner life of the Triune God. It is the reality that expresses itself in the economic life. Though LaCugna concurs with Wilson-Kastner and Leonardo Boff that the Latin non-hierarchical understanding of the perichoretic Trinity provides a basis for feminist and liberation theologies, LaCugna finds their methodology wanting. Charging that the Latin approach is a "noneconomic methodology," LaCugna maintains that such an approach limits perichoresis only to intra-divine life, without recourse to the economic life. For LaCugna, the starting point of perichoresis is not the intra-divine relations, but the economy of salvation. As the mystery of one inclusive communion of both human and divine persons, LaCugna sees perichoresis as a "divine dance" between the Triune God and the creation in which humanity is drawn into the divine life as a beloved partner through the incarnation and life of Jesus Christ. As LaCugna writes, "It is the life of communion and indwelling, God in us, we in God, all of us in each other."[97] In her estimation, the perichoretic Trinity repudiates any separation between divine life *ad intra* and *ad extra*, providing "a dynamic model of persons in communion based on mutuality and interdependence."[98]

As Moltmann also sees it, the Trinitarian history of God's relationships of perichoresis corresponds to the eternal perichoresis of the divine persons in their opening of themselves for reception and unification of the entire creation. Thus, for him, the perichoretic unity of the Triune God, which is the fellowship with and in God, is so wide open as to embrace and unite itself with the entire creation. The Trinitarian unity "must consequently be understood as a *communicable* unity and as an *open, inviting unity, capable of integration*."[99] As a dynamic unity, creation and humanity are incorporated into the unity of the Triune God. Echoing Moltmann that the divine unity is integrating and inclusive, Boff argues that perichoretic unity embraces all people and history. The divine mutual self-giving and receiving love of the three persons of the Trinity is the foundation of our communion, of our fellowship with God and one another. Through the power of the Holy Spirit, we are drawn into a divine fellowship of love and unity of the Triune God whose goal is to transform all human relationships and the whole of the world into their triune image. Boff writes, "Through being an open reality, this triune God also includes other differences, so the created universe enters into communion with the divine."[100] As a communion of love, the divine persons seek to embrace the whole of creation, which emerges from their desire not to live alone in their fabulous communion, but to seek companions in communion and love with the creation. Hence, the entire creation exists in, and reflects, the Trinity, and is a "receptacle capable of holding the manifestation of the Trinity."[101]

Therefore, the creation, incarnation, and redemption of the world and its eschatological consummation by the Triune God in Christ and Spirit are the fulfillment of God's need for communion and unity with the world and humanity. "Creation is a fruit of God's longing for his Other and for that Other's free response to the divine love," Moltmann writes, "That is why the idea of the world is inherent in the nature of God himself from eternity."[102] As a perichoresis, the Trinitarian God and humanity and the world are mutually interdependent such that one cannot exist apart from the other.[103] In this relationship, the three persons of the Trinity relate reciprocally, both to each other and to the world.[104] The unity of persons of the Trinity is the point of encounter where God and humanity mutually indwell in, and co-exist with, each other in one mystery of communion and interdependence. Thus, unlike Barth, LaCugna, and Pannenberg, Moltmann suggests, "God 'needs' the world and man. If God is love, then he neither will nor can be without the one who is his beloved."[105]

Therefore, the economic life does not faintly mirror obscured intra-divine relations, but is a true revelation of God's perichoretic life of communion with Christ and Spirit, in which God shares God's inner life with creation. God and creation are inseparable through perichoresis. LaCugna writes,

> The life of God is not something that belongs to God alone. *Trinitarian life is also our life*. . . . There is one life of the triune God, a life in which we graciously have been included as partners.[106]

She argues that Christians "are made sharers in the very life of God, partakers of divinity as they are transformed and perfected by the Spirit," which is divinization and glorification.[107] God exists concretely as divine persons in communion with humanity such that the Trinity is "God's life *with us and our life with each other*. It is the life of communion and indwelling, God in us, we in God, all of us in each other."[108]

The fact that the perichoretic unity of God finds expression in the reciprocal relation between God and the world and humanity does not mean that God ceases to be God or the latter ceases to be what they are. No way! As Pannenberg rightly sees it, the unity of God does not exclude, but includes the world, which is the object of God's kingdom. The Triune God relates to the world out of his sheer love for the world. As God's love is God's *ousia* itself, Pannenberg sees love as the Spirit with which the divine persons love each other and the world without abrogating the distinction between them. Pannenberg writes, "Divine love in its

The new hermeneutics of the Trinity   155

trinitarian concreteness . . . embraces the tension of the infinite and the finite without setting aside their distinction."[109] This is a very crucial point. God and the world and humanity remain distinct despite their radical unity. God's freedom is not compromised either. "Because God is love, having once created a world in his freedom," Pannenberg contends that God "finally does not have his existence without this world but over against it and in the process of its consummation."[110]

Pannenberg also refuses to concur with Moltmann and Boff that the divine unity can be based on perichoresis because perichoresis, which presupposes another basis of unity, can only manifest it. Pannenberg writes,

> The persons are not first constituted in their distinction, by derivation from the Father, and only then united in perichoresis and common action. As modes of being of the one divine life they are always permeated by its dynamic through their mutual relations.[111]

Nonetheless, he concurs that the essence – unity – of the Trinitarian God cannot be isolated from his historical actions in the economy as if God is "untouched by the course of history and inaccessible to all creaturely knowledge."[112] Divine action, which is God's self-realization in the world, incorporates the creatures into eternal fellowship of the divine persons without alteration of their eternal being. Pannenberg claims that the common action of the divine persons in the economy not only brought creation and history into existence, but also retrospectively impacted the inner life the Triune God. According to Pannenberg, the Father, in creating "the world and sending his Son and the Spirit to work in it, has made himself dependent on the course of history."[113] Such dependence is not to be construed as absolute, for "the eschatological consummation is only the locus of the decision that the [T]rinitarian God is always true from eternity to eternity."[114] What Pannenberg refutes with this claim is the idea which posits "divine becoming in history" as though the essence of the Triune God were simply the result of a historical process which attains actuality only in the eschatological consummation. For Pannenberg, the dependence of God's being on the eschatological consummation of the kingdom does not change, but confirms the eternal veracity of his deity.

The perichoretic unity of the Triune God, according to which the whole of creation is incorporated into the Trinitarian divine life of God, is an eschatological reality. Thus, the unity of the persons of the Trinity has an open future. Such a future lies with the ultimate inclusion of the entire creation and humanity into the perichoretic communion at the eschaton. As Moltmann sees it, the perichoretic unity of the Triune God will be consummated in the eschaton with the eventual union of not just the Son with the Father, but also the Triune God with the world through the Spirit's work of glorification and unification. This eschatological consummation of the Trinitarian history of God is thus bound up with the consummation of the Trinitarian life of the Triune God in itself.[115] The two, which coincide and determine each other, as matter of fact, resolve the tension between the economic and immanent Trinity. The world and humanity, which have already become integral part of the Triune God in Christ through the Spirit

156   *The new hermeneutics of the Trinity*

in the economy of salvation, are and will be constitutive of the immanent Trinity. Moltmann writes, "When everything is 'in God' and 'God is all in all,' then the economic Trinity is raised into and transcended in the immanent Trinity."[116] Kärkkäinen gets Moltmann right when he views this consummation as God's eternal way of indwelling the creation, "a desire that is already present in the act of creation when God, in his love, reaches out to the Other. This is the eschatological perichoresis, 'mutual dwelling,'" according to which, the entire creation will be the new dwelling place of the Triune God.[117]

But this perichoretic unity of the Triune God should not be understood as something that lies in the distant future. Rather, it is an ongoing reality breaking from the future into the present creation. The "when" in Moltmann's claim should not be misconstrued merely as human time, suggesting everything is not yet in God. But seen as God's (not humanity's) time, it is clear that everything is already in God. This is because all time – past, present, and future – are actual realties to the Triune God. In God, eternity and time coincide and impact each other. God embraces time and is impacted by time without being bound by it. In other words, time is never a confinement for the Triune God even when God is deeply involved in time. Hence, the eschatological consummation of the unity of the Triune God is only a confirmation of the ongoing Trinitarian perichoresis of God with the cosmic community in the economy of salvation. I affirm with LaCugna that in this framework "there is neither an economic nor an immanent Trinity; there is only the *oikonomia* that is the concrete realization of the mystery of *theologia* (knowledge of God in Godself) in time, space, history, and personality."[118] The Triune God with cosmic community is the Triune God *ad intra* and vice versa. The eschatological consummation of the divine-creation communion translates to an eternal Trinitarian doxology where the Triune God is and will be glorified and adored forever and ever.

What does this new Trinitarian hermeneutic mean for our everyday life in the world? How can we interpret and organize our Christian and social life in accordance with the doctrine of Trinitarian communion? What this new hermeneutics of the communion of the Trinity faces in this regard is colossal, and to these pragmatic ethical consequences we now turn.

The Trinitarian communion: a moral ideal

The new Trinitarian theology is not an abstract speculation about the Triune God, but has radical ethical implications for real-life situations. It is a critical reflection on the Triune God as concretely revealed in Christ and the Spirit with revolutionary moral consequences for our life and every dimension thereof. First, the new Trinitarian theology radicalizes how we understand our life in light of the life of the Triune God. The affirmation of contemporary Trinitarian theology, according to which the life of the Triune God does not exclusively belong to God alone, but includes our life,[119] is a critique and a moral model for our life. As a critique, it challenges every Christian life lived in isolation from God and fellow humanity. As a model, the new Trinitarian theology liberates us from our exclusive lifestyle

The new hermeneutics of the Trinity 157

into living a life of communion with the Triune God, with others and with God's own creation, as shown to us in Christ and the Spirit. Such a life of communion with God and the other, lying at the heart of the Christian faith, epitomizes our participation in the life of God: "Divine life is therefore also *our* life. The heart of Christian life is to be united with the God of Jesus Christ by means of communion with one another."[120] The new Trinitarian theology helps to understand that our life finds fulfillment not in isolation, but in a life of communion lived out and shared with God and the other in every facet of human existence.

Second, the new Trinitarian theology also has a far-reaching bearing on our ecclesiastical system. The perception of the Triune God as three co-equal perichoretic persons in communion is a critical ethical model for restructuring of the Church. The church's structure and leadership style is often influenced by its own perception of God. A non-Trinitarian monotheistic perception of God, for example, has resulted in the church evolving a stratified structure in which power and privilege is concentrated in the hands of an individual or a group of individuals, to the exclusion of other members of the church. Such clerical monotheism perpetuates oppressive and hierarchical leadership models in the church according to which the bishop is regarded as the sole representative of Christ to whom all of God's people must bow, an idea which led to the emergence of the hierarchal structures.[121] But a church that lives out Trinitarian communion will evolve egalitarian structures which promote equitable participation of all for the common good of the church. In such a church, Moltmann contends, the Trinitarian principles of "concord," "dialogue," "consensus," and "harmony" triumph over the monarchical principle of "power," "authority," and "obedience." It is also the brotherhood and sisterhood of the community of Christ and not the church's hierarchy which defines and guarantees its unity. Moltmann writes,

> Here the unity of the Christian community is a trinitarian unity. It *corresponds* to the indwelling of the Father in the Son, and of the Son in the Father. It *participates* in the divine triunity, since the community of believers is not only fellowship *with* God[,] but *in* God too.[122]

Third, new Trinitarian thinking impacts our socio-political system. According to LaCugna, Trinitarian theology "transforms the political and social forms of life appropriate to God's economy."[123] The Triune God as revealed in Christ and the Spirit rebuts any social and political order based on non-Trinitarian understandings of God, which justifies oppression in the world. The construal of God as a Trinity of co-equal persons in communion is a paradigmatic model that will help to create a just and democratic political system of government in the world. As a doctrine of freedom, Moltmann argues that the Trinitarian theology calls for a social understanding of God which corresponds to an egalitarian view of the community of humanity: "The Trinity corresponds to a community in which people are defined through their relations with one another and in their significance for one another, not in opposition to one another, in terms of power and possession."[124] In such a socio-political perichoretic system of government, people will

158 *The new hermeneutics of the Trinity*

possess everything in common (excluding their irreplaceable personal identities), and thus, there will not be a privileged or marginalized class. In other words, perichoretic political power is shared, not concentrated in the hands of few. The perichoretic understanding of state political power is the antithesis of totalitarianism and any form of political absolutism. Thus, political leaders who draw inspiration from the perichoretic *arche* of the Triune God would be democrats rather than dictators, liberators rather than oppressors, servants rather than rulers.

Fourth, the perichoretic communion of the Trinity critiques human socio-economic systems such as libertarian capitalism, which dispossesses the masses, and socialism, which undermines distinctions among people. The communion of the Trinity calls for a socio-economic system characterized by freedom, justice, equality, mutual sharing, and reciprocity on the basis of unity in diversity. The Trinitarian communion is thus an inspiration for restructuring of the socio-economic system of human society, which provides a leveling field for both individual and collective ownership of property. Boff writes, "The sort of society that would emerge from inspiration by the trinitarian model would be one of fellowship, equality of opportunity, generosity in the space available for personal and group expression."[125] One's personal interest will not threaten, but promote the collective interest of the society and, thus, the gulf between the haves and the have-nots will be significantly bridged. In this society, no one would be excluded; all would participate in contributing and enjoying the commonwealth. Boff argues that only such a society where its "social fabric is woven out of participation and communion of all in everything can justifiably claim to be an image" of the Triune God.[126] Thus, any society that evolves hybridized perichoretic socio-economic and political system which integrates elements of empowering libertarian capitalism and socialism would profit investors without exploiting proletariats, and promote personal well-being without neglecting public welfare of the society.

Fifth, because there is no domination whatever in the perichoretic communion of the co-equal divine persons, the idea of the perichoretic communion of the divine persons *ad extra* and *ad intra* is the moral norm for human male-female relationships in society. The Trinitarian communion critiques all forms of gender prejudice that subordinate women to men. It liberates women and men to relate to each other as equal partners created in God's image to participate in the divine life of communion. LaCugna argues that the Trinity makes it abundantly clear that

> Subordination is not natural but decidedly *un*natural because it violates *both* the nature of God and the persons created in the image of God. Jesus Christ, who is the economy of God, is the one in whom there is no longer male nor female, free nor slave, Jew nor Gentile.[127]

The new Trinitarian doctrine invites patriarchal families and societies to embody egalitarian mutual relations that promote equal participation in decision-making as well as sharing of resources after the pattern of the perichoretic Trinitarian communion of God. Thus, patriarchy, the rule of men over women, as we shall see later in Chapter 5, contradicts the perichoretic *arche* of God as preached and lived

The new hermeneutics of the Trinity 159

by Jesus Christ. Wherever and whenever God's perichoretic *arche* is, patriarchy is banished once and for all from the family of the Triune God. The two are mutually exclusive and contradictory and thus cannot co-exist. LaCugna writes,

> The household of the patriarch is not the household of God. In God's new household the male does not rule, God rules together with us, in solidarity with the poor, the slave, the sinner. Male and female are equal partners in God's household.[128]

Both serve each other, others, and above all, the Triune God.

Finally, since women (and men) cannot be truly liberated from the patriarchal oppression without the liberation of the earth, the perichoretic communion is a promising model for establishing right human relationship with the earth. The perichoretic communion of the Triune God is not just with humanity, but with the whole earth, thus motivating the transformation of human domination of the earth. Instead of perceiving the earth as an object to be exploited for human enrichment, the perichoretic theology of the Triune God calls for the human perception of the earth as a fellow subject to be loved, maintained and cared for, in the fashion of the Triune God.

When the Triune God declared after creation that everything was "very good," this does not mean that what was created was "perfect" and hence does not require any further improvement. On the contrary, the world was not created "perfect," but "very good" so as to give ample room to humanity to constantly deploy its power and creativity to make it better than it was first created. Thus, the destruction of the earth by whatever human means not only disparages the perichoretic presence of the Triune God in the world, but also undoes the "very good" work of the Triune God. The earth is the eschatological dwelling place of the Triune God. Hence, the way humanity can image the Triune God in its relationship with the world is not only to respect the perichoretic presence of the Triune God in everything created, but also recognize the right of the earth to justice and care as human rights. In this way, the cry for justice and liberation by the earth would be granted and human life, bound up with the existence of the earth, safeguarded:

> Special human rights to life and existence are valid only as long as these human beings respect the rights of the earth and of other living things. . . . Anyone who disregards the rights of the earth threatens coming generations and the survival of humanity.[129]

Summary and conclusion

The new hermeneutics of the Trinity is one of the most amazing developments in contemporary theology. What is fascinating is that it insists on God's self-revelation in Christ in the economy of salvation rather than the *theologia* (God in Godself) as the authentic starting point for any valid Trinitarian hermeneutics of God. The Triune God, who is inscrutable, is epistemologically accessible

160   *The new hermeneutics of the Trinity*

in the economic life where the Triune God is revealed as a Trinity of Persons in their inner life. The Triune God in Godself is identical with the Triune God revealed in the economy of salvation and vice versa. Nonetheless, it is only in the economy of salvation and not the *theologia* that we come to know of the Triune God as the "Creator," "Redeemer," and "Sustainer" of humanity and the world. Therefore, the economy is the epistemological "doorway" into the inner life of the Triune God, which otherwise remains inaccessible. Here accessing the inner life of the Triune God means that the Triune God is neither three modes of being nor manners of subsistence of one and the same personal God. Rather, the Triune God is the actual Trinity of loving Persons in communion. But this is not just an epistemological revelation of the Triune God. Rather, the economy retroactively constitutes God's intra-divine life from eternity to eternity. To analyze the *ordo cognoscendi* of the Triune God in the economy is nothing but to explicate the *ordo essendi* of the inner life of the Triune God.

With the economy as the only normative starting point for a legitimate Trinitarian hermeneutics, this leaves us with no option but to begin our critical analysis of the doctrine of the Triune God with the Trinity of Persons and not abstract unity of God. Though the economy includes the entire action of the Triune God from creation to its consummation, the Triune God of distinct and mutual Persons, is perceived specifically in Jesus' proclamation of the kingdom, his cry of abandonment on the cross, and in human society. This "bottom up" hermeneutical approach is the antithesis of the traditional hermeneutics, which often perceives the Triune God first and foremost in *theologia* and secondarily in the economy. The divine persons are each unsubstitutable, constituted by their communal relationship with each other. Each is a *sine-qua-non* for the personality and divinity of the others. That is, the divine persons cannot truly be personal and divine apart from each other. Such an idea of mutually dependent persons of the Triune God, permeating each other without undermining the irreplaceable identity of each other, is at odds with the traditional idea that the Father alone is the source of the divine persons, an idea which not only precludes reciprocity among the divine persons, but also creates hierarchy in the life of the Triune God and thus in human and non-human cosmic society.

To obviate this danger of subordination, we have demonstrated that the personal relationship between the divine persons as revealed in the economy of salvation must be seen as reciprocal. The order, according to which the Father begets the Son and breathes the Spirit, is irreversible. But the Father does not only beget the Son and breathe the Spirit, but equally makes his deity dependent on the Son's work of establishing his kingdom in the world, and the Spirit's work of consummating the kingdom. These reciprocal relations between the divine persons, which is not seen in relations of origin, find complete expression in the economy, where the Father hands over the kingdom to the Son and the Son hands it back to the Father in final consummation, even as the Spirit creates communion between them through raising Jesus from the dead and incorporating humanity and the world into the communion. Thus, the *arche* of the Triune God is not the mere eternal rule according to which Father begets the Son and breathes the Spirit in Godself, it is the reciprocal *arche* rooted and revealed in the Jesus Christ and the Spirit in the economy which incorporates humanity and the entire world as co-partners.

The unity of the Triune God does not lie either in the commonality of the origin of the divine persons, which is the person of the Father, or their possessing identical divine nature, which is substance or singularity of divine subject in God. Such a conception of divine unity is abstract and at best monadic unity. The practical unity of the Triune God does not lie exclusively in inner perichoretic union and fellowship of the divine persons themselves. Instead, it lies in personal diversity, a real communion of these distinct persons that incorporates the whole cosmic community. The unity of the persons is communicable, integrative, and open, such that their fellowship includes humanity, history, and the whole of creation. The unity of the Triune God is an ongoing and eschatological reality.

To speak of the unity of God in Trinitarian terms is not to say that God is independent of the world or that God has no actual relationship with the world and humanity. Rather, it is to speak of the ongoing and eschatological union and fellowship that the Triune God has established with the world in Jesus and the Spirit. Humanity and the world, which are the objects of God's love, are forever incorporated into the inner united life of the Triune God, who out of loving freedom has decided in Christ and the Spirit never again to live unaccompanied, in a divine self-sufficient eternal pavilion apart from them. The Lover is forever united with his beloved, that is, the world. As an indestructible union, which has come to stay, there is nothing whatever in eternity or in time that can ever put it asunder. That is the Triune God's unbreakable promise to humanity and the world. Any unity of the Triune God that falls short of this is a non-Trinitarian unity of God!

As a final point, the new hermeneutics of the doctrine of the Triune God undertaken on this basis has radical moral consequences for Christian faith and life. It is not just a critique of all forms of abstract monotheistic understanding of God, which justify authoritarianism and hierarchy in the church and cosmic society. It is also a prototype for constructing just and egalitarian faith and political community in accordance with the vision of the non-hierarchical divine community of the Triune God. Apolitical or religious community inspired by the Triune God will develop inclusive structures in which the members have unproblematic access to its power and resources. At this juncture, we must ask what this new Trinitarian understanding of God would mean for Africa. How does it specifically transform the African tradition of community in the Nigerian context?

Notes

1 Karl Rahner, *Theological Investigations*, trans. Kevin Smyth, vol. 4 (Baltimore, MD: Helicon Press, 1961), 113.
2 Catherine Mowry LaCugna, *God for Us: The Trinity and Christian Life* (San Francisco, CA: HarperSanFrancisco, 1991), 221.
3 Wolfhart Pannenberg, *Systematic Theology*, trans. Geoffrey W. Bromiley, vol. 1 (Grand Rapids, MI: Eerdmans, 1991), 273.
4 Ibid., 300.
5 Ibid., 298.
6 Ibid., 296.
7 Jürgen Moltmann, *The Trinity and the Kingdom: The Doctrine of God*, 1st ed. (Minneapolis, MN: Fortress Press, 1993), 19.

162 *The new hermeneutics of the Trinity*

8 Ibid., 65.
9 Ibid., 64. Emphasis in the original.
10 LaCugna, *God for Us*, 22.
11 Ibid., 211. Italics in the original.
12 John Zizioulas, *Being as Communion: Studies in Personhood and the Church* (Crestwood, NY: St. Vladimir's Seminary Press, 1985), 17. Emphasis in the original.
13 In new the Trinitarian hermeneutics of the Trinity, there is no distinction between the *ordo essendi* (order of being) and the *ordo cognoscendi* (order of knowing), even though the former often precedes the latter. The two coincide and are two aspects of the same indistinguishable reality. That is to say, God in his revelation is who God is *in se* and vice versa. God exists in the *ordo essendi* as eternal Triune God, but we come to know God in the *ordo cognoscendi* through his economy. In the *ordo cognoscendi*, our analysis of the economy of God is often linked to the immanent life of God in the *ordo essendi* from eternity.
14 LaCugna, *God for Us*, 223. Italics in the original.
15 Leonardo Boff, *Trinity and Society*, trans. Paul Burns (Eugene, OR: Wipf & Stock Publishers, 1988), 95.
16 Moltmann, *The Trinity and the Kingdom*, 161; Pannenberg, *Systematic Theology*, 329.
17 Pannenberg, *Systematic Theology*, 259–63.
18 Ibid., 308.
19 Ibid., 310.
20 Ibid., 264.
21 Ibid., 267.
22 Ibid., 272.
23 Ibid., 335–6.
24 Moltmann, *The Trinity and the Kingdom*, 22. Emphasis in the original.
25 Ibid., 31.
26 Ibid., 81.
27 Ibid., 161.
28 Ibid., 83.
29 Ibid., 80.
30 Ibid. The question of the death of God is a difficult dilemma to resolve. This is because in the Trinity, the Son is not God in isolation from the Father and the Spirit, but in communion with them. Thus, the word "God" could be used to refer to a particular person of the Trinity as well as entire persons of the Triune God or the unity of their communion. As a result, the death of God may mean either the death of the God the Son alone or the whole of the Triune God or the breakdown of the unity of their communion. The last option appears to be most plausible solution to the dilemma.
31 Pannenberg, *Systematic Theology*, 314.
32 Ibid. Italics in the original.
33 Ibid., 315.
34 Moltmann, *The Trinity and the Kingdom*, 56.
35 Boff, *Trinity and Society*, 118.
36 Ibid., 119. Emphasis in the original.
37 Ibid., 6–7.
38 Ibid., 120.
39 Ibid., 118.
40 LaCugna, *God for Us*, 301. Italics in the original.
41 Ibid., 243.
42 John Zizioulas, *Communion and Otherness: Further Studies in Personhood and the Church*, ed. Paul McPartlan (London: T&T Clark, 2006), 5.
43 Moltmann, The *Trinity and the Kingdom*, 172.

The new hermeneutics of the Trinity 163

44 Ibid.
45 Ibid., 173.
46 Pannenberg, *Systematic Theology*, 320.
47 Ted Peters, *God as Trinity: Relationality and Temporality in Divine Life* (Louisville, KY: Westminster/John Knox Press, 1993), 138. Emphasis in the original.
48 Ibid. Emphasis in the original.
49 Pannenberg, *Systematic Theology*, 319.
50 Zizioulas, *Being as Communion*, 16. Italics in the original.
51 Ibid., 41.
52 Zizioulas, *Communion and Otherness*, 154.
53 Zizioulas, *Being as Communion*, 46.
54 Ibid.
55 Zizioulas, *Communion and Otherness*, 122.
56 Ibid., 123.
57 Ibid., 137–40.
58 Moltmann, *The Trinity and the Kingdom*, 165.
59 Ibid., 166.
60 Ibid., 92–3. Emphasis in the original.
61 Though Moltmann categorically claims the doctrine of the Trinity challenges political and clerical monotheism, which promote political or patriarchal domination and ecclesiastical hierarchy, the absence of reciprocity from his ontology of relations of origin in God calls into question his Trinitarian critique of political or patriarchal and ecclesiastical absolutism.
62 Pannenberg, *Systematic Theology*, 322–3.
63 Veli-Matti Kärkkäinen, *The Trinity: Global Perspectives* (Louisville, KY: Westminster John Knox Press, 2007), 121.
64 Boff, *Trinity and Society*, 121.
65 Ibid., 146.
66 LaCugna, *God for Us*, 276. Italics in the original.
67 Ibid., 400.
68 Ibid., 398. Emphasis in the original.
69 Ibid., 354.
70 Ibid., 399. Italics in the original.
71 Ibid., 400. Emphasis in the original.
72 Pannenberg, *Systematic Theology*, 303f.
73 Ibid., 311–12. Emphasis in the original.
74 Ibid., 319.
75 Ibid., 312.
76 Ibid., 313.
77 Ibid.
78 Ibid., 315.
79 Ibid., 320.
80 Ibid., 324.
81 Ibid., 325.
82 Zizioulas, *Being as Communion*, 40–1.
83 Zizioulas, *Communion and Otherness*, 5.
84 Ibid., 159.
85 Thomas Aquinas, *The "Summa Theologica" of St. Thomas Aquinas*, trans. Fathers of the English Domican Province, 2 ed., vol. 1 (London: Burns Oates & Washbourne, 1920), 1, 28, 2.
86 Karl Barth, "The Doctrine of the Word of God," in *Church Dogmatics*, ed. Geoffrey William Bromiley and Thomas F. Torrance, vol. 1 (London: T&T Clark International, 2004), 353.

164 *The new hermeneutics of the Trinity*

87 The comprehensive debate about whether or not the Triune God "needs" the world and humanity to be one is certainly a larger issue beyond the scope of this book. At any rate, as we shall see later in this chapter, the idea of divine need is used in the new Trinitarian theology to contradict the abstract classical doctrine of God, which claims that the unity of God is self-sufficient in and of itself devoid of the world and humanity. The Triune God's need for the world and humanity does not imply that God is deficient; rather, it is the need that springs from God's superabundance and overflowing love.

88 Barth, "The Doctrine of the Word of God," 354.

89 Moltmann, *The Trinity and the Kingdom*, 19.

90 Ibid., 96.

91 Ibid., 150.

92 Ibid., 157, 175.

93 Ibid., 175.

94 Boff, *Trinity and Society*, 150.

95 Ibid., 128.

96 LaCugna, *God for Us*, 272.

97 Ibid., 228. LaCugna contends that though the philosophical evidence for translating the word "perichoresis" as "the divine dance" is scarce, the use of that metaphor is effective in expressing the unity of the Triune as persons in communion. See ibid., 271–2.

98 Ibid., 270.

99 Moltmann, *The Trinity and the Kingdom*, 149. Emphasis in the original.

100 Boff, *Trinity and Society*, 3.

101 Ibid., 227.

102 As cited in Kärkkäinen, *The Trinity*, 106.

103 As we will see later, God is free not to create in Godself, but having created the world, God's freedom consists in God's relationship with the world. The loving God, who does not respond to the loving response of humanity (by which humanity loves God in return through serving the neighbor and the whole creation), is a bound, and not a free God. In fact, it's in this reciprocal response that God impacts and is impacted by the world and humanity.

104 Moltmann, *The Trinity and the Kingdom*, 98. The Triune God takes delight in having a reciprocal relationship with the world and humanity. This is the mystery of the incarnation and the cross, which, though real, continues to elude our human understanding! As a delightful reciprocal exchange, the Triune God in Christ and the Spirit takes on the sin of the whole of the world in return in order to bestow God's own righteousness on humanity and the world.

105 Ibid., 58.

106 LaCugna, *God for Us*, 228. Emphasis in the original.

107 Ibid.

108 Ibid. Italics in the original.

109 Pannenberg, *Systematic Theology*, 446.

110 Ibid., 447.

111 Ibid., 385.

112 Ibid., 332. It is very important to know that, unlike Moltmann, who rejects the use of the traditional concept of essence to express the unity of God, Pannenberg does not, but rather, he recasts it in terms of relational category.

113 Ibid., 329.

114 Ibid., 331.

115 Moltmann, *The Trinity and the Kingdom*, 126; Pannenberg, *Systematic Theology*, 330.

116 Moltmann, *The Trinity and the Kingdom*, 161.

117 Kärkkäinen, *The Trinity*, 112.

118 LaCugna, *God for Us*, 228.

119 Ibid., 1.
120 Ibid.
121 Moltmann, *The Trinity and the Kingdom*, 201.
122 Ibid., 202. Italics in the original.
123 LaCugna, *God for Us*, 16.
124 Moltmann, *The Trinity and the Kingdom*, 198.
125 Boff, *Trinity and Society*, 151.
126 Ibid.
127 LaCugna, *God for Us*, 398.
128 Ibid., 394.
129 Jürgen Moltmann, *God for a Secular Society: The Public Relevance of Theology* (Minneapolis, MN: Fortress Press, 1999), 132–3.

Bibliography

Aquinas, Thomas. *The "Summa Theologica" of St. Thomas Aquinas*. Translated by Fathers of the English Domican Province. 2 ed. Vol. 1. London: Burns Oates & Washbourne, 1920.

Barth, Karl. "The Doctrine of the Word of God." In *Church Dogmatics*, edited by Geoffrey William Bromiley and Thomas F. Torrance. Vol. 1. London: T&T Clark International, 2004.

Boff, Leonardo. *Trinity and Society*. Translated by Paul Burns. Eugene, OR: Wipf & Stock Publishers, 1988.

Kärkkäinen, Veli-Matti. *The Trinity: Global Perspectives*. Louisville, KY: Westminster John Knox Press, 2007.

LaCugna, Catherine Mowry. *God for Us: The Trinity and Christian Life*. San Francisco, CA: HarperSanFrancisco, 1991.

Moltmann, Jürgen. *God for a Secular Society: The Public Relevance of Theology*. Minneapolis, MN: Fortress Press, 1999.

———. *The Trinity and the Kingdom: The Doctrine of God*. 1st ed. Minneapolis, MN: Fortress Press, 1993.

Pannenberg, Wolfhart. *Systematic Theology*. Translated by Geoffrey W.Bromiley. Vol. 1. Grand Rapids, MI: Eerdmans, 1991.

Peters, Ted. *God as Trinity: Relationality and Temporality in Divine Life*. Louisville, KY: Westminster/John Knox Press, 1993.

Rahner, Karl. *Theological Investigations*. Translated by Kevin Smyth. Vol. 4. Baltimore, MD: Helicon Press, 1961.

Zizioulas, John. *Being as Communion: Studies in Personhood and the Church*. Crestwood, NY: St. Vladimir's Seminary Press, 1985.

———. *Communion and Otherness: Further Studies in Personhood and the Church*. Edited by Paul McPartlan. London: T&T Clark, 2006.

5 An authentic African tradition of community

In Chapters 1 and 2, I related the Trinitarian relationality to the African concept of community, and critiqued forces destructive of genuine African community: the patriarchal complex, the Big Man syndrome, and ethno-religious nepotism. In this final chapter, I seek to recast the expression of the African spirit of community (in church and society) from these forces, and recast it according to the liberating gift of the Triune God. Drawing on the new Trinitarian hermeneutics, I will argue that the Triune God's perichoretic (mutual interpenetrating) gift of communing and transforming humanity and all of creation frees and empowers Africans to accompany the Triune God in liberating the African community from its systemic problems. Here there is a fusion of horizons between the recasting of the African tradition of community and the new Trinitarian hermeneutics of God. Rather than critiquing the African community, the new Trinitarian hermeneutics emphasizes that the Triune God frees Africa from structural evils.

In the first part of this chapter, I will explore Martin Luther's Eucharistic theology and the perichoretic life of the Triune God, showing how the Triune God shares and communicates the divine perichoretic life through the Eucharist with humanity and the cosmic community. In parts two, three, and four, I will indicate how the new Trinitarian hermeneutics of Triune God might rescue the African expression of community from the patriarchal complex, the Big Man syndrome, and ethnic and religious nepotism. In the fifth part, I will develop a perichoretic approach to theological education as an emancipatory practice for rescuing and recasting the African concept of community.

The Lord's supper and the perichoretic life of God

In Chapter 4, I argued that the new hermeneutics of the Trinity is not simply abstract speculation about the inner life of the Triune God, but it is rather the relational perichoretic character of the Triune God incarnated with radical social implications. But still missing is how this perichoretic life of the Triune God is shared and communicated to us so that we might live out its social implications in real life.

Many of the developers of the new Trinitarian hermeneutics of God perceive the persons of the Triune God simply as a moral, ideal model of divine community that we are to live up to in church and society. This becomes a new law, which

Authentic African tradition of community 167

cannot be fulfilled faithfully by Christians, thereby leading them to despair. But perceiving God's perichoretic communion as a promising gift (which they can grasp by the grace of Christ in the power of the Spirit), abolishes the demand and thus the despair. The perceptions of the Triune God's perichoretic communion as a gift does not accomplish this, but the persons of the Triune God themselves, deep in their communion, do so. As a gift themselves, the persons of the Triune God in their superabundant fellowship with humanity and the world accomplished by Christ on the cross and bestowed by the Spirit at Pentecost liberate and empower Christians to faithfully live out God's own perichoretic life in real-life situations.

The perichoretic life of the Triune God, which does not exclude but includes humanity and the world, is communicated sacramentally to us in the Eucharist in, under and through the bread and wine. Whenever we partake of the bread and wine, a communion which Luther calls "*synaxis*" in his 1519 essay "The Blessed Sacrament of the Holy and True Body and Blood of Christ, and the Brotherhoods," is enacted between God in Christ and the Spirit and us. As a result, Luther argues, "all the spiritual possessions of Christ and his saints are shared with and become the common property of [the one] who receives this sacrament."[1] He claims that the Eucharist is a tangible, effective sign from God that we are not only united with Christ and his all saints, but also that we possess everything in common with them, including their lives and sufferings. But this is more than only a Christological communion; it is a Trinitarian one, for in the Holy Communion, the Triune God communicates God's entire perichoretic life to us, communing with us in Christ and the Spirit, drawing humanity and the world into the eschatological kingdom. The whole of creation, which is the fruit of God's abundant love and freedom, shares in the Trinitarian communion.

Human and non-human realities are, therefore, equal partakers of God's life of communion. Though non-human realities share in this communion passively, they are not excluded from it. In a way, they share it through humanity, which has been entrusted with the responsibility to care and preserve them from human destruction. As God's earthly means of sustaining us both physically and spiritually, our participation in the Eucharist is a call to care for neighbor and to preserve the whole of creation, without which this sustenance is sacramentally impossible. Such perichoretic Trinitarian communion that takes place in the Eucharist is an ongoing and eschatological reality. As a Trinitarian communion, the Eucharist is not only the exclusive celebration of God's communion with the church, but also an inclusive eschatological celebration of God's ongoing communion with the whole of creation, "for where you eat and drink of this cup, you proclaim the Lord's death until he comes" (1 Cor. 11:26).

Thus, Christ institutes the celebration of the Eucharist as a public event. In his 1526 essay "The Sacrament of the Body and Blood of Christ – Against the Fanatics," Luther contends that the proclamation of the Eucharist is not to be done privately among Christians alone. "Rather, it is to be done publicly before the multitude, for those who do not know of it," that is, in order that they might come to know and participate in it.[2] There is thus a missionary dimension and dynamic to the Eucharist.

168   *Authentic African tradition of community*

Such Trinitarian hermeneutics of the Eucharist also revolutionizes our understanding of the real presence of Christ in the bread and wine. The incarnation is a historical event with retrospective impact. That is, the incarnation has introduced human nature into the inner life of the Triune God. The Triune God forever is impacted by the incarnation of the Son, as evident in God's perichoretic unity with humanity. Thus, on the account of the hermeneutics of the perichoretic divine unity, it is not Christ alone who is really present in, with, and under the sacrament of the Eucharist, but also the entire Trinitarian communion of God. The Triune God is actually present in the bread and wine of the Eucharist through Christ in the power of the Spirit. In other words, Christ is not present in the Eucharist apart from the Father and the Spirit.

Such communal presence of the Triune God in the bread and wine shows that the Triune God is not an abstract God detached from humanity and the world, but rather, the Triune God is intrinsically bound to humanity and the world as a whole, and thus, indwells them. The Triune God is "habitable." As Luther notes, God inhabits and is inhabited by humanity and the world through the Eucharist. When we say, sacramentally speaking, that *created things* are capable of containing the infinite, we do not simply mean that bread and wine are capable of being indwelt by the Triune God, but also that the efficacious redemptive benefit of the Eucharist is infinite and communicated. That is, the Holy Communion is not just proclamation of the forgiveness of our personal sin and that of the church. It is the proclamation of the forgiveness of the sin of the whole world. This sin certainly includes every systemic evil or egoism that destroys the flourishing of human and spiritual community. Luther argues,

> The blessing of this sacrament is fellowship and love, by which we are strengthened against death and all evil. . . . Thus by means of this sacrament, all self-seeking love is rooted out and gives place to that which seeks the common good of all; and through the change wrought by love there is one bread, one drink, one body, one community.[3]

All structural evils that cause any forms of social division and oppression among humanity are defeated at table of the Eucharist. Those who participate in the Eucharist experience individual and collective transformation, a transformation that spurs them to live for, in, and with the needy neighbor and the world that groan for redemption. As we share in God's perichoretic gift through the sacrament of the Eucharist, the Triune God empowers us through the Word to live out the social implications in every sphere of our human life. It is against this backdrop that the new Trinitarian project of recasting the practice of the African community from systemic problems can be appreciated. Thus, we, unlike other African theologians, are not calling for contextualization according to the Bible so to speak, but re-contextualization of the divine and human African community according to God's gift of Triune communion to which the Bible bears witness.

This re-contextualization is the Triune God's act of restoring humanity and all of creation spiritually and materially to a shared perichoretic life where

Authentic African tradition of community 169

forgiveness, peace, justice, and freedom reign on earth as in heaven. The Triune God has started this re-contextualization in Christ through the Spirit on the cross. This transformation is not just a past historical event; it is indeed an experiential and eschatological reality. In fact, it is the in-breaking of the future of the Triune God into the present African community and the whole world!

The Triune God is the starting point of this re-contextualization. Though the re-contextualization is entirely the work of the Triune God, God does not desire to do it apart from us, or else St Paul would not have wasted his time and resources going about preaching this gospel of transformation. As Luther submits in his *The Bondage of the Will*, God

> does not work in us without us, because he has created and preserved us that he might work in us and we might cooperate with him, whether outside his Kingdom through his general omnipotence or inside his Kingdom by the special virtue of his Spirit.[4]

In other words, salvaging the African community from systemic problems and distortions is the work of the Triune God, which African Christians are able to share in by the power of the Spirit. They participate in this transforming gift as part of the overarching mission of the Triune God in the world.

Dismantling the patriarchal complex

The Trinitarian communion of the Triune God provides a solid and down-to-earth foundation for liberating the African tradition of community from the patriarchal ideology. Dismantling the patriarchal complex is inexorably bound with liberation of the patriarchal hermeneutics of God. The patriarchal African community cannot be radically transformed into non-patriarchal community in Africa unless Africans completely transform their perception of God. In as much as they continue to perceive God in patriarchal terms, male-female relationships will continue to be patterned along a patriarchal model that embraces patriarchy as divine injunction. Such perceptions of God, which often divinize masculinity, distances femininity from God. As Michelle A. Gonzalez argues, "As long as God is imaged exclusively as male, men will be viewed as closer to the divine. Exclusively male God-language divinizes masculinity."[5] But the new Trinitarian hermeneutics of God rooted in Christ and the Spirit shows the Triune God is not gender-prejudiced, but rather, a gender-inclusive God. As the hermeneutics that affirms an all-encompassing perception of God, the Trinitarian communion of God rescues any African patriarchal conception of God that sanctions the domination of men over women. It calls for an inclusive perception of God that embraces feminine perceptions of the Triune God. This does not mean that human perception of God should be impersonal. Rather, feminine personal perceptions of God should be viewed just as valid as the male perceptions of God. The masculine naming of God should not be absolutized, but remain open to be enriched and transformed by the feminine personal appellations of God. The Trinitarian communion of God liberates

170 *Authentic African tradition of community*

men and women from the legacy of African community, which justifies hierarchy among genders and affirms patriarchy as the right order of divine creation.

Second, the Triune God cures the patriarchal infection by overturning every religious assumption that subordinates the piety of women to men in Africa. The Triune God rooted in Christ and the Spirit affirms that every human being who is saved by grace through faith is a priest. As priests, men and women who are baptized, regardless of their sex, race and vocation, not only have direct access to the Triune God through Christ in the Spirit without the aid of human intermediary, but also they are co-heirs with Christ with equal rights to inherit every spiritual and material blessing, and to intercede for themselves and for others before God. Thus, the patriarchal hermeneutics of God, which perceives men as the divine archetype through which women could live religious lives only by submitting to the shackles of male domination, contradicts this scriptural witness to the priesthood of all believers. To liberate the African community from the legacy of patriarchy is to rescue the community from the popular religious belief that measures women's religiosity in terms of their absolute submission to men. To rescue men from the patriarchal oppression of women in Africa is to challenge them to rethink the male-dominated hermeneutics of God that often privileged them over women. Therefore, the assumption that determines the faith of woman by her absolute submission to man in marriage and society is false and idolatrous.

Third, to recast the African patriarchal notion of community into a community free from the patriarchal complex, I argue for the new Trinitarian deconstruction of patriarchal biblical hermeneutics that appeals to the Scriptures to justify male supremacy in the church and society. The Scriptures have often been utilized to endorse patriarchal evil, upholding male ascendancy and female oppression. This Trinitarian deconstruction of the patriarchal hermeneutics of the Scriptures calls for reinterpreting Scriptural texts. Patriarchy is removed from the lens of the Trinitarian communion of God. Scriptural texts that are shaped and constructed from the patriarchal point of view are to be critiqued and recast in light of an "unpatriarchal" Trinitarian communion that dismantles, rather than empowers, patriarchal structures. I, therefore, concur with Oduyoye, who contends:

> We cannot use scripture *any more* to legitimize the non-inclusion of femaleness in the norm of humanness. To be authentic, Christian *new Trinitarian* theology *of God* must promote the independence of distinctive beings and stand by the principles of inclusiveness and independence *of women.*[6]

The most important question to raise in this Trinitarian hermeneutics of deconstruction is not what the Scriptures say about patriarchy, but rather, what the Triune God, to which the Scriptures bear witness, accomplished over and against patriarchy.[7] What the Triune God has accomplished in Christ and the Spirit is the normative parameter for deconstructing patriarchal biblical texts, which are often used to dehumanize women within and outside the church. The Triune God has inaugurated in Christ a new perichoretic human household in society that is a healthier alternative home to a patriarchal household. This perichoretic new household not only celebrates and embraces diversity, but is rooted in reciprocity rather than dominance, in equal partnership rather than hierarchy and, most importantly, in mutual love rather than fear between men and women.

Thus, pseudo-Pauline patriarchal male-privilege discourses imploring a husband to love his wife and the wife to submit to her husband should not be interpreted to mean definitive and exclusive roles, as though love and submission are diametrically opposed to each other in marriage. Having reciprocal obligations, a husband and wife should mutually love and respond to each other in accordance with the gift and paradigm of the perichoretic new household of God. In this perichoretic household, men do not rule over women or in isolation from them. God rules this new household by making room for human collaboration inclusive of men, women, and all who are oppressed. Seen in this light, the egalitarian familial order of the relationship between man and woman as equal partners replaces every hierarchical relationship in the African family and in the larger community that sees the man as the boss and the head, while the woman is the servant and the follower.

Fourth, the deconstruction of male-privileged biblical narratives alone cannot rescue the African tradition of community from the patriarchal syndrome. There is also need to deconstruct the distinction of social gender roles between men and women that are culturally and socially constructed and transmitted through socialization, but are often endorsed by the church and society as divine order. To the extent that the rigid social gender roles used to empower men and to suppress women remain unchallenged, the African communal tradition cannot be liberated from the patriarchal complex. Though in some ways, men and women may embody enduring distinct sexual identities, the distinct social gender roles assigned to them by the society are not fixed, and thus changeable. As these functional gender roles are matters of nurture rather than nature, they ought to be relativized to embrace perichoretic mutuality, shared responsibility, and democratic decision-making between genders in keeping with the perichoretic life of the Triune God. Assigning greater responsibility and near absolute power to the African male over against the African female in the family, church, and the society in virtue of their distinct genital embodiment is unjust and life-denying for women as people created in the image of the Triune God. Therefore, shared humanity, mutual dialogue, negotiation, and consensus, not the human genital embodiment, which the African male acquires by chance, should be the basis of sharing power and responsibility between men and women both within and outside the family.

Finally, the Triune God calls for living out under the inspiration of the Spirit the gender-inclusive perichoretic life of the Triune God in the church and society. To live out the gender-inclusive life of the Triune God is to struggle for gender-inclusive power structures in the church, government, private and public corporations in Africa. To live out the gender-inclusive life of the Triune God means also to stage a public protest against harmful cultural patriarchal practices that dehumanize and oppress African women. The African church and society that truly lives out the gender-inclusive life of the Triune God will respect and defend gender equality as an inalienable right of every human being. In other words, the African community can only claim to be liberated from patriarchal sin through living out the gender-inclusive life of the Triune God when it confesses and repents of the injustice committed against women on the basis of their innate sexual and childbearing roles. Therefore, the Trinitarian communion of God is an inspiration for women to become "social deviants," as the saying goes, subverting not only every traditional patriarchal norm that impinges on their rights, but also demanding attitudinal and structural changes in the family, church, and society that affirm the right and dignity of the body and humanity of women.

Because the liberation of women from patriarchal oppression is intertwined with the liberation of the earth from patriarchal domination, I argue for the liberation of the ecosystems in Africa from the patriarchal degradation perpetrated by human beings who assume a dominant position over the creation. As such, the Trinitarian communion of God entails a view of stewardship, rather than ownership, of creation. This understanding of the Trinitarian God calls for ecological and environmental justice, care, conservation, and protection against harmful human consumer practices for the sake of women and posterity.

African church and society cannot be truly non-patriarchal in the fashion of the Triune God without a balanced ecosystem. This is because any imbalance in the ecosystem exacerbates the exploitation and oppression of women. As R. R. Ruether argues, the domination of women and of nature in the Third World is inexorably linked. The impoverishment of the latter invariably entails the impoverishment of the former and vice versa. "Deforestation," for example, "means women walk twice and three times as long each day gathering wood; it means drought, which means women walk twice and three times farther each day to find and carry water back to their huts."[8] This is a clear-cut daily reality of the vast majority of African rural women. Thus, unless nature is truly liberated from the undue Big Human exploitation, the oppression of these women by men is bound to persist both in church and society.

The true Big Man: newariga diksen

I previously explored how the Big Man syndrome infiltrates and impacts African church and society, obstructing the realization of the spirit of African community. This syndrome is not part of the legacy of the African tradition of community, but rather, it is the legacy of colonialism perpetuated today by African Big Men/ Women. Therefore, recasting the African tradition of community via the gift of the perichoretic communion of the Triune God calls for salvaging the community from the Big Man syndrome. The new Trinitarian hermeneutics of God is essential in this.

The hermeneutics of the Triune God, who in Christ and the Spirit completely communes with the world and humanity, especially with those who exist at the margins, enlightens us to recognize how the true Big Man operates in such a way that is consistent with the perichoretic life of the Triune God. It is not the new Trinitarian hermeneutics of God that helps to understand a true Big Man, but the

Authentic African tradition of community 173

Triune God in communion, who illuminates our hearts and minds in Christ and the Spirit to understand the true Big Man. The new Trinitarian hermeneutics of God is simply our human attempt to perceive and articulate the authentic character of this authentic Big Man/Woman, based on the biblical witness to God and God's image in human being. This witness shows that the authentic Big Man is God in God's own Triune communion as rooted in Jesus Christ, who, being in the form of God, did not consider equality with God something to be grasped, but emptied himself, taking the form of a servant with us (Phil. 2:6–7).

As authentic Big Persons, the Triune God did not take the form of a slave in order to exercise typical sovereign lordship. Rather, as "the Son of Man," the Triune God rooted in Christ "did not come to be served, but to serve, and to give his life as a ransom for many" (Mk. 10:45). Challenging his disciples, who argued among themselves about who should be first (that is, the Big Man of the group), Jesus said that the true Big Man is not a lord or king who uses coercive power to oppress and maintain dominance over their subjects, but the servant who serves the people: "whoever wants to become great among you must be your servant" (Mk. 10:44). This does not mean that the Triune God assumes a form of slave to become master-servant in Christ for humanity to imitate. According to D.E. Fredrickson, the trouble with this moral theory of imitating divine self-limitation is that it

> [s]ets a moral standard of humility before the poor and marginalized, which they are, structurally, never able to live up to but to which they perpetually are held accountable by those who have power and privilege and who have comforted their own consciences by telling tales of sacrifice in the imitation of the obedience of the Son of God.[9]

Indeed, all our human attempts at imitating the example of the Triune God's servanthood will inescapably end in despair and failure; we do not have the *will* to imitate God's apart from divine grace. But God took the form of servant in and with us through Christ that we might be made true servants of God and neighbor in the power of the Spirit. In doing this, the Triune God has inaugurated a new community of humanity where the members are mutual servants of each other. Instead of exercising authoritarian lordship over humanity, the Triune God as the authentic Big Persons in communion, does the opposite, that is, God sets us free from egoism and hubris in order that we may serve God through serving our neighbor. That is exactly who a true Big Man/Woman is, for he or she does not lord absolute power over the people, but freely and reciprocally liberates, empowers and serves the people rather than self as a gift of the Triune God's liberating perichoretic communion. The true Big Man/Woman is thus at the same time a free lord and a dutiful servant.

Luther explicated this revolutionary understanding of the true Big Man, that is, a lord, in his 1520 treatise "The Freedom of a Christian." Here he contends that the Christian is not just "a perfectly free lord of all," but also "a perfectly

174 *Authentic African tradition of community*

dutiful servant of all." He argues that though the Christian is lord, that is, Big Man through justification by faith alone in Christ, the Christian is also servant to their neighbor. As Luther writes,

> Although the Christian is thus free from all works, he ought in this liberty to empty himself, [and] take upon himself the form of a servant . . . to serve, help, and in every way deal with his neighbor as he sees that God through Christ has dealt and still deals with him."[10]

As a servant, Luther argues that justification by faith inspires a Christian who is a true Big Man not to serve oneself, but the neighbor. That is to say, delivering love and justice to the neighbor is a measure as well as a way of life for a true Big Man/Woman. He writes,

> A Christian lives not in himself, but in Christ and in his neighbor. Otherwise, he is not a Christian. He lives in Christ through faith, in his neighbor through love. By faith he is caught up beyond himself into God. By love he descends beneath himself into his neighbor.[11]

Suffice it to say that Trinitarian communion of God transforms the position of the true Big Man from the highest stratum of the society to its lowest echelon. This paradoxical position of the true Big Man as a servant at the margin of the society can rightly be expressed in the Nigerian context by the Chamba[12] metaphor "newariga diksen," which literally means, "Big Man is a garbage site." Though the adage may sound weird and even offensive to a Western audience, it is wise counsel that is often given to a newly elected or appointed leader in northern Nigeria. Unpacking what "garbage site" is and its characteristics in Africa is crucial for unearthing the significance of the metaphor in question. "Garbage site" is usually a place at the fringes of the house or the village where unwanted household wastes are dumped. As a dumping ground, garbage site is first and foremost always open, not just to accept all kinds of trash, but is open to every member of the household and the community who want to dispose of their trash. Therefore, the garbage site is accessible and an un-discriminating site.

Second, though some garbage constitutes a hazard to the environment, other garbage is an invaluable source of nutrients. The decomposed compost garbage materials that accumulate over time can be used as fertilizer to enrich the productivity of the soil. As fertile ground, the garbage or its decomposing waste materials are used to grow the crops, which supply the food on which the household and the village depend daily for survival. Thus, garbage site is a source of livelihood and empowerment. As such, it is not uncommon to see the poor, homeless, and the most vulnerable members of the community sifting through the garbage for valuable materials, which they may find and sell to middle men who recycle them at local factories. The garbage site is the place that provides hope for the hopeless and those who exist at the margins of the society.

Authentic African tradition of community 175

As a final characteristic, the garbage site is not a natural place. That is, it does not just occur. It is the members of the household and the community who create garbage for their benefit. As a human-made place, though the garbage site often stinks, it provides an essential service to the community, a space where waste materials, which would have littered and polluted the community and environment, are discarded to keep the community healthy and clean, and thus a mark of godliness. As a "servant," garbage site serves the community by dialectically bearing the burdens of not only its cleanliness, but also its filthiness. Hence, the expression "newariga diksen."

In effect, the garbage site of the society is the preferential locus of God's presence in the midst of God's own people in the world, and to neglect such a location is to neglect Godself. The Triune God as constituted in Christ and the Spirit relocates the position of the true Big Man/Woman from the most exalted corridors of power to the "diksen" of the society as the appropriate locus of their vocation. The relocation turns the garbage site of the society to a seat of service and not a place of domination, because it is where the true Big Man/Woman shares their power and authority to serve with the marginalized people. As a result, the pyramidal hierarchy that distances the true Big Man/Woman from the people is dismantled and becomes a level ground. It is at the "diksen" that the true Big Man/Woman can access and be accessible to all victims of injustice, such as the poor, outcasts, and oppressed, who groan daily for freedom at the fringes of the society. Such an encounter avails the Big Man/Woman of the opportunity to experience the pain of those at the margins of the society and to work with them for their total liberation. The liberation that occurs at this site is total not just because it embraces the oppressor and the oppressed, but because it is the climax of liberation. There is no other liberation left beyond the one taking place at this garbage site of the society. It is both experiential and eschatological liberation.

As the servant and not lord of the people, the Triune God also empowers the authentic Big Man/Woman to bear the burden of the people as a gift of the Triune God at the garbage site of the society. Bonhoeffer argues,

> God is a God who bears. The Son of God bore our flesh. He therefore bore the cross. He bore all our sins and attained reconciliation by his bearing. That is why disciples are called to bear what is put on them.[13]

As the Triune God bears the burden of our sin, brokenness, and suffering with Christ in the Spirit, so a true Big Man/Woman is to bear the suffering, criticisms, and problems of the people. The true Big Man/Woman, who is "diksen," is called to bear rather than to inflict injustice on the people. To bear injustice not only is to eschew committing injustice, but also to bear the burden for administering justice and mercy. The authentic Big Man/Woman is to bear the burden of executing distributive justice as the gift of God's perichoretic communion. The bigness of the person in power is not about using the state power and resources to advance one's own rule and glory, but rather, it is about bearing the burden of serving with

176 *Authentic African tradition of community*

the people and liberating them from systemic problems that oppress and infringe on their fundamental human rights. As a "diksen," the authentic Big Man/Woman is to empower the weak and the homeless and to give hope to the hopeless and the vulnerable members of the society. The concern of the authentic Big Man/ Woman should not be how to take advantage of the people, but how to promote their well-being.

The implications of the gift of true communion of the Triune God with humanity as it impacts the Big Man syndrome in Africa is enormous. First, Africa needs to cultivate and practice a perichoretic Big Man/Woman system of leadership in which victims of injustice and oppression are engaged fully in making policy decisions. Referring to such perichoretic leadership as the "participatory golden rule," Gary Simpson argues,

> Decision makers must be consequence takers; and vice versa, consequence takers must decision makers. Those who bear the impovering, dispossessing consquences of economic [and political] policy must be full participants with an effective voice in decision-making processes, procedures and bodies.[14]

To have an effective voice in decission-making in a democractic setting like Nigeria is to let the voice and choice of the people rather than the Big Man/Woman prevail in making public policies and deciding who should govern. This requires transparent, free, and fair elections and meticulous obedience to the rule of law, which gurantees the inalienable human rights of the people. The situation where the voice of the Big Man/Woman in power often dominates every public policy decision and the choice of who should lead the people are the antithesis of a participatory perichoretic system of governance.

Second, the true meaning of the authentic Big Man/Woman as "newariga diksen" calls for reviewing and effective eliminating of existing laws that either promote or aid and abet the Big Man/Woman syndrome in Nigeria.[15] One such law that is overdue for review is the immunity law, which not only absolutizes the power of the elected executives, but also protects them from any criminal and civic charges in a court of law while in office, no matter the criminal and civic misconduct they commit. Hence, Nigerian legislators need to remove the immunity clause as enshrined in the 1999 constitution. The current penalties for corruption, economic, and financial crimes are also not strict enough and out of step with the scale of these crimes. For instance, the present punishment for corruption and financial and economic crimes is between two and seven years of imprisonment.[16] In contrast, these white-collar crimes must carry a sentence of life imprisonment or capital punishment. Last but not least in weight, strong laws are urgently needed that guarantee the existence of a truly independent and incorruptible judiciary, that is, a judiciary that enforces the laws dealing with high-profile corruption, and economic and financial crimes without interference from the executive branch of the government. The current laws, which subordinate the judiciary to the executive branch, need to be repealed. A new law should be made to provide for the institutional and financial independence of the judiciary.

Finally, living out what the Trinitarian communion of God means is that the church in Africa needs to relocate itself from its comfort zone to the garbage site of society to break bread and share wine with the homeless, the poor, and the oppressed. Such relocation of the church will spur the church leadership not only to distance itself from the Big Men/Women, but also reclaim its critical prophetic voice. As God's earthly means of publicity, church leaders can now be in a better place to speak the truth in love that will unsettle the powers that inflict oppression and injustice on the African people. Their critical prophetic admonishment will instill in the political leaders fear of God that is not just the beginning of wisdom, but also the pillar of just and incorruptible rule.

This critical prophetic publicity is necessary because, despite God's rule over the earth through secular law, human beings (and particularly, ministers of the Word) must carry out God's critical engagement with rulers. As Gary Simpson rightly argues,

> [W]hile publicity's rebuke comes from God, God does not work immediately, but rather, through earthly means. God rebukes "mediatedly." In this sense, publicity is the vehicle that instills the fear of the Lord, which is the beginning of wisdom and wise politics.[17]

But only church leaders with impeccable moral integrity and incorruptible lifestyles will be able to stand in God's congregation, exercise such critical authority of divine publicity, and be heard. As Luther implores bishops and preachers hesitant to rebuke secular rulers:

> Observe, however, that a preacher by whom God rebukes the gods is to "stand in the congregation." He is to "stand"; that is, he is to be firm and confident and deal uprightly and honestly with it; and "in the congregation," that is, openly and boldly before God and people.[18]

For Luther, unless the Word puts secular leaders to death and raise them to newness of life in Christ, they cannot be made authentic Big Men/Women.

Since Africa is a multi-party state, unless church leaders steer clear of partisan politics, they cannot remain at the vanguard of critical divine publicity. Though maintaining political neutrality does not prevent church leaders from voting for any candidate of their choice during elections, no clergy involved in partisan politics can have the "objective" voice to speak *with* and *for* God and the voiceless. When they speak, the Big Men/Women in power can easily misconstrue their prophetic voice as merely the voice of political opposition. But there is a clear-cut difference between the two voices; unlike the voice of the opposition, which is politically biased and subjective, and meant to seize the political power of the state, the critical prophetic public voice of church leaders is politically engaged yet does not seek to rule directly. Rather, it intends to deracinate systemic evil in the entire political system that undercuts good governance, justice, and rule of law.

178   *Authentic African tradition of community*

As a dangerous prophetic enterprise, public prophetic resistance of the powers of injustice and corruption no doubt will provoke a stiff reaction and persecution from the powers that be and the church itself. It will also cost precious time, money, relationships, and maybe even the life of church leaders. Only church leaders and members who are convinced of the risks of losing these treasured resources by the power of the Spirit will be willing to engage the temporal powers of corruption, injustice, and oppression. Such church leaders and members can productively serve as God's appointed earthly means of a critical prophetic voice of resistance in the African society, not caring about the controversy and unpopularity that their critical public prophetic engagement might provoke in the country, even among their counterparts and church members.

The Trinitarian communion of God resists all oppressive Big Man/Woman ideology and rule. African Church leaders informed by the fear of the Triune God and love of the neighbor should also spontaneously organize and partake in robust public resistance against Big Men/Women who perpetrate systemic injustice and blindly plunder the public treasury. Gone are the days when church leaders should construe public resistance against an unjust government as the exclusive business of the civil society. Though the institutional separation between the church and state should be maintained, as Luther taught in his 1523 essay "Temporal Authority: To What Extent It Should Be Obeyed,"[19] such separation does not mean the church should approve unjust and corrupt Big Man/Woman governance. Therefore, those African clergy who resist participating in peaceful public demonstrations against unjust and ungodly government on the grounds that such peaceful demonstrations are reserved only for civil society and have nothing to do with the church need to liberate themselves from this erroneous belief! The visible solidarity with and participation in non-violent public protest against tyrannical Big Man's/Woman's rule is neither a breach of law and order nor an aberration of their "sacred" function. It's a divine call. A church leader who participates in a non-violent demonstration against the corrupt and unjust Big Man/Woman government and is willing to go to jail until just order and rule is restored demonstrates not only a perfect obedience to the law, but also ultimately fulfills his or her critical public pastoral vocation. The stark failure to do this means the clergy are promoting or cooperating with evil.

Apart from critical prophetic engagement with corrupt and unjust rule of the Big Man/Woman, the participation of the church in the gift and paradigm of the Triune God will also spur the African church to jettison a hierarchal style of leadership and receive a non-hierarchal and inclusive perichoretic gift of leadership. Viewed in terms of perichoretic equal divine persons in communion, the church in Africa would be an ecclesial community of equal brothers and sisters where openness, consensus, and accessibility to others are fundamental ingredients for clergy-laity relations. The African church that receives and embodies the gift of the Triune God's perichoretic communion, to paraphrase Boff, would be "a church that is more communion than hierarchy, more service than power, more circular than pyramidal, more loving embrace than bending the knee before authority."[20] In such egalitarian and all-inclusive church leadership, the priesthood of all believers finds comprehensive expression as all believers have equal opportunity to share in ecclesial leadership and authority. As the perichoretic *arche* of the Triune God is distributive, the power and authority of the church will be evenly distributed among its members without any oppressive hierarchy. Hence, no clergy empowered by the Triune God can arrogate power to himself or herself or use it to dominate the church and perpetuate one's glory and self-interest. As servants and not bosses of the church, clergy will work together with the laity as equal partners in the vineyard of the Triune God, serving God by serving the neighbor at the "diksen" of the society. Every believer's spiritual gift is identified, appreciated, and harnessed for the building up of the body of Christ and the neighbor. Such an egalitarian, inclusive, and participatory church can rightly be called the embodiment of the Triune God!

The gift of ethnic and religious diversity

Ethnic and religious nepotism is the last but not least in weight of the tripartite systemic issues plaguing the spirit of African communality that has to be redressed for that spirit to find full expression in the church and society. To this end, ethnic and religious exclusivism, which is the fundamental basis of ethnic and religious nepotism, needs recasting according to the gift of perichoretic communion and inclusive unity of the Triune God. As I have established previously, ethnic and religious nepotism often manifests itself in the instrumentalization of ethnic nationality and religion for personal gain and aggrandizement. Addressing this instrumentalization is an aspect of recasting the ideology of ethnic and religious exclusivism.

Therefore, the corollary of the Trinitarian communion of God's unity is that it frees and empowers the diverse ethnic nationalities to transcend their ethnic parochialism and sentiment to embrace each other as members of one universal community of the Triune God. What binds people together irrespective of their ethnic differences in this global community of the Triune God is the fact that everyone is created in the image of God. As people who bear the image of the Triune God, ethnic diversity does not threaten, but affirms the unity of humanity in the world. To be human in the image of the Triune God is to be a rooted cosmopolitan human being who puts behind one's ethnic parochialism in order to be a citizen of the cosmos. Interpersonal relationships are not constrained by racial, tribal, or geographical boundaries. To be a communal person in Trinitarian terms is to be open to the other, to accept and respect the other as oneself.

The diversity in unity in the Triune God is a gift, hence, our ethnic diversity is not a curse, but a rich gift that empowers and promotes national unity and mutual welcoming. Ethnic otherness is part of the very good gift of God's economy of creation to Africa. As Ferdinand Nwaigbo writes about Nigeria,

> Like a flowing water of life, ethnicity is a free gift of God to Nigerians. As a free gift, ethnicity is a source of thanks to the Almighty God for the splendour of creation, a source of praise for the marvels which God has accomplished among the people of Nigeria through His divine act of creation.[21]

180   *Authentic African tradition of community*

It is through re-imaging ethnic diversity, which is a gift of the Triune God, that Africans will experience genuine communion with God and one another. Africans bear faithful witness to their true humanity when they live out the life of the perichoretic communion and otherness that exists in the Triune God. To be preoccupied with our ethnic identities is to ignore the essential human feature that makes us human, namely, the image of the Triune God. African multi-ethnic societies, when transformed by the communion of the Triune God, will live out an inclusive form of inter-ethnic communion: all ethnic groups living with and relating to each other without discrimination or domination, resorting to dialogue rather than violence in addressing their differences and grievances. To establish inter-ethnic trust, peace, and justice, the Trinitarian communion of God calls for the sharing of the state power and resources among various ethnic nationalities in the fashion of the shared communion of the Triune God.

The instrumentalization of ethnicity only for personal interest is a perversion of the gift of ethnic otherness. This otherness is part of the goodness of God's own creation, and violations should be punishable by law. The key to dealing with this is creating a *functional* separation of power and the rule of law so as to prevent the dominant ethnic groups or those in power from using state power and resources to the benefit of one group at the expense of minority groups. Like the dominant ethnic groups, every minority ethnic group, no matter how small, must be granted the natural right to hold any responsible and influential national leadership position. Rather than playing the ethnic politics of winner-takes-all for the dominant groups, the Trinitarian communion of God promotes the perichoretic politics of winner-shares-all with the ethnic minorities. Our national goal of building a just and egalitarian African community cannot be realized unless the human equality and dignity of every ethnic nationality is affirmed, in the fashion of the Triune God, without subsuming them into the dominant groups. This is because it is in the freedom of the minority groups that the dominant groups will also find their freedom. Hence, we can have a free and egalitarian Africa.

The gift of the Trinitarian communion of God also frees and empowers the African church as an icon of the Triune God to reclaim the essence of the church as a Catholic multi-ethnic community, which the Triune God intended it to be at its inception, today, and at the eschaton. The Triune God did not intend the church to be a closed ethnic/racial community, otherwise Jesus would not have commissioned the disciples to embark on a global cross-cultural mission with the Triune God. As such, the existence of an ethnic/racial church undercuts the trans-ethnic desire of the Triune God. The Trinitarian communion of God liberates closed ethnic/racial churches within and outside Africa to open up their doors, membership, and fellowship to those ethnic groups who are irreducibly different from them. An inter-ethnic church which is gifted and empowered by the Triune God is not only a church where the blood of Jesus Christ is thicker than the blood of ethnic relation, but also where believers' loyalty to Christ transcends their loyalty to their ethnic group. As the Triune God desires, ethnic diversity is to be celebrated rather than instrumentalized, harnessed to build up rather than to destroy and divide the Church. Every member is loved and cared for not because of their ethnic identity,

Moreover, led by the Spirit, everyone's gift is discerned, welcomed, appreciated, and utilized regardless of his or her ethnic otherness. Ethnic nepotism is banished once and for all in any multiethnic church, which lives out the inclusive perichoretic life of the Triune God.

The unity of the Trinitarian communion of God that affirms God's open ongoing and eschatological communion with the whole humanity and cosmic community – including all religious groups – calls into question religious nepotism caused by exclusive religious particularism. This challenges the *vicious* expression of religious exclusivism often responsible for causing religious intolerance and rioting, for instance, in Nigeria. Such a boundless and omnipresent perichoretic communion of the Triune God with humanity and the world transcends all human-made religious boundaries to incorporate all religious faiths into the divine life.

This does not, however, mean that the two dominant Nigerian religions for example, need to relinquish their peculiarity by surrendering "their particularist claims to truth in favor of the universalism of truth," as Moltmann suggests world religions should do.[22] Suggesting that the two dominant religions need to surrender their particularistic claims to truth is impractical. Rather than surrendering their particularistic exclusive claims to truth, the two dominant religions should be free to maintain and express such particularity within the confines of their own religion insofar as much as such expression does not harm the members of the other religious group. This free wholesome retention and expression of religious peculiarity is very important in a multi-religious society. Even "interfaith mutuality," as Lamin Sanneh argues, "presumes religious committedness or at least the validity of particularity[,] . . . for denying one religion, even our own, does not increase religious tolerance."[23]

Religious nepotism is a caustic expression of religion in the public sphere stemming from the irresponsible and prejudicial mixture of religion and politics, for instance, in Nigeria. Though the gift of the Triune God's perichoretic communion embraces the entire world, the Triune God does not abolish, but affirms, the distinction between religion and state. To freely exercise religious particularity within the boundaries of one's religion is to accept the soft separation of state and religion as a gift of God's two ways of ruling the world. According to Luther, God rules the world through two separate governments, the secular and the spiritual, both of which are divinely instituted for the preservation of the world. The secular government preserves temporal righteousness and therewith-physical life through wielding the sword and law, while the spiritual government promotes spiritual righteousness and therewith-eternal life by preaching the Gospel. Contending the two governments must not be mixed up, but rather, must carefully be distinguished, Luther argues, "both must be permitted to remain; the one to produce righteousness, the other to bring about external peace and prevent evil deeds. Neither one is sufficient in the world without the other."[24]

The Triune God desires that the two governments, which need to function separately but complementarily, must not interfere with the affairs of each other. Each must function within its own boundaries without the one seeking unnecessarily to

182 *Authentic African tradition of community*

control and dominate the other. Luther argues that the temporal government, for example, must not "extend too far and encroach upon God's kingdom and government . . . for God cannot and will not permit anyone but himself to rule over the soul."[25] Thus, Luther warns secular and spiritual leaders not to coerce people with draconian laws into believing this or that faith against their will. Faith is a free act and should not be imposed on the people. The people have the absolute freedom to decide for themselves which faith to hold unto, under the inspiration of the Spirit as the Gospel is preached [or as the Quran is recited]. Nonetheless, this non-interference in the affairs of each other does not mean that the secular government should condone the lawless practice of religion or that the spiritual government should tolerate lawless secular government. Rather they should act as checks and balances on each other lest either become lawless. Therefore, the African political and religious leaders need to heed Luther's teaching of public theology and embrace God's two distinct ways of ruling the world as part of the Triune God's gift of perichoretic communion, a crucial distinction, which is virtually absent from the African tradition of community.

What this implies is that the government and the church, while operating separately and complementarily in Africa, need to respect and safeguard the religious freedom of the people as a fundamental human right. Moltmann accurately writes that

> the religions must learn to respect individual religious liberty as a human right, and in this framework to act tolerantly towards one another, and to be prepared for dialogue. To cling to the [harmful] divergences and contradictions between the religious groups would make them enemies of the human race.[26]

A religion that is the enemy of humanity and the whole of creation is the enemy of God, and therefore, a false religion. The Christian faith rooted in God as constituted in Christ and the power of the Spirit champions the cause of the marginalized and preserves rather than destroys human and non-human life. Peaceful religious co-existence does not mean merely an absence of religious violence, but rather, the presence of religious freedom, a freedom in which religious bodies recognize each other's particularity and respect the freedom of their followers to practice or change their faith without persecution. Freedom of religion also includes the right to be employed and be promoted devoid of any religious consideration.

The situation where certain people are denied employment and traditional leadership in northern Nigeria unless they convert to Islam is a threat to religious freedom. The situation where some converts to Christianity from Islam or vice versa are persecuted by immediate family and members of their religious group is a denial of their religious freedom, and hence a mark of religious intolerance.

Because the Triune God rules the world through secular law, to curtail public religious nepotism and establish a peaceful and inclusive multi-religious society, the practice of religion should be subject to the rule of law. Practicing religion according to the rule of law in a multi-religious Nigerian society for example, calls, first of all, for the strict application of Section 10 of the 1999 constitution, which prohibits any government, federal or state, from adopting any official religion.[27] Such a prohibition, when enforced, will not only provide a neutral ground for every religion to thrive without fear of persecution from the state, but also restrain those in power from using state power and resources to support their religion and its members to the exclusion of non-members for political patronage. The states that have already violated this constitutional provision in northern Nigeria should be called to account, compelling them to uphold the provision. Second, those who instrumentalize religion for personal enhancement by preaching intolerance, hate or war against non-members should be brought to justice. Unless the government is deliberate and passionate about enforcing this with impartiality, God's desire to establish a just and peaceful multi-religious society in Africa will continue to be elusive.

As a final point, government should check the lawless practice of religion often responsible for religious violence, and provide specific guidelines according to which religious groups can propagate and live out their faith.

Perichoretic theological education

In the preceding sections, I have explored ways by which the African tradition of community in Africa can be rescued from the tripartite systemic problem of the patriarchal complex, the Big Man syndrome, and nepotism in line with the egalitarian and inclusive life of the Triune God. In this section, I will articulate a perichoretic approach to theological education as an emancipatory practice for rescuing and recasting the African model of community. I will specifically explore what perichoretic theological education is and how it can be taught as an emancipatory practice for recasting the African church and society.

The new Trinitarian hermeneutics of God rooted in Christ and the Spirit in the economy of salvation, which has radical consequences for restructuring African community, also provides a solid foundation for rethinking the practice of theological education in Africa. The practice of theological education, largely centered on God, the Bible, and the church, usually has three objectives. The first objective is spiritual formation. Rooted in the perichoretic communion of God, who spiritually forms believers, theological education is also designed to impart in students such spiritual formation in Christian faith and life. As such, the institutions of theological education are spiritual nurseries where Christ forms and transforms the spiritual lives of students for service in the church and society.

Academic formation is another objective of theological education. As training in academic excellence, theological education is intended to transmit a body of knowledge rooted in God, scripture, and the church to students for the attainment of academic competence and critical inquiry. It is not enough for people to lay claim to a divine calling to the pastoral ministry. Such a divine calling must be accompanied by an academic training of the mind that not only reflects critically on complex scriptural questions, but also analyzes and interacts with theological claims in light of the Bible. It involves equipping students with the much-needed academic skills of analyzing contemporary issues affecting the church and society and how they can academically address these issues from theological and scriptural standpoints.

Theological education is not only transformative and informative, but also practical. That is, it is also intended for ministerial formation. As a bridge between theory and practice of theological education, ministerial formation prepares students for practicing pastoral ministry. It inculcates in students the essential virtues of honesty and integrity necessary for being leaders of the church of God. Therefore, the spiritual and academic formation in theological education is not an only end in itself, but also a means to an end. The end is to train students for ordination as ministers of Word and Sacrament within and outside the church. Such ministerial formation involves equipping students with the professional expertise for dealing with the dynamic changing of the pastoral needs and challenges of the Christian congregation.

Perichoretic theological education is that form of pastoral education that weaves these three objectives of theological education into a whole for training effective ministers of God's Word and Sacraments. This means giving equal status to three objectives in our theological institutions. These objectives mutually permeate each other so that encountering one in our theological institutions invariably means encountering the other two. This permeation makes the three-fold objective distinct without separation and united without confusion, rooted in the communal unity and diversity of the Triune God.

A perichoretic approach to theological education empowers and promotes a participatory system of theological learning, according to which the chapel as well as the classrooms are equal centers of theological education, so students integrate the knowledge of the head with the knowledge of real-life situations. Perichoretic theological education ensures that what is learned in the classroom, for example, the dynamics of the new Trinitarian hermeneutics of God, stands at the core of preaching in the chapel, and what is preached in the chapel is lived out both within and outside the classroom. Such emancipative participatory practice of perichoretic theological education not only liberates students from being simply passive "bank accounts" into which teachers deposit knowledge, but also empowers them freely to take initiative and assume personal responsibility for learning and applying what they have learned in the seminary to structural issues affecting both the church and society.

We, therefore, need a perichoretic approach to theological education in Africa that incorporates the three dimensions of the pastoral training program into a holistic training of pastors who not only will effectively administer God's Word and Sacraments, but who also will be critical of contemporary structural evils inimical to the well-being of the church and society. We need to maintain a balance between spiritual and academic requirements for admission of students to our theological institutions. In this way, theological institutions can select students who are not only spiritually and cognitively exceptional, but also are practically passionate about pastoral ministry and social transformation of the community.

The new Trinitarian hermeneutics of the Triune God can radically impact the status, place, and teaching of the doctrine of the Trinity in theological institutions. Barth gives the doctrine of the Trinity a place of prominence in his work *Church Dogmatics* by placing it at the prolegomenon before any other doctrines. Barth argues that there is no way that the significance of scripture, which is usually examined first and foremost in Christian theology, can be justified unless the God whose revelation makes the Scripture holy is made clear beforehand.[28]

Theological institutions in Africa should follow suit. They should embark on theological curricular change that places the new hermeneutics of the Trinity at the forefront of their systematic theological curriculum rather than somewhere after the doctrine of God's oneness. Seminary professors need to teach the Trinity first to students before any other doctrines, even though the doctrine of the Trinity includes other Christian doctrines. They need to teach it from the standpoint of salvation history with its transformative impact on the church and society rather than as abstract speculation. To teach the new Trinitarian theology is to teach the perichoretic communion of the egalitarian God as a gift for critiquing and salvaging the African practice of community from the three-fold systemic evil that we have examined. To teach the Trinitarian understanding of God is teach an open communion of the Triune God that frees and empowers humanity and the whole cosmic community to share in the divine life:

> The Trinity is ultimately therefore a teaching not about the abstract nature of God, nor about God in isolation from everything other than God, but a teaching about God's life with us and our life with each other [and with all the cosmic community].[29]

Summary and conclusion

In this concluding chapter, I have drawn conclusions from my attempt to rescue and begin recasting the African tradition of community according to the liberating gift of the Trinitarian communion of the perichoretic life of God. As the persons of the Triune God share their perichoretic life with us in the Eucharist, the Triune God indwells, and is indwelled by humanity and the world. Not only is every personal and systemic force of egoism inimical to the African spirit of community, but also Christians are transformed and empowered to live out the radical implications of the perichoretic life of the Triune God in church and society. As the Triune God works in and with Africans to transform their community, the Triune God as a democratic, just, and inclusive communion is a gift, and paradigm for this transformation.

In order to liberate African church and society from the patriarchal complex, I argue we must dismantle patriarchal hermeneutics of God, Scripture, religious beliefs, traditional gender roles, and structures that dehumanize women. Apart from arguing for gender-inclusive and liberating hermeneutics of God and scripture, I contend that the Trinitarian communion of God not only ends oppressive

186 *Authentic African tradition of community*

male-female relationships, moving toward mutual dialogue rather than dictatorship, and equal partnership rather than hierarchy, but also establishes gender-inclusive power structures that affirm the rights, humanity, and dignity of women.

As for the Big Man syndrome, I argued for retrieving the notion of "newariga diksen" (Big Man is a garbage site) as the true Big Man. The true Big Persons of the Triune God themselves, deep in their communion, help us to perceive the right status of the true Big Man/Woman. They help us to relocate the position of the Big Man/Woman from the highest echelon of the society as the seat of power to the garbage site of society as the appropriate place of service. This humble site is where the true Big Man/Woman takes on the burden of the people and not vice versa. There the authentic Big Man/Woman is made not a despot, but a burden-bearing vulnerable servant. This servant serves along with the marginalized and excluded people, sharing their suffering while maximizing the liberating gift of the Triune God. As "diksen" (garbage site), the true Big Man/Woman bears the burden of dispensing justice that protects and promotes the rights and well-being of the people. That is, the true Big Man/Woman does not inflict injustice or exercise domineering power over the people; the authentic Big Man/Woman shares power, liberates, empowers, and uplifts rather than oppresses the people. The authentic Big Man/Woman pours himself or herself out as a libation to the people, sacrificing their life and comfort at the garbage site of the society, which is the altar of service for the sake of the people.

Reclaiming "newariga diksen" as the true Big Man/Woman calls for a perichoretic system of leadership in which those who bear the consequences of the misrule of Big Man/Woman are accorded full rights and an effective voice in making public decisions. Such perichoretic leadership works effectively when it is based on a *functional* separation of powers and rule of law that not only guarantees and enforces the fundamental human rights of the people, but also implements strict punishment for corruption, and financial and economic crimes.

The liberating perichoretic communion of God also retrieves for the church the authentic meaning of Big Man, that is "newariga diksen." The true meaning of the Big Man/Woman repositions the church from its comfort zone to the "diksen" of the society, as the locus of celebrating communion with the oppressed, the poor, and the most vulnerable members of the society. The Triune God prefers always to be present at the "diksen," standing in solidarity and communion with the oppressed and excluded. Not only empowering church leaders to keep their distance from corrupt and unjust Big Men/Women, this God also inspires them to reclaim their critical prophetic ministry as the voice of God and the voiceless. At this "diksen," the Triune God spurs them on to spontaneously initiate and participate with groups in civil society in non-violent public protest against the corruption and injustices of the Big Man/Woman's rule.

The ethnic diversity in Africa is the reflection of the diversity in the Triune God. Thus, the ethnic diversity is the gift of the Triune God's economy of creation. As there is mutual relation and unity in the Triune God with diversity, the Trinitarian communion of God empowers the diverse ethnic communities to commune, co-exist, and embrace one another as the gift of the Triune God. This ethnic diversity should be utilized as the gift of God's economy of creation for building up rather than tearing apart the church and society. The instrumentalization of ethnic identity for dominating and excluding some people from enjoying state power and resources is not only a perversion of the goodness of creation, but also a denial of the inclusive character of the Triune God. Therefore, the currently closed ethnic Christian churches and societies should welcome those who are different from them into their folds, as empowered by the perichoretic communion of God.

To rescue African society from religious nepotism, informed by the destructive ideology of religious exclusivism that breaks community, I argue for an inclusive Trinitarian understanding of the Christian faith that affirms rather than denies the free retention and expression of the uniqueness of Christ. The perichoretic communion and unity of the Triune God in Christ and the Spirit includes all humanity, regardless of religious belief. This should empower the church to cultivate and live out an inclusive understanding of Christian faith that welcomes rather than demonizes non-Christians. What this means is that the church should freely maintain and propagate its exclusive religious particularity within its boundaries without inflicting harm to the members of other religious groups. Therefore, not only should those who preach and engage in actions of harmful religious exclusion, hate, and war against adherents of other religions be brought to justice, but also political leaders who use state power and resources to support their religion to the exclusion of others.

The Triune God's two distinct ways of ruling the world need to be accepted as part of God's gift of perichoretic communion. Again, in that spirit I argue for the strict enforcement of the 1999 constitutional provision that prohibits any government from adopting any official religion and guarantees religious freedom of individuals to hold, renounce, and change their religion without fear or threat of persecution from the members of their immediate family and faith community.

This Trinitarian communion also calls for perichoretic theological education. This is a theological education where the three aspects of pastoral education mutually permeate each other as a holistic education for training pastors and other leaders of the church. Such perichoretic theological education will produce holistic pastors who are not only effective ministers of the Word and Sacraments in the church, but God's critical earthly means of socio-economic and political transformation of the African society. This calls for the revision of the theological curriculum to give the new hermeneutic of the Trinity a central place in theological education.

An authentic African tradition of community is that which lives out the just, egalitarian, and inclusive life of the Triune God. That is, a community that promotes individuality without individualism, communality without patriarchy, and multi-ethnic and religious communion and diversity in unity, without nepotism and discrimination. This authentic community that is rooted in the functional separation of powers and rule of law must uphold and guarantee justice, equity, and the inalienable human rights of all its citizens regardless of their gender, ethnicity, and religion. In such a community, the true Big Men and Women are "diksen," who do not live as lords over the people, but as vulnerable servants who bear the

188　*Authentic African tradition of community*

burden of serving the people along with the marginalized and oppressed at the garbage sites of the community. This kind of authentic African community can properly be called the embodiment of the perichoretic communion of the Triune God! This is the fruit of receiving and living out the liberating gift of the perichoretic communion of the Triune God in Africa and the whole world.

Suggestions for further research

This book has been designed to recast an African notion of community in Africa consistent with the egalitarian, just, and inclusive communion of God. Undoubtedly, this is an ambitious project. Though I have utilized every source at my disposal to accomplish the project, I do not think I have done enough justice to the subject under investigation. Hence, this book is far from being perfect. I must admit the subject of the book is quite dense. I suggest that future writers narrow the subject for an exhaustive analysis. They can specifically undertake narrow, but thorough, study on a topic like "The Significance of the New Trinitarian Theology, the Big Man Syndrome and the Rule of Law in Africa," and/or "The Significance of the New Trinitarian Theology for Rescuing the Patriarchal Complex in Africa."

Finally, there are matters arising in the course of this writing which are larger than the scope of this book, and which need further research. One of these is whether or not the Triune God needs the world and humanity. The divine work of creation, incarnation, redemption, and eschatological renewal of the world and humanity strongly suggests that the world and humanity are more than just temporal partners of the Triune God. Suggesting that the world and humanity are temporal and eternal partners of the Triune God calls for rethinking the classical notion of divine aseity. What also needs further research is the comprehensive analysis of the new Trinitarian understanding of the extent of the Triune God's atonement and its radical implications for recasting the dogma of religious exclusivism in Africa. The question needs to be exhaustively answered if the perception and attitude of the church and its members toward non-Christians is to be changed for peaceful religious co-existence, mutual relation, and tolerance to prevail among the multireligious communities in Africa.

Notes

1　Martin Luther, "The Blessed Sacrament of the Holy and True Body and Blood of Christ, and the Brotherhoods, 1519," in *Luther's Works*, ed. E. Theodore Bachmann and Helmut Lehmann, vol. 35 (Philadelphia, PA: Muhlenberg Press, 1960), 51.
2　Martin Luther, "The Sacrament of the Body and Blood of Christ – Against the Fanatics, 1526," in *Luther's Works*, ed. Abdel Ross Wentz and Helmut Lehmann, vol. 36 (Philladelphia, PA: Muhlenberg Press, 1959), 349.
3　Luther, "The Blessed Sacrament of the Holy and True Body and Blood of Christ, and the Brotherhoods, 1519," 67.
4　Martin Luther, "The Bondage of the Will," in *Luther's Works*, ed. Philip S. Watson and Hulmut Lehmann, vol. 33 (Philadelphia, PA: Fortress Press, 1972), 243.
5　Michelle A. Gonzalez, *Created in God's Image: An Introduction of Feminist Theological Anthropology* (Maryknoll, NY: Orbis Books, 2007), 162.

Authentic African tradition of community 189

6 Mercy Amba Oduyoye, *Daughters of Anowa: African Women and Patriarchy* (Maryknoll, NY: Orbis Books, 1995), 181. Emphasis added.
7 See Gary M. Simpson, "'You Shall Bear Witness to Me': Thinking with Luther About Christ and the Scriptures," *Word & World* 29, no. 4 (2009): 380–8.
8 Rosemary Radford Ruether, "Ecofeminism," in *Feminism and Theology*, ed. Janet Martin Soskice and Diana Lipton (New York, NY: Oxford University Press, 2003), 29.
9 David E. Fredrickson, *Eros and the Christ: Longing and Envy in Paul's Christology* (Minneapolis, MN: Fortress Press, 2013), 155.
10 Martin Luther, "The Freedom of a Christian, 1520," in *Luther's Works*, ed. Harold J. Grimm and Helmut T. Lehmann, vol. 31 (Philadelphia, PA: Muhlenberg Press, 1957), 366.
11 Ibid., 371.
12 The Chamba are an ethnic group found predominantly in the northeast of Nigeria and some parts of Cameroon, Ghana, and Togo.
13 Dietrich Bonhoeffer, *Discipleship*, edited by Geffrey B. Kelly and John D. Godsey (Minneapolis: Fortress, 2001), 90. See also Gary M. Simpson, "'God Is a God Who Bears[:]' Bonhoeffer for a Flat World," *Word & World* 26, no. 4 (2006): 419–28.
14 Gary M. Simpson, "Africa Is the Lord's and Fullness Thereof: Praise Be to God," in *"So the Poor Have Hope, and Injustice Shuts Its Mouth:" Poverty and the Mission of the Church in Africa*, ed. Karen L. Bloomquist and Musa Filibus Panti (Geneva: The Lutheran World Federation, 2007), 159.
15 For more discussion, see Ibrahim Bitrus, "Disturbing Unjust Peace in Nigeria Through the Church and Legal Reforms: The Contribution of Luther's Critical Public Theology," in *On Secular Government: Lutheran Perspectives on Contemporary Legal Issues*, ed. R. W. Duty and M. A. Failinger (Grand Rapids, MI: W. B. Eerdmans Publishing Co., 2016).
16 See Federal Government of Nigeria, Economic and Financial Crimes Commission (Establishment) (EFCC) Act 2004 (Abuja: EFCC, 2004).
17 Gary M. Simpson, "Retrieving Martin Luther's Critical Public Theology of Political Authority for Global Civil Society," in *Theological Practices That Matter*, ed. Karen L. Bloomquist, vol. 5 (Minneapolis, MI: Lutheran University Press, 2009), 163.
18 Martin Luther, "Commentary on Psalm 82," in *Luther's Works*, ed. Jaroslav Pelikan, vol. 13 (Saint Louis, MO: Concordia Publishing House, 1956), 49.
19 Martin Luther, "Temporal Authority: To What Extent It Should Be Obeyed, 1523," in *Luther's Works*, ed. Walther I. Brandt and Helmut T. Lehmann, vol. 45 (Philadelphia, PA: Muhlenberg Press, 1962).
20 Leonardo Boff, *Trinity and Society*, trans. Paul Burns (Eugene, OR: Wipf & Stock Publishers, 1988), 154.
21 Ferdinand Nwaigbo, "Re-Imaging Ethnicity and the Task of Christian Church Leadership in West Africa Sub-Region: The Nigerian Experience," in *Ethnicity and Leadership in West African Sub-Region*, ed. Ferdinand Nwaigbo, Jude Asanbe, Camillus Umoh, Onyema Anozie, Thaddeus Guzuma, John Gangwari, Innocent Ejeh, Austin Echema, and Emmanuel Nwaoru (Port Harcourt, Nigeria: CIWA Publications, 2004), 68.
22 Jürgen Moltmann, *God for a Secular Society: The Public Relevance of Theology* (Minneapolis, MN: Fortress Press, 1999), 133.
23 Lamin O. Sanneh, *Piety and Power: Muslims and Christians in West Africa* (Maryknoll, NY: Orbis Books, 1996), 8.
24 Luther, "Temporal Authority," 92.
25 Ibid., 104–5.
26 Moltmann, *God for a Secular Society*, 133.
27 The Federal Government of Nigeria, *Constitution of the Federal Republic of Nigeria (Promulgation) Decree 1999* (Abuja: The Federal Government of Nigeria, 1999), 24.
28 Karl Barth, "The Doctrine of the Word of God," in *Church Dogmatics*, ed. Geoffrey William Bromiley and Thomas F. Torrance, vol. 1 (London: T&T Clark International, 2004), 300.
29 Catherine Mowry LaCugna, *God for Us: The Trinity and Christian Life* (San Francisco, CA: HarperSanFrancisco, 1991), 1.

190 *Authentic African tradition of community*

Bibliography

Barth, Karl. "The Doctrine of the Word of God." In *Church Dogmatics*, edited by Geoffrey William Bromiley and Thomas F. Torrance. Vol. 1. London: T&T Clark International, 2004.

Bitrus, Ibrahim. "Disturbing Unjust Peace in Nigeria Through the Church and Legal Reforms: The Contribution of Luther's Critical Public Theology." In *On Secular Government: Lutheran Perspectives on Contemporary Legal Issues*, edited by Ronald W. Duty and M. A. Failinger. Grand Rapids, MI: W. B. Eerdmans Publishing Co., 2016.

Boff, Leonardo. *Trinity and Society*. Translated by Paul Burns. Eugene, OR: Wipf & Stock Publishers, 1988.

Bonhoeffer, Dietrich. *Discipleship*. Edited by Geffrey B. Kelly and John D. Godsey. Minneapolis, MN: Fortress, 2001.

The Federal Government of Nigeria. *Constitution of the Federal Republic of Nigeria (Promulgation) Decree1999*. Abuja: The Federal Government of Nigeria, 1999.

———. Economic and Financial Crimes Commission (Establishment) (EFCC) Act 2004. Abuja: EFCC, 2004.

Fredrickson, David E. *Eros and the Christ: Longing and Envy in Paul's Christology*. Minneapolis, MN: Fortress Press, 2013.

Gonzalez, Michelle A. *Created in God's Image: An Introduction of Feminist Theological Anthropology*. Maryknoll, NY: Orbis Books, 2007.

LaCugna, Catherine Mowry. *God for Us: The Trinity and Christian Life*. San Francisco, CA: HarperSanFrancisco, 1991.

Luther, Martin. "The Blessed Sacrament of the Holy and True Body and Blood of Christ, and the Brotherhoods, 1519." In *Luther's Works*, edited by E. Theodore Bachmann and Helmut Lehmann. Vol. 35. Philadelphia, PA: Muhlenberg Press, 1960.

———. "The Bondage of the Will." In *Luther's Works*, edited by Philip S. Watson and Hulmut Lehmann. Vol. 33. Philadelphia, PA: Fortress Press, 1972.

———. "Commentary on Psalm 82." In *Luther's Works*, edited by Jaroslav Pelikan. Vol. 13. Saint Louis, MO: Concordia Publishing House, 1956.

———. "The Freedom of a Christian, 1520." In *Luther's Works*, edited by Harold J. Grimm and Helmut T. Lehmann. Vol. 31. Philadelphia, PA: Muhlenberg Press, 1957.

———. "The Sacrament of the Body and Blood of Christ – Against the Fanatics, 1526." In *Luther's Works*, edited by Abdel Ross Wentz and Helmut Lehmann. Vol. 36. Philladelphia, PA: Muhlenberg Press, 1959.

———. "Temporal Authority: To What Extent It Should Be Obeyed, 1523." In *Luther's Works*, edited by Walther I. Brandt and Helmut T. Lehmann. Vol. 45. Philadelphia, PA: Muhlenberg Press, 1962.

Moltmann, Jürgen. *God for a Secular Society: The Public Relevance of Theology*. Minneapolis, MN: Fortress Press, 1999.

Nwaigbo, Ferdinand. "Re-Imaging Ethnicity and the Task of Christian Church Leadership in West Africa Sub-Region: The Nigerian Experience." In *Ethnicity and Leadership in West African Sub-Region*, edited by Ferdinand Nwaigbo, Jude Asanbe, Camillus Umoh, Onyema Anozie, Thaddeus Guzuma, John Gangwari, Innocent Ejeh, Austin Echema, and Emmanuel Nwaoru. Port Harcourt, Nigeria: CIWA Publications, 2004.

Oduyoye, Mercy Amba. *Daughters of Anowa: African Women and Patriarchy*. Maryknoll, NY: Orbis Books, 1995.

Ruether, Rosemary Radford. "Ecofeminism." In *Feminism and Theology*, edited by Janet Martin Soskice and Diana Lipton. New York, NY: Oxford University Press, 2003.

Sanneh, Lamin O. *Piety and Power: Muslims and Christians in West Africa.* Maryknoll, NY: Orbis Books, 1996.

Simpson, Gary M. "Africa Is the Lord's and Fullness Thereof: Praise Be to God." In *"So the Poor Have Hope, and Injustice Shuts Its Mouth:" Poverty and the Mission of the Church in Africa,* edited by Karen L. Bloomquist and Musa Filibus Panti. Geneva: The Lutheran World Federation, 2007.

———. "'God Is a God Who Bears[:]' Bonhoeffer for a Flat World." *Word & World* 26, no. 4 (2006): 419–28.

———. "Retrieving Martin Luther's Critical Public Theology of Political Authority for Global Civil Society." In *Theological Practices That Matter,* edited by Karen L. Bloomquist. Vol. 5. Minneapolis, MN: Lutheran University Press, 2009.

———. "'You Shall Bear Witness to Me': Thinking with Luther About Christ and the Scriptures." *Word & World* 29, no. 4 (2009): 380–8.

Index

Abioje, Pius Oyeniran 58n23
abundant ix, 6, 56, 118, 140, 151, 167
Achebe, Chinua 39, 59n47, 117
Action Group (AG) 18
Adepoju, Adunola 59n34
Alabi, Mojeed Olujinmi A. 59n43
Alemazung, Joy Asongazoh 44, 60n64, 62
appropriation 88, 91
Aquinas, Thomas xii, 68, 81, 92–7, 106,
    121, 127n142, 128n146, 128n151,
    128n154, 129n200, 131, 163n84, 165
Arche 144, 147–8, 158–61, 179
Aribisala, Femi 34, 41, 58n20, 59n54, 62
Asogwa, Chika 40, 59n48, 62
Athanasius 68–71, 89, 120, 124n3,
    124n7, 124n8, 124n9, 124n11, 124n19,
    131, 149
Augustine 68, 81, 87–92, 96–7, 101,
    106, 121, 127n108, 127n112, 127n113,
    127n120, 127n127, 129n200, 131
authentic: African Christian Theology 29;
    African perception 22; African tradition
    of community x, 5, 187–8; African
    understanding of the community 9;
    Big Man 173, 175–7, 177; Christian
    doctrine 73; contribution 110; new
    hermeneutics of the Trinity 7; starting
    point 159; Trinitarian hermeneutics 10,
    134; Trinitarian understanding 47
authority 4, 23n12, 35, 40, 42, 47, 50,
    54, 157, 175, 177–9, 189n17, 189n19,
    189n24, 190–1
Awoniyi, S. 50, 61n86, 61n92, 62

Barth, Karl xii, 68, 97, 100–6, 108, 122,
    129n188, 129n189, 129n191, 129n193,
    129n200, 129n211, 129n212, 130n214,
    130n215, 130n216, 131–2, 135,
    151, 154, 163n86, 164n88, 165, 185,
    189n28, 190

Basil 68, 71–5, 124n23, 125n30, 125n31,
    125n32, 125n35, 125n36, 131–2
begotten 69, 71–3, 78, 83, 87, 89, 125n50,
    149; begotteness 79
Biafra 20
Big Man 33–5, 39, 44, 47, 53–4, 56,
    173–6, 178, 186; Big Man syndrome
    ix, xii, 6, 10, 22, 28, 33–9, 42–5, 56,
    165–6, 172, 176, 183, 186, 188; True or
    Authentic Big Man 172–6, 186
Bitrus, Ibrahim x–xv, 59n41, 62, 129n211,
    130n216, 132, 189n15, 190
Blanchard, Lauren Ploch 61n94, 62
Boer, Jan H. 44, 60n66, 62
Boff, Leonardo 4, 10, 23n14, 26,
    134, 137, 141–2, 146–7, 153–5,
    158, 162n15, 162n35, 163n64,
    164n94, 164n100, 165n125, 165, 178,
    189n20, 190
Boko Haram 37, 52–3, 57, 61n93, 61n94,
    62, 64
Bonhoeffer, Dietrich 9, 24n24, 26, 175,
    189n13, 190–1
Brantlinger, Patrick 17, 25n48, 26
Burns, Alan 18, 23n14, 23n53, 26
Burton, Richard F. 17, 24n24, 25n47

Cappadocians 88, 88–9, 91, 120;
    Cappadocian Fathers 68, 71–2, 120
Carl, Harold F. 87, 127n103, 132
Carling, Joergen 59n35, 63
Central Legislative Council 18
Christ xii, xiii, 2–3, 5, 6, 15, 23n19, 33,
    39–40, 45, 49, 51, 55, 67, 69, 76, 82,
    84, 87, 89, 93, 96, 98–9, 101–3, 105,
    107, 114, 117, 120, 122–3, 125n55,
    134–40, 145, 147–8, 151, 153–5,
    157–9, 161, 164n105, 167–70, 172–5,
    177, 179–81, 183, 187, 188n1, 188n3,
    188n7, 190–1

Index 193

colonialism x, 16, 22, 32, 43–5, 47–8,
54–6, 60n64, 60n66, 60n68, 62, 64, 172
communal 2, 10–16, 22, 44, 55–6,
60n58, 71, 77, 79, 92, 105, 110–12,
134, 139–40, 142, 152, 160, 168, 179,
184; communality xii, 12, 13, 110–12,
179, 187
communion ix–x, 1–6, 23n8, 27, 40, 49,
53, 56–7, 73–4, 77, 82–3, 90–1, 98,
105, 112, 121, 134, 136–9, 141–61,
162n12, 162n30, 162n40, 163n50,
163n52, 163n53, 163n55, 163n82,
163n83, 163n89, 165, 167–8, 173,
176, 180–1, 185–6, 188; perichoretic
communion x, 2, 4, 6, 8, 9, 10, 13,
24n18, 28, 31, 33, 55, 155, 158–9,
167, 173, 175, 178–9, 182–3, 185–8;
Trinitarian communion x–xiii, 1, 3–10,
33, 45, 134, 136, 144, 146, 149, 152,
157–8, 167–70, 172, 174, 177–8,
180–1, 185, 187
communotheism 110, 123
confession x, 8–9, 105, 138
constitution 18–19, 21, 38, 77, 176, 183,
189n27, 190; constitutional immunity
38; constitutional provision 51, 183, 187
contemporary: African theology 29;
African Trinitarian theologians/
thinkers 68, 109, 123; Catholic theology
106; theology 6, 68, 97, 128n164,
129n182, 132, 133–4, 159; Trinitarian
theologians/thinkers xii, 8; Trinitarian
theology xii, 8, 10, 135, 156
correlation 8, 16, 28, 111, 123, 141
corruption 19, 20–1, 35–6, 39, 41, 44, 56,
58n28, 59n43, 60n65, 62, 63, 133, 176,
178, 186
Crampton, Edmund Patrick Thurman 54,
62n98, 63
creation ix, 4, 6, 10, 13, 15, 18, 20, 22,
23n2, 32, 48, 55, 67, 70–1, 73, 76–7,
81–3, 87, 88, 90–2, 94, 102, 115,
121, 134, 137, 139, 149, 151, 153–60,
164n103, 166–70, 172, 179–80, 182,
186, 187–8
crimes 35, 37, 58n28, 63, 176, 186,
189n16, 190
Crowder, Michael 17, 25n49, 25n56, 26,
60n67, 63
Cunliffe-Jones, Peter 35, 58n24, 63
Cunningham, David S. 7, 24n19, 26

Daley, Brian E. 125n54, 126n59, 132
Daniella, Coetzee 29, 49n3, 63

democracy 19, 30, 37, 39, 42, 44, 58n21,
59n46, 60n60, 61n73, 62, 64–5
Dickson, Kwesi A. 1, 11, 23n4, 24n26, 26
Dictatorship 21, 37, 186
doctrine of the Trinity 1–10, 22, 23n1,
23n9, 24n15, 26, 48, 50, 53, 57,
67–8, 70–1, 73, 81–2, 86–8, 90–2,
94, 96, 97–134, 124n6, 124n13,
125n31, 125n34, 126n24, 127n103,
127n125, 128n173, 129n182,
129n190, 129n204, 130n214,
131n265, 131–7, 139, 145–60,
162n7, 163n61, 163n86, 164n87, 165,
185, 189n28, 190
domination xiii, 6, 10, 29, 31–2, 43, 45,
52, 54–5, 144, 148, 158–9, 163n61,
169–70, 172, 175, 180
drama ix–xii

Ebegbulem, Joseph C. 60n72, 63
Eboh, Simeon Onyewueke 46, 60n71, 63
Economic and Financial Crimes
Commission (EFCC) 35
economic Trinity 87, 96, 100, 102, 108,
122, 135
economy 6, 30, 35, 44, 59n49, 66, 77,
83–6, 88, 91–2, 105–7, 122, 134–7,
142, 145–8, 155, 157–8, 160–1,
162n13; Economy of Creation 67, 71,
76, 81, 83, 121, 179, 186–7; economy
of salvation 1, 4–6, 10, 23n1, 70, 73,
75, 77, 84, 86–8, 92, 96, 100, 107–8,
111, 121, 134–6, 146–7, 153, 156,
159–60, 183
eschatology 124
Esse Commune 93
essence 10, 51, 69–71, 73–5, 77,
80, 84–6, 88, 91–5, 98, 107, 118,
125n55, 125n56, 135, 142, 151, 155,
162n112, 180
ethnicity 47, 60n71, 61n76, 63, 65,
179–80, 187, 189n21, 190
Eucharist 6, 116, 167–8, 185; Eucharistic
xiii, 116
Eunomius 71–2, 75, 78–80, 89, 125n37,
125n40, 125n55, 132

Falola, Toyin 21, 25n60, 26, 51, 60n68,
61n83, 61n88, 61n90, 61n96, 63
father 3, 5, 9, 15, 25n52, 68–105, 107–9,
111–13, 115–16, 120–1, 125n50,
125n56, 127n112, 134, 136–40,
142–61, 162n30, 168
Fawehinmi, Gani 34

194 *Index*

Filibus, Musa P. 49, 61n80, 63, 189n14, 191
Fortman, Edmund J. 67, 70–1, 83, 85, 87, 90–1, 124n1, 124n16, 124n24, 125n39, 16n63, 126n65, 126n77, 126n81, 126n83, 126n89, 126n96, 127n104, 127n106, 127n132, 127n136, 128n162, 132
Fredrickson, David E. 173, 189n9, 190
freedom 2, 10, 12, 16, 24n24, 26, 37, 54–5, 96, 140–2, 144, 149, 151, 155, 157–8, 161, 164n103, 167, 169, 175, 180, 182, 187; Freedom of a Christian 173, 189n10, 190

Gadamer, Hans-Georg 8, 24n22, 26
Galloway, Allan D. 60n67, 63
garbage site 174–5, 177, 186, 188
gender: inclusive 146, 171–2, 185–6; inequality 29–33, 55, 57n2, 57n9, 64, 146, 171; prejudice 158, 169; role 30, 55, 171, 185; sensitive 119
gift ix, x, 10, 31, 33, 45, 55, 57, 74, 82, 89–91, 94, 107, 166–9, 171–3, 175–6, 178–88
Gnostics 81, 121
Godhead 12, 68–71, 73–4, 76, 78–84, 86–7, 90, 93–4, 96, 107, 112, 120–1, 124n19, 127n112, 139
Gonzalez, Michelle A. 169, 188n5, 190
gospel 12, 45, 49, 55, 125n55, 128n181, 132–3, 169, 181–2
government 17–21, 25n52, 30, 32–8, 41–2, 44, 48, 52–4, 56–7, 62, 77, 157, 171, 176, 178, 181–3, 187, 189n15, 189n16, 189n29, 190
Great Muntu 112–16, 123
Gregory of Nazianzen 71, 78–80, 125n46, 125n48, 125n49, 125n50, 125n51, 125n52, 125n53, 125n54, 125n55, 125n56, 125n56, 125n57, 125n58, 126n59, 126n60, 126n61, 125n62, 132–3
Gregory of Nyssa 68, 72, 75–7, 125n37, 125n40, 125n42, 125n43, 132
Grenz, Stanley J. 8, 103, 132
Gumi, Sheikh Abubakar 51, 61n87, 63
Gyekye, Kwame 2, 13, 23n5, 24n37, 26

Hansen, Guillermo C. 74, 94, 124n6, 125n33, 127n112, 128n145, 128n153, 132

Harden, Blaine 33–4, 58n17, 63
Hausa 18, 23n12, 32, 46, 48
Hegel, Georg Wilhelm Friedrich 16–17, 25n45, 26, 100–1; Hegelian 101, 109, 113, 122, 140, 142
hermeneutics of God/Trinity ix, 1, 5–10, 22, 23n1, 24n15, 26, 29, 45, 56, 68–9, 81, 88, 92, 103–4, 108, 113, 119–20, 122–3, 130n50, 131n264, 132–7, 141–2, 148, 156, 159–60, 166, 168–70, 172–3, 183–5
hierarchy 4–5, 7, 16, 40, 42, 56, 78, 95, 110, 111, 114, 145, 146, 148, 157, 160–1, 163n61, 170–1, 175, 178–9, 186
homoousion 71–2
Hopkins, Dwight N. 13, 24n34, 34n36, 26
Human Rights Watch 58n28, 63
hypostases 71, 73–7, 79–80, 88, 104, 120–1, 143, 144; hypostasis 71–4, 76, 120–1, 143, 150

ideology x, 29, 30, 32, 45, 51, 57, 57n3, 58n13, 63–4, 169, 179, 187
Igbo 18–20, 33, 46, 48
Iheukwumere, Emmanuel O. 44, 60n65, 63
Ikuenobe, Polycarp 14, 24n34, 25n41, 26, 60n58, 63
immanent Trinity 81, 87, 96, 102, 107, 122, 135, 155–6
incarnation 70, 83, 94, 106, 115, 122–3, 137, 153–4, 164n104, 168, 188
Independent Corrupt Practices and the Other Related Offences Commission (ICPC) 35
individualism xiii, 13–14, 16, 22, 43, 109, 145, 150, 187
injustice 4, 9, 30, 36–7, 41, 55, 56, 172, 175–6, 177–8, 186, 189n14, 91
Innocent, Eme Okechukwu 59n37, 63
Irenaeus 68, 81–3, 121, 126n63, 126n66, 126n68, 126n69, 126n71, 126n73, 126n78, 132–3
Irobi, Emmy Godwin 47, 61n74, 64
Isichei, Elizabeth 25n51, 25n55, 25n57, 26
Islam 23n31, 50–1, 54, 57, 60n66, 62, 182
Izuakor, Levi I. 45, 60n68, 64
Izugbara, C. Otutubikey 32, 58n13, 64

Jenkins, Philip 42, 60n56, 64
Jenson, Robert W. 101, 103, 128n181, 129n190, 132

Jesus 2–3, 41, 74, 82, 84, 88, 98, 101–3, 107, 117, 122–3, 125n55, 134–42, 145, 147–9, 153, 157–61, 173, 180
Johnson, Alaba 58n30, 64
Jonathan, Goodluck 21, 52, 53

Kant, Immanuel 97–8, 128n170, 128n171, 132
Kariatlis, Philip 74, 125n31, 125n34, 132
Kärkkäinen, Veli-Matti 8, 28, 57n1, 64, 92, 97, 112, 127n140, 127n167, 130n248, 132, 146, 156, 163n63, 164n102, 164n117, 165
Katsina, Aliyu Mukhtar 38, 59n39, 64
Kelly, John Norman Davidson 81, 90, 124n13, 126n64, 127n125, 127n126, 132
kingdom of God 32, 40, 45, 55, 86, 111, 121, 138, 145, 154, 182
Kombo, James Henry Owino 24n15, 26, 68, 109, 112–16, 123, 130n250, 132
Kukah, Mathew H. 35, 58n29, 64

LaCugna, Catherine Mowry 5, 10, 24n16, 26, 92, 106, 121–2, 125n38, 127n138, 127n143, 128n145, 130n217, 131n277, 133–7, 142, 146–8, 153–4, 156–9, 161n2, 162n10, 162n14, 162n40, 163n66, 164n96, 164n97, 164n106, 164n118, 165n123, 165n127, 165, 189n29, 190
Lamb, David 47, 61n75, 64
Lassiter, James E. 60n63, 64
Lawson, John 82, 126n68, 133
leadership xii, 4, 20, 22, 23n12, 34, 35, 39, 40–2, 44, 46, 49, 55–6, 59n53, 63, 157, 176–80, 182, 186, 189n21, 190
Lergo, Tunga 48, 61n78, 64
Letham, Robert 70, 91, 124n17, 124n21, 127n135, 133
liberation 4, 44–5, 58n23, 59n49, 59n51, 62, 66, 124, 124n6, 125n33, 127n112, 128n145, 132, 141, 153, 159, 169, 172, 175
love ix, xii, 8–9, 41, 45, 51, 55, 69–70, 81, 90–2, 94–5, 97, 108, 119, 124, 135, 137, 139–44, 147, 151, 153–6, 159, 161, 164n87, 164n103, 167–8, 171, 174, 177–8, 180
Luther, Martin 6–7, 24n17, 24n20, 24n23, 26, 58n22, 59n41, 62, 65, 166–9, 173–4, 177–8, 181–2, 188n1, 188n2,

188n3, 188n4, 189n6, 189n10, 189n15, 189n17, 189n18, 189nn19, 189n20, 190; Lutheran x, xiii, xiv, 3, 49, 59n41, 62, 189n14, 189n15, 190–1
Lutheran Church of Christ in Nigeria (LCCN) xiii, 49

Majawa, Clement 59n46, 64
Makama, Godiya Allanana 29–30, 57n2, 57n9, 64
Marcion 81
marriage 30, 170–1
Mbachirin, Abraham Terumbur 18, 25n50, 26, 49, 61n82, 64
Mbiti, John S. 11–12, 14, 24n27, 24n30, 24n33, 24n40, 26, 29, 114
Mbuvi, Andrew M. 116, 131n265, 133
military 19–22, 45
mission 40, 55, 95–6, 169, 181
modalism 23n9, 91, 97, 105, 108–9, 121–2, 135, 142
modes of being 3, 74, 103–5, 130n215, 142, 151, 155, 160
Moltmann, Jürgen 10, 45, 60n69, 64, 86, 103–4, 108–9, 129n205, 129n207, 130n233, 133, 134–7, 139–40, 142–3, 146, 148, 152–7, 162n7, 162n16, 162n24, 162n34, 163n43, 163n58, 163n61, 164n89, 164n99, 164n104, 164n112, 164n115, 164n116, 165n121, 165n124, 165n129, 165, 181–2, 189n22, 189n26, 190
monarchy 15, 78–80, 84–8, 93, 111, 116, 120–1, 145–50
monotheism 3, 10, 23n9, 73, 84, 103–4, 110, 114, 135, 139, 145–6, 151–2, 157, 163n61
moral ideal xiii, 166
Mtetwa, Sipho 13, 24n38, 26
Mugambi, J. N. Kanyua 3, 23n9, 36
Mwoleka, Cristopher 2, 23n8, 27
mystery x–xii, 2–3, 7, 71, 76, 106, 114, 117, 119, 129n209, 133, 135–7, 139, 141, 153–4, 164n104

Nadaswaran, Shalini 36, 59n36, 64
National Council of Nigeria and the Cameroons (NCNC) 18
National Party of Nigeria (NPN) 20
nepotism xiii, 6, 10, 16, 19, 28, 46–51, 53–4, 56–7, 166, 179, 181–3, 187
newariga diksen 174–6, 186
Northern People's Congress (NPC) 18

196 *Index*

noumenon 98, 122
Nwaigbo, Ferdinand 60n71, 63, 179, 189n21, 190
Nyamiti, Charge 24n15, 27
Nyiawung, Mbengu D. 42, 59n55, 65

Obirin Meta 118–20, 123
Oborji, Francis Anekwe 13, 24n32, 27
Odeyemi, Jacob Oluwole 61n76
O'Donnell, John J. 104–5, 129n209, 133
Odumosu, Olakunle F. 36, 58n31, 65
Oduyoye, Mercy Amba 31, 57n10, 65, 170, 189n6, 190
Ogbonnaya, A. Okechukwu 3, 11–12, 24n15, 24n25, 24n29, 27, 68, 109–16, 123, 130n236, 130n240, 133
oikonomia 84, 111, 135, 137, 156
Okure, Teresa 42, 60n57, 65
Omotola, J. Shola O. 29, 31, 57n5, 58n12, 65
ontology 74, 80–1, 92, 113, 144–6, 163n61
Onyeozili, Emmanuel C. 39, 59n44, 65
oppression ix, 20, 29–30, 41, 44–5, 55–6, 145–6, 157, 159, 168, 170, 172, 176, 177–8
ordo cognoscendi 137, 160, 162n13
ordo essendi 137, 160, 162n13
Orobator, Agbonkhianmeghe E. 68, 109, 116–20, 123, 131n266, 133
orthodox x, 71, 97, 99–101, 106, 109, 117–18, 120–1, 147, 150
Osamwonyi, Omozuwa Gabriel 41, 59n52, 65
ousia 68–9, 71, 73–80, 103, 120, 125n50, 154

Palmer, Timothy P. 34, 58n22, 65
Pannenberg, Wolfhart 8, 10, 24n21, 27, 71, 86, 89, 91, 104, 124n18, 127n119, 127n137, 129n206, 130n226, 133–5, 137–40, 142–3, 145–6, 148–50, 154–5, 161n3, 162n16, 162n31, 162n46, 163n49, 163n62, 163n72, 164n109, 164n112, 164n115, 165
Parrat, John 11, 24n28, 27
patriarchy ix, xii–xiii, 29, 31–3, 55, 57n3, 63, 64–5, 158–9, 169–70, 187, 189n6, 190
People's Democratic Party (PDP) 21
perichoresis x, 6, 23n2, 56, 76, 92, 120–1, 134, 146, 148, 150, 152–6, 164n97; perichoretic communion ix–x, xiii, 2,

4–6, 9–10, 13, 24n18, 24n23, 28, 31, 33, 55, 158–9, 167, 172–3, 175, 178, 180–3, 185–6, 187–8; perichoretic human household 170–1; perichoretic leadership 176, 186; perichoretic life ix, 16, 154, 166–7, 171–2, 181, 185; perichoretic theological education 7, 184, 187; perichoretic Trinity 12, 153; perichoretic unity 153–6, 168
person: authentic big persons 173, 175, 186; in community 11–15, 21, 23n5, 24n37, 25n44, 26, 33, 38; divine persons 1–3, 12, 13, 70, 73, 75–9, 84–6, 88–9, 91–2, 94–6, 97, 99, 104, 107, 111–12, 121, 134–5, 138–61; divine persons in communion 3, 145, 154, 178; internally displaced persons 53; monarchical big persons 56; persons of the Triune God 6, 15, 23n2, 28, 108, 160, 162n30, 166–7, 185, 186
persona 86, 103, 121, 142; *personae* 85–6, 89, 91, 108, 121
Peters, Ted 8, 108, 130n233, 133, 143, 163n47, 165
phenomenon 35, 98, 122
pneumatomachii 71
police 20, 37, 39, 58n25, 59n38, 65
poverty 30, 36, 56, 58n31, 59n34, 62, 65, 189n14, 191
Prestige, George Leonard 86, 126n99, 133
procession 74, 76, 79, 90, 92, 94–7, 147, 150
prosopon 71, 105
Protectorate 17–18
Protestant x, 40, 106
publicity 177

Quran 51, 182

Rahner, Karl 61, 93, 96–7, 106–19, 122, 127n144, 128n163, 130n218, 130n224, 130n225, 130n227, 130n232, 133, 135, 161, 165
recanting: African Church and Society 183; African tradition of community xiii, 2, 8, 22, 67, 112, 145, 166, 168, 172, 183, 185; doctrine of the Trinity 97, 103, 108; ethnic and religious exclusivism 179, 188
re-contextualization 168–9
redemption 8, 50, 67, 70, 76, 81–3, 86–7, 96, 98, 102, 122, 136–7, 154, 168, 188
regula fidei 81

Index 197

revelation 4, 36, 77, 86, 94, 100–4, 107, 111, 122, 135–6, 145, 147–8, 154, 160, 162n13, 185; God's revelation 67, 93, 99, 101, 105, 121, 135, 136, 148; God's self-revelation 67, 97, 103, 105, 120, 122
Ritschl, Albrecht 100
Rodney, Walter 32, 43, 58n14, 60n62, 61n77, 65
Rojas, Maria 32, 58n16, 65
Roman Catholic x, 35
Ruch, E. A. 15, 25n45, 27, 42, 60n59, 65
Ruether, Rosemary Radford 173, 189n8, 190
rule of law 5, 38–9, 56, 59n42, 64, 176–7, 180, 182, 186–8

Sacrament 4–6, 8, 15, 22, 33, 167–8, 184, 187, 188n1, 188n3, 190
Sampson, Isaac Terwase 61n85, 61n89, 61n91, 65
Samuel, Oni 30, 32, 34, 57n6, 58n15, 58n21, 60n60, 65
Sanneh, Lamin O. 181, 189n23, 191
Schleiermacher, Friedrich 68, 97–101, 122, 128n173, 128n174, 129n200, 133
Setiloane, Gabriel M. 2, 23n7, 27
Shutte, Augustine 13, 24n35, 27
Simpson, Gary M. xiii, 176–7, 189n7, 189n14, 189n17, 191
society xii, 4–7, 10, 14, 15, 20, 23n12, 24n14, 26, 28–35, 39, 42–6, 48–50, 54–6, 59n36, 60n58, 60n69, 61n84, 62, 64, 67, 105, 109, 119, 124, 134, 141–2, 144, 146–7, 158, 160–1, 162n15, 162n35, 163n64, 164n94, 164n100, 165n125, 165n129, 165, 166, 170–2, 174–9, 181–7, 189n17, 189n22, 190, 191
son 3, 5, 9, 15, 51, 68–92, 94–6, 99, 102, 104–5, 108, 111–15, 120–1, 125n50, 125n51, 125n53, 125n56, 126n66, 127n112, 133, 135–40, 142–52, 155, 157, 160, 162n30, 168, 173, 175
spirit xii, 2–6, 8–9, 15–16, 22, 23n9, 23n11, 33, 40, 45, 55, 67–8, 70–92, 94–100, 102–5, 107–17, 120–3, 124n25, 125n35, 125n42, 125n46, 125n49, 125n50, 125n56, 125n58, 126n62, 126n66, 127n112, 131–2, 134, 136–57, 160–1, 162n30, 164n104, 167–73, 175, 178, 181–3, 187
submission 31–2, 36, 55, 170–1

subordination 80, 82, 110–12, 138, 146–8, 158, 160; subordinationism 71, 82, 87, 88, 91, 111–12, 116, 121, 135, 146–7
substance 68–74, 80–1, 84–9, 91–3, 95, 110–11, 120–1, 125n50, 129n200, 136–7, 141–7, 150–2, 161
suffering 14–15, 44, 139–40, 167, 175, 186
Sule, Ahmed Olayinka 59n53, 65
synaxis 167
systemic evil x, 4–5, 7, 9, 57, 168, 177, 185

taxis 76, 145, 147
terrorism 53, 57
Tertullian 68, 81, 83–7, 110–12, 121, 126n79, 126n82, 126n84, 126n90, 126n97, 126n100, 127n103, 127n105, 127n107, 130n249, 132–3
tritheism 74, 77, 103–4, 108–9, 112, 117, 121, 129n200, 141–3
Triune God ix, xii, 16, 22, 23n2, 24n23, 28–9, 31, 33, 39, 45, 49, 55–7, 67–8, 71, 73, 75–86, 88–96, 99, 102, 105–13, 115–24, 124n1, 124n16, 124n20, 124n22, 125n39, 126n63, 126n65, 126n77, 126n81, 126n83, 126n89, 126n90, 127n104, 127n106, 127n124, 127n132, 127n136, 128n162, 128n164, 128n173, 129n187, 129n192, 129n202, 129n209, 132, 133–61, 162n13, 162n30, 164n87, 164n104, 166–73, 175–88

unbegotten 72, 89
Unity Party of Nigeria (UPN) 20

Vähäkangas, Mika 2, 23n6, 27
vestige xiii, 1, 24n18, 90, 102, 105

War Against Indiscipline (WAI) 20
Welch, Claude 99–100, 129n182, 133
Wiredu, Kwasi 60n58, 66
word 4–7, 22; *see also* Sacrament

Yoruba 18, 21, 43, 46, 48

Zalanga, Samuel 40, 59n49, 59n51, 66
Zizioulas, John 10, 134, 137, 142–7, 150, 162n12, 162n42, 163n50, 163n52, 163n53, 163n55, 163n82, 163n83, 165